# Independence Years

*By the same author:*

*The Irish Question 1840–1921*  (1940, 1965, 1975)

*The Commonwealth Experience*  (1969, 1982)

*Constitutional Relations Between Britain and India: The Transfer of Power 1942–7*  (Editor-in-Chief, 12 vols., 1967–82)

*The Unresolved Question: The Anglo–Irish Settlement and its Undoing 1912–72*  (1991)

*Nationalism and Independence, Selected Irish Papers*  (1997)

# Independence Years

## The Selected Indian and Commonwealth Papers of Nicholas Mansergh

*Edited by*
Diana Mansergh

*Foreword by*
Sarvepalli Gopal

OXFORD
UNIVERSITY PRESS

# OXFORD
UNIVERSITY PRESS

YMCA Library Building, Jai Singh Road, New Delhi 110001

Oxford University Press is a department of the University of Oxford. It furthers the
University's objective of excellence in research, scholarship, and education
by publishing worldwide in

Oxford New York

Athens Auckland Bangkok Bogota Buenos Aires Calcutta
Cape Town Chennai Dar es Salaam Delhi Florence Hong Kong Istanbul
Karachi Kuala Lumpur Madrid Melbourne Mexico City Mumbai
Nairobi Paris Sao Paolo Singapore Taipei Tokyo Toronto Warsaw

with associated companies in Berlin Ibadan

Oxford is a registered trade mark of Oxford University Press
in the UK and in certain other countries

Published in India
By Oxford University Press, New Delhi

ISBN 019 564847 1

Typeset at Wordsmiths, Saraswati Vihar, Delhi 110034
Printed in India at Saurabh Print-O-Pack, Noida
Published by Manzar Khan, Oxford University Press
YMCA Library Building, Jai Singh Road, New Delhi 110 001

# Foreword

The Commonwealth of Nations is a rare phenomenon in world affairs which has endured in the twentieth century because of its flexibility and adaptation to the rapidly changing times. Starting off as a British Commonwealth of Nations it consisted for the most part of countries with a majority British community. The Balfour Declaration of 1926 emphasized common allegiance to the Crown as the symbol of unity of the organization. The only exception was Éire (the Irish Free State). As a mother country herself she had little in common psychologically or culturally with the other overseas dominions, the majority of whose inhabitants were immigrants from Britain. She was also not reconciled to the fact that she was the first nation in the British empire to be divided on religious grounds—six mainly Protestant counties of Ulster which remained with Britain and twenty-six southern Catholic counties in the Irish Free State, which all had, by the Act of 1920, equal status in the Council of Ireland. There was no room for compromise between unity and autonomy, and in Ireland, as later in India, the basic issue was the presence of a large religious minority determined not to submit to majority rule of the other creed. Even after partition, this has continued to this day in both countries as a festering sore. Chagrined by this settlement, Éire restricted herself to external association with Britain and the Commonwealth, and showed no spontaneous loyalty to the Crown. Even external association was a brittle concept, as was demonstrated by Éire remaining neutral in the Second World War.

Éire had, therefore, much in common with India and Pakistan, who attained independence in August 1947. They acquired dominion status as a shorter and quicker route to freedom, but would they follow the Irish precedent or remain happily on the old terms in the Commonwealth? India was unwilling to swear allegiance to the Crown and was unshaken in her determination to be a sovereign republic. This was natural, as she had her own traditions and more affinity with Éire than with the older dominions. So to suit India and in the wake of the good will that marked the transfer of power, the concept of the Commonwealth was revised as no longer involving allegiance to the Crown but accepting it as a symbol and as the head of the Commonwealth. Ironically, this was in April 1949 and almost coincided with Éire's departure from the association. Had the settlement come earlier, de Valera no doubt would have approved.

It was now a multiracial Commonwealth, for India was followed by Pakistan and Ceylon on similar terms, and the non-white populations of Asia formed the majority. The only exception in Asia to joining was Burma (Myanmar) but several other Asian and African states were, in the coming years, to accede and the centre of gravity moved away steadily from London. As a result, the organization has today become one of the main junctions of international affairs, taking great interest in regional problems and far removed from its earlier conventional status and procedures under the Balfour Declaration.

Nicholas Mansergh was a pioneer historian of the changing Commonwealth and these essays show him keeping pace with the times. Born and educated in Ireland, he was sympathetic to her attitude of remaining for several years in the organization but studiously keeping apart from even the basic concept of external association. This was the first sign of the drift away from the rigid definition of dominion status and Jawaharlal Nehru, later to be the first prime minister of free India, and always a student of international affairs, had been attracted by the courageous Irish stand. He had, in the twenties and thirties, opposed dominion status for India as representing not independence plus but independence minus. Mansergh had watched the gradual transform- ation of the young radical republican leader who wished to have nothing to do with Britain, into the saviour of the Commonwealth in 1956 against the wishes of conservative leaders like Raja- gopalachari. Mansergh visited India at the time of the Asian Relations Conference on the eve of independence in March 1947 and was impressed by a senior Congressman's remark that New

Delhi, for all its splendour, had the drawback of much of it having been imposed by alien rule. He visited India and Pakistan twice again thereafter and kept in touch with the rapidly changing scenario.

Has, as Mansergh later asked, the Commonwealth a future and can it retain its vitality? His optimism is convincing. It has been developing on non-racial lines with a basic adherence to parliamentary democracy which has taken root in different climates. Even a shift to military dictatorships in certain countries has proved temporary. The withdrawal of South Africa, one of the founding nations, in 1961 marked a clear stage in the evolution of an association very different from that at the time of its origin; and South Africa later had to revert to majority rule before it could return. The later development of the Commonwealth along these lines and no longer pro-colonial and pro-West, would not have surprised but given satisfaction to Mansergh.

S. Gopal

# Editor's Preface

Nicholas Mansergh had intended to collect in one volume some of his many scattered essays and papers, as soon as he had finished his last full-scale book, *The Unresolved Question: The Anglo-Irish Settlement and its Undoing*. But Yale University Press, who published it in 1991, had to do this posthumously. A selection of his Irish papers, 'Nationalism and Independence', which I made later, was published by Cork University Press in 1997. The present volume is my attempt to make such a collection of his Indian and Commonwealth papers.

It was in January 1942 that an appeal to Churchill was led by Sir Tej Bahadur Sapru for 'a single bold stroke' of 'far-sighted statesmanship' to break the constitutional deadlock in India. This was concerned with the transfer of power from British to Indian hands. In fact it was 'mainly concerned with the far more difficult issue of what Indian hands'. In response to this appeal, a first step was the sending of the Cripps Mission to India. Glimpses of the unfolding of the subsequent story are contained in these pages, but for those who require a detailed, documented account there are the twelve volumes of the British documents, *India: The Transfer of Power 1942-47* (HMSO 1970-83). The editing of these documents took fifteen years and Nicholas Mansergh, with full assistance, was Editor-in-Chief (1968-83).

Mansergh paid his first visit to India in 1947 as an observer at the Asian Conference in New Delhi. For him 1947 also marked the beginning of his twenty-three years as a Commonwealth Professor, momentous years of development and expansion for the Commonwealth. Three times he was a Visiting Professor at the Indian School of International Affairs in New Delhi and he attended the Commemorative Asian Conference in 1987. His impressions and insights are rooted in the time in which they were written and do not fail to convey with freshness and immediacy the prevailing atmosphere and climate of opinion of those days.

Cambridge                                          DIANA MANSERGH
January 1999

# Acknowledgements

My greatest debt is to Professor Gopal for so generously lending his name to this volume and for writing a Foreword. I also thank most warmly Dr Lionel Carter for his valuable help and advice during the preparation of the book. To Professor Peter Clarke and my sons, Philip, Martin and Nicholas and my son-in-law Paul Gilbert, I am most grateful for all their help and support in a variety of different ways.

The essays are reprinted by the kind permission of the original publishers whose names appear in the Table of Contents and some of them also at the chapters' end.

There has been very little alteration to the text of these writings and where necessary they should be read in relation to the date of their publication.

Mrs S. French of Fulbourn, who has typed the whole book, has my best thanks again for all her help.

# Contents

## Part II. The Commonwealth in Asia

## Part III. Reappraisals

## Part IV. Retrospect

## Epilogue. India in the 1950s

# Part I. Independence—The Transfer of Power with Partition—Commonwealth Membership

# 1

# The Prelude to Partition:
# Concepts and Aims in Ireland and India*

'In this matter, when among other voices the voice of manifest right cries out against us to Heaven, I must acknowledge that never in my life have I suffered pangs like these, that I feel shame to show my face.'[1] The writer was the Empress Maria Theresa; the recipient her Chancellor Kaunitz; the occasion the first partition of Poland in 1772. Posterity remembers the Great Frederick's cruel gibe about the Empress who wept while she took, but remained little mindful of her foreboding that untold suffering would come to later generations because of a partition urged upon her for reasons of state. 'Placet', she said in yielding to them, 'since so many great and learned men will have it so: but long after I am dead it will be known what this violating of all that was held sacred and just will give rise to.'

The eighteenth-century enlightenment was affronted by the perpetration of so cynical an act. 'On partage savamment les royaumes, comme autrefois on divisait les sermons', protested Horace Walpole

*The 1976 Commonwealth Lecture. This was part of the Memorial in Cambridge to Field Marshal Smuts—a former student at Christ's College, who after the Second World War was elected Chancellor of the University. A Smuts professorial chair and a lecturership were also founded and the author was the first Smuts Professor of the History of the British Commonwealth (1953–70). Later he was invited to give this lecture.

1. *Cambridge Modern History*, vol. VI, *The Eighteenth Century* (Cambridge, 1925), p. 630.

to Madame du Deffand,[2] and he might have added, what the perpetrators of the partition well understood, that kingdoms, like sermons, were the more digestible when divided into three parts. Partition itself became a pejorative term, the *Annual Register* in 1807 being unable to postulate any more damning interpretation of the Tilsit agreement than that it constituted a partition of Europe itself, carved out between Buonaparte and Alexander, in which the latter 'fell into the snares of the Italian, with an imbecility bordering on insanity.'[3] In more recent times the word itself suffices to stir resentment among liberals, and antagonism among Nationalists—other than those for whom a partition is, or has been, a condition of their separate statehood.

In any enquiry into the nature of partition the point of departure must needs be the word itself. In political parlance it has no single, or simple, connotation. In the case of Poland, it meant the partitioning of an ancient kingdom in three phases into three parts, each part being absorbed into the polity of a powerful and predatory neighbour; for the Turkish Empire before the First World War it meant chiefly, as it may in South Africa,[4] progressive partition from within through the re-emergence of nationalities, Greeks and Bulgars, Romanians and Serbs, long subjected by conquest to alien rule, while the 'partition of Africa', a phrase that is itself to be used with some caution by historians—Professor Sanderson's 'The European Partition of Africa'[5] is more indicative of what happened—meant historically the division, not of a political, but of a geographical entity by powers either actually or by derivation, e.g. the South African colonies and republics, external to it.

The phenomenon of partition in this century has had two further

---

2. Letter of 13 April 1773. See *Supplement to the Letters of Horace Walpole*, ed. Paget Toynbee (2 vols.: Oxford, 1918), vol. 1, p. 213. The passage in the letter continued, *'et l'on massacre le peuple avec autant de sang-froid qu'on les ennuyait. Voilà un siècle de lumières.'*

3. *Annual Register, 1807*, pp. 271-3.

4. The distinguishing feature in the South African case is the contemplation of partition as an objective of government policy; see the exposition of the purposes of the Promotion of Bantu Self-Government Act 1959 by government spokesmen, notably Dr Verwoerd, in the *South African House of Assembly Debates*, vol. 101, 1959, cols. 6001-8, 6018-19 and 6214-27.

5. *Journal of Imperial and Commonwealth History*, vol. III, no. 1 (1974).

manifestations, both international in origin and consequence. The first was particular, namely the partition of Palestine to make possible the re-creation of a Jewish state; the second a product of great-power tensions, namely the partition of states along what came to be known after the First World War as the international frontier, and which after the Second World War ran through Korea, Vietnam and Germany.

While set in this wider background, the scope of this enquiry is limited to what, by contrast with the international, may be described as a domestic i.e. within a single polity, dimension. Within such a classification two kinds of partition may be identified. The first is to be seen when states once separate then unified—for example, Belgium and Holland, Sweden and Finland, Sweden and Norway again pulled apart. In such cases clearly there is a form of partition, but in so far as the pulling apart is related to previously existing and distinct historical, linguistic or ethnic identities, the term itself is infrequently applied,[6] the reason being that it subsumes the existence of a partitioner and when division is by domestic accord, albeit deriving from domestic discord, that role remains unfilled. It is not so, however, in the second case, that of partitions which arise when dependencies unified either previous to, or under, imperial rule divide, or are divided, in the process of becoming once more independent. In such situations, the withdrawing imperial authority, short of unconditional abandonment, as by the Portuguese of Angola, must in the last resort, and may much earlier, decide to whom power is to be transferred; and if it be to more than one successor authority, then it must in so doing assume at the least some measure of general responsibility for the consequent partition. In such an eventuality the outgoing imperial power, by necessary constitutional enactment providing for transfer,[7] must also make provision for partition. In law, therefore, there is a partitioner and the term partition is consistently used of the outcome.

6. This is also true of Pakistan, geographically divided since its inception in 1947, and partitioned in a political sense with the constitution of a separate state, Bangladesh, in January 1972.

7. See the Government of Ireland Act, 1920 (10 & 11 Geo. V c. 67), the Irish Free State Constitution Act, 1922 (13 Geo. V c. 1, session 2) and the Indian Independence Act, 1947 (10 & 11 Geo. VI c. 30).

The partition of Ireland and of India belongs to this last category. At the time of partition both countries were within a single polity, the British imperial system, and in each case the partition coincided with a transfer of power, albeit limited in the Irish case, to indigenous authorities. The common denominator was thus more than partition; it was partition and a transfer in a triangular political context. My principal purpose is to consider the interplay of ideas and forces in such a triangular setting with particular regard to the extent to which the setting itself may have influenced the tactics, conditioned the responses or limited the range of options open to the three parties or protagonists, irrespective of, or superimposing upon the otherwise great differences in the histories and circumstances of the countries so partitioned.

In the two instances under consideration the triangle had as its base a nationalist majority, who cherished the theory of one nation and sought to restore, or establish, its independence as a unit; as one side a minority who, when faced with the prospect of rule by the majority community, formulated a two-nation theory, or its near-equivalent; and as the other, the imperial power predisposed to holding the balance, but only for so long as that might be to its own advantage, within the limits of its resources and consistent with its image of its world role. The political strategy pursued by each party to the triangle was designed to ensure the fulfilment of its conceptual aim, itself conditioned in varying degree by assessment of economic or other interests, and the more closely in any particular case that strategy was tied to literal realization of concept, the less flexible it became. Theory and practice in such circumstances were apt to be more closely intertwined than essays in detailed historical reconstruction, with their discounting or neglect of the ideological, often allow.

In respect of the first party in the triangle, the concept was one of restored independence to a country long under alien subjection. In Ireland after 1916, and more especially after January 1919, the goal was symbolized in a particular constitutional form—the republic; in India the aim was more generally expressed first as *Swaraj*, and later as *Purna Swaraj*, i.e. the complete independence on which the Congress resolved on 22 March 1940. The freedom sought in each case was for a country deemed, like Mazzini's beloved Italy, to have been endowed by Providence with its own irrefutable boundary marks. In Ireland throughout the period of frustrated demand for self-rule that ran from Parnell to Pearse,[8] from the exponent (and exploiter) of constitutionalism to the protagonist of physical force, none among nationalists abated the claim to coincidence of nation, state and island—that best mannered of parliamentarians, John Redmond reacting to a suggestion of partition by denunciation of it as 'an abomination and a blasphemy', while uncompromising revolutionaries believed with Pearse that it were better for a man that he had not been born than that he should sacrifice one iota of a national claim that rested upon the foundation of its territorial integrity. In India, the Indian National Congress, which, as Gandhi succinctly put it to the Round Table Conference in 1931, claimed 'to represent the whole of India',[9] were the exponents of that self-same one nation theory, a nation that in their case stretched from the Himalayas to Cape Comorin, possible partition being equated with outrage, or, in Gandhian phraseology, with 'the vivisection' of Mother India. The principle of a united India, Maulana A.K. Azad, the President of the Congress, and Jawaharlal Nehru told Sir Stafford Cripps in the course of his Indian mission early in 1942, was one for which they were prepared to go to almost any length[10]—the qualifying 'almost' indicating an attitude less rigid than the Irish and foreshadowing (if that is not reading too much into a word) Congress acquiescence, on 3 June 1947, in partition as the price of independence, though it is right to recall that in the resolution approving such acquiescence the All-India Congress Committee declared:

Geography and the mountains and the seas fashioned India as she is, and no human agency can change that shape or come in the way of her final destiny . . . when the present passions have subsided, India's problems will

8. By happy coincidence each has been the subject of a biography of unusual interest since this lecture was delivered, i.e. F.S.L. Lyons, *Charles Stewart Parnell* (London, 1977), and Ruth Dudley Edwards, *Patrick Pearse: The Triumph of Failure* (London, 1977).

9. *Indian Round Table Conference* (2nd session), 7 September to 1 December 1931, *Proceedings of the Federal Structure and Minorities Committee*, Cmd 3997, p. 390.

10. N. Mansergh and E.W.R. Lumby (eds.), *India: The Transfer of Power 1942–47* (London, HMSO 1970), vol. 1, no. 496.

be viewed in their proper perspective and the false doctrine of two nations in India will be discredited and discarded by all.[11]

There was a gap between enunciation, however eloquent or uncompromising, of the concept of one independent nation-state and its realization. In the way there came Ulster, there came Muslim India; there was, not as a constant but as a variable, its actions in no small measure conditioned by the balance of its own domestic political forces, the imperial power. There was also the complexity, itself deriving from the triangular setting, that while the concept was singular, its realization was conditional upon attainment of two goals, independence and unity. The first predicated armed revolt or at the least political pressure upon the imperial power, i.e. a militant stance—Conor Cruise O'Brien has noted how even in Parnellite days *United Ireland*, the party's journal, used the vocabulary of warfare to describe parliamentary debates, Nationalist MPs sharing in 'the exultation of battle' and engaging in 'eager man to man conflicts with the foe';[12] the second a conciliatory tone. In theory the two were reconcilable; in practice as the majority lined up behind their leaders an exhilarating mood of militancy was easily, only too easily, in part deflected to others, who by detachment from, or opposition to, nationalist aims appeared to be providing the arguments and the obstacle most likely to frustrate their attainment. The pursuit of autonomy without prejudice to unity was not, and is not, psychologically an easy assignment, as many others in Europe,[13] Asia and Africa were also to learn.

It is often suggested, or implied, that both the Irish and Indian national movements had a choice between seeking to conciliate the minority community by recognizing its deep-felt need for safeguards and attempting to impose upon it the will of the majority by rigid insistence on the fact that after all it was the majority. Theoretically that may be so, but the exercise of that choice in practice either way was so fraught with risk that there was bound to be ambivalence and reservation in the making of it.

Historically, however, the outline of the answers given was

11. Quoted in V.P. Menon, *The Transfer of Power in India* (Bombay, 1957), p. 384.

12. C.C. O'Brien, *Parnell and His Party 1880–1890* (Oxford, 1957), p. 81, n. 2.

13. Cyprus is in mind especially.

clear enough. Faced with the problem of recalcitrant minorities, the majority nationalist parties in Ireland and India sought, as part of their campaign for self-government, to organize and demonstrate electorally their overall representational strength. In Ireland, Parnell, that master of tactics, embarked on a policy of electoral invasion, intended to consolidate support for Home Rule in the North and to convey the impression of its inevitability. The policy was crowned with significant success. Of the eighty-nine contested Irish seats in the election of November 1885, the Nationalists won eighty-five with Ulster returning eighteen Nationalists as against seventeen Unionists. Here, if required, was convincing and conclusive evidence that there was no question of a united Northern province resisting Home Rule. The Congress victories in the provincial elections in British India in 1937, based upon a well-organized mass movement, seemed to point to a similar conclusion—there was no natural or historical area where the electorate was unitedly opposed to the national demand, the potentially separatist Muslim League under the leadership of Mohammed Ali Jinnah in fact not coming near to having a majority in any province, and, overall, winning only 108 out of 482 Muslim seats.[14] There were only two forces in India, Jawaharlal Nehru had claimed in the course of the election campaign—British imperialism and Indian nationalism— and when Jinnah had retorted that there was a third party, the Muslims, Nehru dismissed out of hand the notion of the Muslims in India as 'a nation apart'.[15] Did not the results of the elections go far to vindicate that dismissal?

But here intervened a familiar paradox in politics. In India, as earlier in Ireland, overwhelming electoral victory significantly reinforced the claims for autonomy or independence. But in terms of unity the exact opposite was the case; there nothing failed like success. By giving the appearance of the mobilization of a seemingly external threat; by the militancy of their posture, their language

14. H.V. Hodson, *The Great Divide* (London, 1969), p. 62. There were special factors bringing about the result, by no means least the League's sense of being an elitist grouping, not a popular mass movement, which accounted for its not contesting all the Muslim seats, but they little diminished the impression given.

15. Sarvepalli Gopal, *Jawaharlal Nehru: A Biography* (London, 1975), vol. 1, pp. 223–4.

on the hustings, their ballads or songs—*Bande Mataram* was deemed by some 'a hymn of hate against the Muslims'; by post-election attitudes and actions, the Congress going so far as to organize a 'mass contact' movement among Muslim peasants and workers on the argument that 'even the Muslim masses' looked up to the Congress 'for relief';[16] by their emphasis upon the link between culture and nationality the majority parties contributed significantly to the closing of anti-Home Rule ranks in Ulster and to the Muslims' resolve to mobilize behind the League lest they be reduced to 'mere pages' at the footstool of a Hindu Congress. In both instances the leaders of the minority dramatized the threat—Carson by organizing one great demonstration for Easter Tuesday, 1912, two days before the introduction of the Third Home Rule Bill, and others for the signing of a Solemn League and Covenant pledging resistance to Home Rule, on 28 September that year; Jinnah, reacting sharply to the Congress 'mass contact' campaign, by organizing a mass movement based on the cry 'Islam in danger',[17] followed by the proclamation of a day of national rejoicing when the Congress provincial ministries resigned shortly after the outbreak of war, and later by Black Flag days, culminating in a call to the 'Muslim nation' to direct action 'to achieve Pakistan' on 16 August 1946, a sequel to which was the 'Great Calcutta Killing', reliance being placed throughout on sentiment at the grass roots, the more inflamed because it, too, as in Ireland, stirred the embers of centuries-old religious antagonisms.

Thus it was; might it have been otherwise? Before following along a road signposted with familiar and facile speculation, it is well to underline firstly, that the leaders of the majority parties were overridingly preoccupied with autonomy, or national independence, and secondly, that they had no certainties as to the dimensions of the minority question. It is then instructive to consider the nature of the constraints upon majority strategy operating within triangular confines. If one poses first the hypothesis that the majority nationalist parties had followed policies of conciliation, at critical times, what assurance was there on one level that this

16. Ibid., p. 225.
17. See Percival Griffiths, *The British Impact on India* (London, 1952), p. 340, for the impressions of a contemporary observer.

would not have been interpreted by the faithful as tantamount to abandonment in the face of minority recalcitrance, or menace, of some cherished, even integral, parts of their concept of nationality and, on another level, that it would not have led step by step to the *de facto* recognition of the existence in Ireland, and in India, at the very least of the semblance of a second nation?

If one looks closer for illustration to clothe the issue in concrete terms, one might ask what would have been the consequences in Ireland had John Redmond, leader of the Irish Parliamentary Party before the outbreak of war in 1914, not only yielded, as he did, step by step to pressure to concede the veiled exclusion, i.e. exclusion for a period of years, of some parts of Ulster, but further, bent on conciliation of the minority, had accepted a clean cut, or the naked (to use the terminology of the time) exclusion of all of the province's nine counties, as was proposed by Sir Edward Carson on 21 July 1914, the first day of the Buckingham Palace Conference, and by him commended to Redmond and his principal associate, John Dillon, on the ground that the total exclusion of Ulster was in the interest of the earliest possible unity of Ireland, opinion in the nine counties being so evenly divided that exclusion on such a territorial basis would almost certainly prove short-lived?[18] The answer seems all too clear. The man who by irresolution, most of all on partition, was destined to discredit constitutionalism, destroy the Parliamentary Party, leave a name that became a by-word for political credulity, would have been not only politically ruined overnight, but would then and there have handed over the leadership of the national movement to men who, like Carson—to whose aim they were violently opposed but whose methods they much admired—held policies of conciliation in contempt.

The parting of the ways between conciliation and majority self-assertion is conventionally deemed to have come to the Indian National Congress in the form of a more explicit choice at a given moment in time. The provincial elections of 1937, already alluded to, led, after protracted disputation about governors' powers, to Congress acceptance of invitations to form governments in

18. Redmond Papers, National Library of Ireland, Dublin. Redmond kept a note of the proceedings of the conference which are not on official record.

provinces in which they emerged as the majority or largest party. Were they in provinces either with substantial Muslim populations or where special factors existed, as in the United Provinces,[19] to be single-party governments? Or were independent Muslims to be invited to serve? Or were Congress–League coalitions to be formed (as would indeed have been in accord with the general instruction given to governors) to ensure so far as possible that representatives of minorities should be included in provincial governments? The Muslim League entertained insecurely grounded expectations of the last, i.e. coalitions in which they would be partners. But, in fact, though a few individual, non-League Muslims were, Muslim League members were not invited to serve, save only on humiliating conditions, one being that of becoming full members of the Congress. They were deeply offended. But they had not been invited, immediately because the League had fared poorly in the elections, but fundamentally because of the Congress conviction that it represented, and should act as if it did represent, all India. Had not the elections gone a long way to confirming this? Were there not Congress Muslims? (There were, but they were noticeably thin on the ground, despite Nehru's election claim that there were Muslims in the Congress who 'could provide inspiration to a thousand Jinnahs.'[20]) Why should the Congress not take power? What English party that had won a decisive electoral victory would invite its defeated opponents to share in the responsibilities of government? Why form coalitions, notorious for their instability, when there was no need to do so? It was not reasonable to expect it: the Congress leaders did not feel it to be so. In the retrospect of more than twenty years, I went over the ground with two of them, Rajendra Prasad and Jawaharlal Nehru. Prasad, who played a key role in Bihar and Orissa,[21] remained clear in conscience—

19. See Gopal, *Jawaharlal Nehru: A Biography*, pp. 225–7.

20. Ibid., p. 224.

21. There is a detailed explanation of what happened and why in *Rajendra Prasad: Autobiography* (Bombay, 1957), pp. 442–7. He goes so far as to write: 'appointment of Muslim Leaguers as Ministers in Provinces where the Congress had been returned in a majority would have been unconstitutional'. This would, indeed, have been the case where no Muslim Leaguers had been returned, the relevant provisions of the Government of India Act 1935 (26 Geo. V c. 2), pt III, ch. II, sect. 51(2) laying down that

though also still mindful of the claims to office of the party faithful and satisfied that he could have done no other, without running contrary to the spirit of parliamentary democracy and majority rule on which the Congress concept of a future unitary India rested; while Nehru, more sensitive, even troubled about the possibility of an opportunity of Congress–League working cooperation seemingly missed, and largely, as one of his colleagues later alleged, on his responsibility,[22] for ever, was still convinced no other course had been practicable, in principle warranted or even prudent, given the vanity, the personal ambition and the disruptive aims of Jinnah. Others were not so persuaded The Congress, commented Sir Penderel Moon, 'passionately desired to preserve the unity of India. They consistently acted so as to make its partition certain'. And in their rejection of coalitions he discerned the *fons et origo malorum*.[23] His judgement, thus forcefully and felicitously phrased, is widely endorsed both in this particular and in its general formulation.

Historically neither can be viewed in isolation. In seeking to assess the consequences of a particular Congress action—repudiation of coalitions—it is well also to bring into the reckoning the likely consequences of Congress acceptance of them. Over against the gain in Muslim goodwill there would then have had to be set the price to be paid for a concession of all-India principle. Coalitions in the provinces would have implied a coalition when the time

---

ministers had to be members of the provincial legislature save for the first six months after appointment. Since, however, it was Congress policy to appoint single-party governments irrespective of whether there were Muslim League, or, indeed, non-Congress Muslim members or not, any such gloss would have been disingenuous. More probably Prasad was thinking only of convention since he later comments that he was convinced the Congress committed no constitutional impropriety in terms of the British precedents to which they sought to adhere.

22. Maulana Azad considered that Nehru's advice against inclusion of more than one Muslim League minister in the United Provinces to have been a major error attributable to Nehru's 'theoretical bias'. See A.K. Azad, *India Wins Freedom* (Bombay, 1959), pp. 160–2.

23. *Divide and Quit* (London, 1961 ), p. 14. Sir Percival Griffiths' conclusion (*The British Impact on India*, p. 340) was that the Congress was fully within its rights, but had made 'a grave tactical blunder', V.P. Menon's that it was a 'factor which induced neutral Muslim opinion to turn to the support of Jinnah' (*The Transfer of Power in India*, p. 56).

came to form a responsible government at an as yet non-existent responsible, representative centre. Would such a coalition have enhanced the prospect of a unitary independent India? And what might have been the effect overall of such concession upon the unity of the Congress Party itself? Might not conciliation of the minority have had to be paid for in division within the majority? The fact that such questions arise suffices in itself to indicate that, in this as in most other cases, it may be unrealistic to assume that had one thing been different all else would have remained the same. It is in fact improbable. The leadership of constitutional, or quasi-constitutional, national movements is at all times peculiarly vulnerable to allegations by sea-green incorruptibles to its left of retraction from the concept of the independent, unitary nationhood it is there to realize. In Ireland there had been the protagonists of physical force; in India there were the Hindu communalists, as those who were mindful of the later twenties had reason to recall, waiting in the wings. Redmond made some concession of nationalist principle which rested upon majority rule and he fell: the Congress made none and they remained and with them the constitutionalist control of the national movement, albeit precariously, survived.

Sir Penderel Moon's more general judgement upon the course of Congress policy might also *mutatis mutandis*, but with qualification, be pronounced upon Sinn Féin. With at least an equal passion, they desired unity and intermittently rather than consistently acted so as to prejudice its attainment; the greater in particular their insistence upon the Catholic-Gaelic foundation of Irish nationhood, the more acute the Northerners' feeling that they were, and indeed were deemed to be, alien to it. In both countries the majority well understood that liberty must needs be won by sustained effort and a readiness, in both cases impressively forthcoming, for sacrifice in the national cause. But unity in each case, more deeply grounded as it was in concept than in history, was apt to be assumed. Parnell's most recent biographer tells us that the idea 'that Ireland might possibly contain two nations, not one, apparently never entered his head',[24] while as we have seen, that same possibility in respect of India was summarily dismissed by Nehru in 1937. From such assumptions of unity may have

---

24. F.S.L. Lyons, *Charles Stewart Parnell*, p. 623.

derived many of the insensitivities which confirmed partition. But how far did they cause it?

Or to put the question in another way, is there evidence in Ireland or in India to suggest that either at such critical junctures as have been considered or over an extended period of time, greater sensitivity reflected in more conciliatory attitudes on the part of the majority would in fact have produced a different outcome, as distinct from a different and a less, or more, blood-spattered road to the same outcome? To answer that—and it is a question of cardinal importance—one must consider the aims of the second party and then in each case try to assess how far those aims may have imposed constraints upon minority action and reaction, such as may themselves have precluded unity by understanding and peaceful political process.

In both Ireland and India the minority community belonged to a ruling, or a former ruling, race. This was socially in terms of land ownership, economically in terms of control of the levers of industrial power as well as politically a self-evident reality in Ulster; in India it was a legacy, overlaid by nearly two centuries of British rule, but with reminders of one-time dominance in the princely States, the ruler of the greatest of them, Hyderabad, being a Muslim holding sway over a preponderantly Hindu population, and, immediately of more importance, the social standing of the landowning Muslim leadership in the United Provinces and the Punjab. In both Ireland and India this ruling past was psychologically important in that it created a presumption on the part of the minority at least of non-subordination when imperial rule ended. There was a second, and a fundamental factor. Neither Ulster Protestants nor Muslims shared the religion, tradition or, in the case of the Muslims in north-western India, the literature or any of the languages of the majority community. They did not have the same heroes or folk-memories, nor yet the same inner allegiance. To that extent they did not instinctively feel themselves to be part of one nation, their attitude being rather one of aloofness, even in days of quiescence and settled imperial rule.

But were they more than minority communities? The imperial power did not so treat them in governmental terms. Dublin Castle administration, whatever may be thought of it—and James Bryce, as Chief Secretary in 1906, was depressed by the 'intolerable defects

... which made its working inconceivably troublesome and harassing'[25] while Sir Warren Fisher, when, as head of the civil service, he had a look at it in its last phase, summed up his impressions in a sentence, 'the Castle administration does not administer'[26]—was for the whole of Ireland; and, while the map of India was a mosaic of princely States and British-Indian provinces with concessions made to minorities in the latter by way of electoral weightage, unity was the basis and oft-proclaimed goal of British rule—though there was conflict, reflecting part subconscious ambivalence, between unitary profession on the one hand and preoccupation with the development of provincial self-government on the other, it having been persuasively argued[27] that progressive devolution of power to the provinces on the scale on which it took place, while marking an advance towards self-government, also in corresponding and necessary measure eased the way to partition. But while making allowance for such part-contradiction between profession and practice, the overall position remained that the structure of imperial administration subsumed that, if power were to be transferred, it would be in India, as in Ireland, to a central and single successor authority with the carry-over, or addition, of safeguards for minorities. And what was implicit in patterns of government was explicit in terms of economic, social and political realities. Were they to be disregarded, as disregarded they must needs be, were division to succeed to unity? Was Derry to be cut off from its Donegal hinterland, the jute mills of Calcutta

25. Bryce to Goldwin Smith, 16 June 1906, quoted by Patricia Jalland in 'A Liberal Chief Secretary and the Irish Question: Augustine Birrell 1907–1914', *The Historical Journal*, vol. 19, no. 2 (1976), p. 421.

26. Report of Sir Warren Fisher, 12 May 1920. Quoted in Charles Townshend, *The British Campaign in Ireland 1919–1921* (Oxford, 1975), p. 78.

27. R.J. Moore, in *The Crisis of Indian Unity 1917–1940* (Oxford, 1974), p. 316, where he concludes categorically:

There can be no doubt that . . . the method and timing of the devolutionary process exacerbated divisions within India. Britain's no freedom without unity principle placed freedom beyond early reach. The enlistment of Muslim collaborators through the concession of autonomous communal provinces enabled Muslims to entrench themselves in their majority provinces.

from the jute of East Bengal? How did you disentangle Protestant from Catholic in Northern Ireland, Muslim from Hindu in Bengal or Muslim from Hindu and Sikh in the Punjab? Were the services and police, the personnel of government and even the office furniture to be divided? The answer to all of these questions including the last—civil servants were much interested in the fate of the furniture and the files[28]—was to be in the affirmative—which *inter alia* underlines the fact that historically the issue was no more determined by such considerations than it was by the structural implications of imperial administration. On the contrary it was brought to the point of decision in long-range dialectics—the demand of the majority for self-government, or independence, for the whole of Ireland or India being met by the counter-claim of the minority that, by reason of differences in race, community or nation, division should succeed to the unity that had prevailed under imperial rule—with the rhetoric which is so compulsive an element in the appeal of nationalism[29] accentuating the dissociating protest of a counter-nationalism.

In both Ireland and India the contention of the smaller community came to be that it was to be regarded not as a minority but as a distinct and distinguishable entity, and, therefore, not properly to be subjected to the will of the majority. Beyond that, however, there was an important difference. In Ulster the positive Unionist claim was not that the Ulster Unionists constituted a separate nation—though that also was sometimes adumbrated—but rather that they were, and wished to remain, part of another nation. They were in Ireland but not unreservedly of it: of Britain, again

28. I am indebted to Dr J. McColgan for information on this point in his unpublished dissertation, 'The Irish Administration in Transition 1920–22' (UCD, 1976) and to personal impressions in respect of India. See A.K. Azad, *India Wins Freedom*, p. 201 for an indication of the problems relating to files.

29. Pearse, writes his most recent biographer, was convinced that 'it was rhetoric not steady organizing by faceless men that would bring the host of the true Gaels from all the corners of Ireland', R.D. Edwards, *Patrick Pearse: The Triumph of Failure*, p. 160. History has shown his conviction to have been well-founded but the more successful such rhetoric was in giving emotional appeal to abstract concept, the more sharply it marked off those who did not entertain the concept.

with qualification, but not in it. They believed that the Union had been economically beneficial, remained politically and strategically realistic, its continuance moreover being for them something in the nature of a psychological imperative. Far, therefore, from its being their wish to secede, it was their militant intent to remain a part of the United Kingdom. It was 'our cherished position of equal citizenship in the United Kingdom' that 100,000 Covenanters in September 1912, 'this time of threatened calamity', pledged themselves, Carson at their head, to defend by the use of 'all means which may be found necessary to defeat the present conspiracy to set up a Home Rule Parliament in Ireland.'[30] And there they took their stand, with this qualification that while the preservation of their 'cherished position' in the United Kingdom remained a constant, their initial and peculiarly Carsonite (and English Unionist) purpose of defeating Home Rule—the maintenance of the Union in its integrity Carson termed 'the guiding star of my political life'—gave way to the more modest and realistic aim, throughout entertained by the province's indigenous leader, James Craig, and adopted by Bonar Law, the New Brunswicker of Ulster descent who, in November 1911, succeeded Balfour in the leadership of the English Unionist Party, of excluding the province of Ulster, or some part of it, from subjection to a Home Rule Parliament in Dublin dominated by those they regarded as hereditary foes. Either way, it was a case of a minority resolved not to submit to majority rule, but not a case of a minority that conceived of itself as embodying a self-sufficient separate nationhood. To that extent, therefore, the two-nation theory fitted the contention of the minority in Ireland, but only with qualifications such as were not to apply in India. There the counter-assertion to majority claims, when it came effectively in the years 1936–40, was unequivocal. It was that there were two nations, both within the subcontinent and both aspiring to independence. It is to Jinnah, as more than leader in a conventional political sense, of the Muslim League, accordingly and, in the circumstances logically, that one must look for the classic exposition of the two-nation theory.

In his address to the Lahore Conference of the Muslim League

---

30. The text of the Covenant is reprinted in Paul Buckland (ed.), *Irish Unionism* (Belfast, Northern Ireland PRO, 1973), Document no. 119.

in March 1940, Jinnah began with an emphatic repudiation of what he described as a simplistic Hindu and British notion that the differences in India were of a communal character, such as might be resolved by concessions, by safeguards within a unitary state, by giving a more substantial measure of devolution to the provinces or, alternatively, in a federal system with a centre vested, if need be, with minimal powers.[31] On the contrary, in Jinnah's words, it was 'a dream that Hindus and Muslims can ever evolve a common nationality . . .'; they 'have two different religions, philosophies, social customs, literatures. They neither intermarry nor even interdine. Indeed they belong to two different civilizations'. The notion of majority rule in such countries was an irrelevance and a geographic concept of nationhood meaningless. Yet it was not, in this rhetoric, as I believe, that Jinnah was formulating the essence of his case. It was rather in the quiet assertion: 'The problem of India is not of an intercommunal character, but manifestly of an international one and must be treated as such'. By international he meant literally as between nations. From this contention he was not to retreat. In the autumn of 1944, the Viceroy, reporting to the Secretary of State on the causes of the breakdown of recently concluded Gandhi-Jinnah talks, entered into in an attempt to bridge the gulf between the Congress and the League, noted:

Jinnah adhered to 'two nations' theory according to which Moslems are separate nation from Hindus though intermingled with them. He pressed acceptance by Gandhi of the Moslem League's Lahore resolution of March 1940 and made it clear that he would accept nothing less than sovereign Moslem States . . . and demanded . . . relations between Moslem States and the rest of India should be by treaty as between equal and independent powers. Gandhi denied 'two nations' theory.[32]

The Governor of the United Provinces added the further gloss that in the talks neither Jinnah nor Gandhi had abandoned their former ideas, Jinnah emphasizing the two-nation theory and Pakistan more strongly than before and clearly wanting 'this

31. The address is reprinted in N. Mansergh (ed.), *Documents and Speeches on British Commonwealth Affairs* (2 vols.: Oxford, 1953), vol. II, pp. 609–12.

32. N. Mansergh and Penderel Moon (eds.), *India: The Transfer of Power 1942–47*, vol. V, no. 30.

question finally decided before the British leave; Gandhi, though he camouflages his position as usual, aims at a Hindu Raj and adheres to the view that independence must come before a settlement.'[33] Gandhi himself retrospectively confirmed the correctness of his diagnosis in replying to a question posed by Tej Bahadur Sapru, 'Quaid-i-Azam [Jinnah] would have nothing short of the two nations theory and therefore complete dissolution. . . . It was just here that we split.'[34] The heart of the matter was in that last brief sentence. Maulana Azad—and who was better, or more painfully placed to pass judgement than the minority President of the majority national movement—confirmed that this was so. 'Mr Jinnah's scheme', he wrote in a submission to the British Cabinet in April 1946,

is based on his two-nation theory. His thesis is that India contains many nationalities based on religious differences. Of them the two major nations, the Hindus and Muslims, must have separate states. When Dr Edward Thompson once pointed out to Mr Jinnah that Hindus and Muslims live side by side in thousands of Indian towns, villages and hamlets, Mr Jinnah replied that this in no way affected their separate nationality. Two nations, according to Mr Jinnah, confront one another. . . .[35]

Jinnah in formulating the concept of two nations, as against two communities in India, had a practical, over and above a dialectical point to establish. Nations, unlike communities, negotiate as equals, irrespective of size. That is what he wanted to happen *before* power was transferred. And with a lawyer's logic and his own resolute refusal to concede anything inconsistent with his concept of a Muslim nation in India, he built up by stages a position in which at conferences and later in government, the Muslim League demanded and obtained virtual parity[36] with the Congress, the representatives of the minority with those of the majority, on the implicit assumption, at all times repudiated by the Congress, of the separate nationhood of Muslims and Hindus—the Congress nomination of

33. Ibid., no. 33.
34. Ibid., no. 344, annex.
35. A.K. Azad, *India Wins Freedom*, p. 143.
36. In the Interim Government formed on 15 October 1946 the six members nominated by the Congress included by agreement a representative of the Scheduled Castes; the Muslim League being entitled to nominate five without restriction. See V.P. Menon, *The Transfer of Power in India*, pp. 315–16.

its own President, the Muslim, Maulana Azad, as one of its representatives to the Simla Conference 1945 being, in Jinnah's phrase, a 'symbolic affront' to which he retorted by publicly refusing to shake hands with the Maulana, an incident in itself indicative of the constraints deriving from concepts, in this case from the concept that the League represented *all* Muslims, and therefore by logical derivation that Muslims could represent only the League. But while such strict adherence to the implications of a two-nation theory may have been a handicap in negotiations, it did provide at once a *rationale* for intransigence and a base from which to withstand Congress and British pressures for concessions. A more consummate master of the art of political negation even than Carson,[37] Jinnah sought and succeeded, by negation, in ensuring that a transfer of power could take place only on the basis of a two-nation concept.

What validity did the concept possess? Were there two nations in India? Or, for that matter, in Ireland—even though there the doctrine was at no point formulated in all its uncompromising bleakness? Politics, not being a science, offers no answers demonstrably correct. But the questions none the less may be worth posing, if only for their implications. If it were proven, as it cannot be, that in either, or both cases, there were two nations, then, given the temper of twentieth-century nationalism, it would be reasonable to infer that there existed an in-built presumption of partition. If, in turn, that were so, then, to come back to a question posed earlier, it would be reasonable also to conclude that more conciliatory policies, or more understanding attitudes, on the part of the majority, were unlikely to conjure that second nation out of existence. If, on the other hand, it could be demonstrated that there existed not two nations but only majority and minority communities, then partition assumes the guise of an unnatural or contrived division and the burden of responsibility resting on all parties, and on the third by no means least, is correspondingly greater.

The position of the third party, the imperial power, differed

37. It is possibly not altogether coincidental that both were lawyers and that both made their early reputations as members of a minority, outside their later community homelands, Carson at the Irish Bar and as MP for Trinity College, Dublin, Jinnah in Bombay.

from the first and second in one very evident respect—it did not seek, it controlled, the levers of power. *Prima facie* in the exercise of that control it had, in accord with Tacitean precept, an interest initially in becoming, and then in continuing to be a third party, i.e. in creating a situation with partition potential—though by no means necessarily in partition since, when such control was about to be demitted, the balance of advantage might well incline otherwise and towards the constitution of a united, well-disposed successor state. For that, among other reasons, it is less than realistic to look for a consistent pattern of imperial policy, even in one particular triangular situation. An imperial government, unlike a national movement, is not primarily concerned to advance a cause, or bring about the realization of an ideal, but rather to guide and direct affairs in the light of its own pragmatic judgements upon its own best interests. The limitations upon its freedom of action, while very real, are thus ordinarily of a material kind, such as were imposed upon British governments by considerations of security in the Irish and of the world balance of power in the Indian cases; in both by the limits of Britain's military and economic resources; and by obligations assumed, or assurances given, as well as by past actions which had foreclosed otherwise possible options.

But ordinarily also an imperial power is not wholly free from constraints of an ideological or conceptual nature. In the British case, two such constraints may be mentioned. The first, general in its application, was Britain's commitment after the First World War to the idea of a Commonwealth of free and equal nations which progressively tended to limit, or preclude, courses of action inconsistent with its character or advancement. This was evident in the Irish and, of first importance in the Indian case. The second was altogether particular to the Anglo–Irish triangular relationship. It derived from an incident in domestic politics, the association of Whigs and Radicals with the Tories in order to defeat the First Home Rule Bill in 1886. That association was continued thereafter within the folds of a Unionist Party, predominantly Conservative, yet embracing those on the right and the left who had seceded from the Liberals on Home Rule. It was a party which, however adaptable in its responses to changing interests in other fields, had implicit in its very being one unchanging element—support for the Union. That was, in effect, written into its constitution, by virtue of its being the very occasion and bond of its existence. Since the party, with the aid of its in-built majority in the Lords, was in a position to determine Irish policy negatively, when not positively, from 1886 down to the Anglo–Irish settlement 1920-1, its conceptual commitment to the Union imposed a rigidity upon policy rare in the annals of modern British history.

Overall the third party, more particularly as the time of transfer—unwilled by it in the Irish but willed in the Indian case—approached, like the first and the second, one way or another also had limited grounds for manoeuvre—more limited, if I may anticipate my own conclusion, than Prime Ministers, Secretaries of State or Viceroys in the more specious of their utterances liked to suggest, their critics to suppose or historians in their later judgement to imply.

Beyond this, one might venture a general comment. In a triangular pre-transfer of power situation there is, all affinities supposed or actual apart, a tendency for the second and third parties, the minority and the outgoing imperial power, to be drawn together in resistance to the demands of the first, the majority Nationalist Party.[38] Indeed it is close to a law of politics. In part it may be explained in terms of near-coincidence in immediate interest, despite the difference in long-term aims. The imperial power, over and above an in-built and non-rational reluctance to depart, will almost certainly prefer, having rational regard to the safeguarding of its interests, a phased withdrawal, while the first aim of minority parties must be to delay the imperial departure until assured of the realization of their own concepts of their own future. All of these aspects were apparent, with one evident qualification, in the Anglo–Irish and Anglo–Indian situations.

In Ireland the association between the second, minority, party and the third, which for convenience is here termed the imperial power,[39] was manifestly a political factor of first importance, broad community of interests being reinforced by the bonds of kinship. It was not, however, a unifying factor in domestic politics, but, on the contrary, a source of deep party division, one of the great

38. This was evident also in Cyprus.
39. In Irish debates of the Asquith–Lloyd George era 'Imperial' Government (or Parliament) were terms in general use in this context.

English political parties, the Liberal Party from Gladstone to Asquith, being committed as a matter of principle to Home Rule for all Ireland—Asquith affirming in 1912 that 'Ireland is a nation, not two nations, but one nation'[40]—the other, the Unionist Party, to the maintenance of the Union and by necessary inference, to the defeat of Home Rule.

When in November 1911, Bonar Law took over the leadership of the Unionist Party, he reaffirmed this purpose, asserting specifically that he was not interested in the exclusion of Ulster, or some part of it, from the jurisdiction of a Dublin-dominated Home Rule Parliament, but with defeating Home Rule in the interests of the unity of Kingdom and Empire. He could imagine no lengths of resistance, so he declared in a long-reverberating, declamatory utterance at Blenheim on 29 July 1912, to which Ulster could go in such a cause, which he would not be prepared to support. But even in the passionate temper of pre-war politics, and despite the party's ideological commitment to the Union, the English Unionist leadership had perforce to recognize that the claim of a settler minority in northeast Ireland to impose a veto upon the constitutionally expressed wishes of more than three-quarters of the Irish people over an indefinite period of time was so obviously indefensible on ordinary democratic reckoning as to be a source of electoral weakness. With no little equivocation, the party leadership accordingly moved towards a more limited objective—that of ensuring that the minority in the North was excluded from the jurisdiction of a Home Rule Parliament, a course the more easily acquiesced in by reason of an assumption not confined to Unionists that, without Ulster, Home Rule was not viable and that therefore, through such exclusion, the Union might still be preserved. Under pressure of Covenanting campaigning, the threat of a revolt in Ulster, backed by unrelenting English Unionist pressure, the Liberal government yielded step by step and by the outbreak of war conceded the principle of exclusion for a period and for an area yet to be determined. The concession ensured the realization of the Ulster, but not of the English, Unionists' conceptual aim, the Ulstermen, having therewith implicitly established their contention that in Ireland they were not to be treated as a minority but a community apart without

---

40. Roy Jenkins, *Asquith* (London, 1964), p. 279.

thereby, however, in any way weakening, indeed if anything strengthening, the demand for Home Rule elsewhere in Ireland.

The postwar Government of Ireland Bill 1919, by making provision for a settlement on the basis of Home Rule for two parts of a divided Ireland, lent statutory substance to this concept of separateness. 'The new policy', noted Captain Wedgwood Benn in the debate on its second reading, 'is that Ireland is two nations'.[41] Lloyd George equivocated, observing 'Ulster is not a minority to be safeguarded. Ulster is an entity to be dealt with . . . . I am not now going to enter into the question of whether there is one nation or two nations . . . .'[42] The basis of the bill, however, was that Ireland was not one nation. For Ulstermen that sufficed. They had attained their immediate goal and their campaign against subjection to a Dublin-based Home Rule was crowned with success. Unqualified English Unionist backing of their cause at critical moments had been a condition of it. Indeed, it has been claimed that the outcome was, in a particular sense, the handiwork of one man, the Canadian, Andrew Bonar Law. But for his fundamental commitment to Ulster, concludes his biographer, Northern Ireland would not have assumed the form it did.[43] In its own important but limited sense, this is a reasonable contention. Nor is it unfitting. Bonar Law had backed Ulster for itself over and above the Unionist Party's wider purpose—defeating Home Rule—which Ulster's resistance was thought to serve; and though 'diehards' continued to feel bitter resentment at the abandonment of the Union as a whole even to safeguard the position of a cherished part, his was the decisive influence in persuading the main body of Unionists to see as a worthwhile end what had erstwhile been thought of as a means to an end. But form is not substance and the separation of the north-eastern counties from the rest of Ireland is hardly to be thought of as susceptible of explanation in personal terms.

The principle of division accepted, important subsidiary questions remained still open to debate. Chief among them were the area to be excluded and the period of its exclusion. The two were

41. H. of C. Deb., 29 March 1920, vol. 127, col. 1020.

42. Ibid., 31 March 1920, col. 1333.

43. Robert Blake, *The Unknown Prime Minister* (London, 1955). See especially his verdict on p. 531.

interrelated. In respect of area, the whole province of Ulster constituted a historic unit, but it held out no assurance of a settled Protestant majority. Equally, however, so Carson had protested in the aftermath of the 1916 Rising, the Ulster Unionists did not want 'bits of counties here and bits of counties there, a tessellated pavement with a bit in and a bit out', such as partition determined district by district by majority local allegiance would certainly have brought about. On the contrary they demanded a coherent, compact area of six counties. Earlier still, in 1912, an even more compact area of four counties had been proposed and the debate on the Government of Ireland Bill 1919 showed that this possibility had not been altogether forgotten.

Late that year, 1919, the Cabinet reviewed all of these possibilities—the exclusion of the whole of Ulster, of the six counties, or of an area more narrowly defined. But while such was the theoretical range of options before them, there was also the limiting factor that only the Ulster Unionists were willing, or in a position, to run the local, devolved administration that was contemplated in the draft bill. They had their own conditions for running it. Those conditions were firstly lasting exclusion and secondly, to ensure that, a strong preference, conveyed to the Cabinet in December 1919, which was tantamount in effect to a further condition, that the devolution scheme should be applied to what were termed the six Protestant counties, no more and no less.[44] That preference reflected, as Captain Craig later phrased it, an Ulster Unionist conviction that the best way to safeguard Ulster was 'to save as much as we knew we could hold. To try to hold more . . . would seem an act of gross folly on our part.'[45] The Cabinet, despite some lingering glances at the possibility either of excluding all Ulster or of plebiscites, acceded to Ulster Unionist wishes. The upshot was the partitioning of Ireland in such a way that the exclusion of the Unionist minority from an all-Ireland polity created a new Nationalist minority, much smaller in total certainly, but near-identical in its one-third proportion to that Unionist minority which was now to become a majority.

About this Lloyd George made two points in the course of the

44. Cab. 27/68 (15 and 19 December).
45. H. of C. Deb., vol. 127, col. 992.

later negotiations on the Anglo–Irish Treaty. The first was on area: 'The real unit', he told the Irish delegates,

was Ulster. It was an old province and a recognized unity ... but it was felt to be handing over a large Catholic population to the control of the Protestants. There was almost an agreement for the partition of Ulster. Therefore we had to get a new unit ... on the whole, the six-county area had been acceptable to the Nationalists as preferable to a new delimitation of Ulster. True, if you took a plebiscite of Tyrone and Fermanagh, there would be a Catholic majority. ... The alternative would have been a Boundary Commission. There would then have been a more overwhelmingly Protestant majority. In order to persuade Ulster to come in there is an advantage in her having a Catholic population.

The second was on the attitude of the Cabinet to partition. 'We stand neutral,' he said. 'That would be useful', retorted Gavan Duffy, 'if you had not created a partition Parliament.'[46]

On the first point made by the Prime Minister one may reflect that the Ulster Unionists understood better what they had caused to be done than Lloyd George who did it; on the second, one may note that it elicited a realistic comment from a representative of the first party on the advantage to the second of getting matters settled before the withdrawal of the third. So it was that, in the case of Northern Ireland, Jinnah's dream—divide and depart,[47] in that order with the frontiers settled in accord with minority views— was realized. By way of even better measure, as an inducement to the minority to acquiesce in an all-Ireland superstructure, there was acceptance of the principle of parity of representation between minority and majority on the proposed Council of Ireland, a fact which, as Asquith noted, was calculated in itself to weight the scales against the unity the Council was ostensibly designed to promote. And yet, underlying the settlement, there was an assumption in which Jinnah could not have acquiesced. It was, that seems clear from Cabinet records, that partition, in the majority Cabinet view, was a temporary expedient rather than a lasting division, it being expressly recorded therein that the unity of Ireland was the

46. Thomas Jones, *Whitehall Diary*, ed. K. Middlemas (3 vols.: Oxford, 1969–71), vol. III, p. 131.

47. In the Irish case it was the Dublin Castle administration that departed; the sovereignty of Westminster, despite devolution, remaining unimpaired in the six counties.

long-term aim.[48] That was not consistent with a concept of two nations, but rather of one that was temporarily divided. The definition of the Irish Free State as initially co-terminous with the whole of Ireland in the subsequently negotiated Anglo–Irish Treaty indicated the same line of thinking.

The first part of the Irish settlement, the Government of Ireland Act 1920, was determined by two sides of the Irish triangle, the British and the Ulster Unionists, the second at one remove so to speak, there being in Lloyd George's later excusing phrase no one to negotiate with on the third, the Nationalist side, with Sinn Fein in revolt. In December of the following year the second part of it, the Anglo–Irish Treaty 1921, was negotiated again by two of the three, but a different two, Sinn Fein and the British government. The former knew what they wanted, an all-Ireland republic, but had not defined, short of that, what they might settle for; the latter had obtained in Northern Ireland one long-standing objective, the safeguarding of the position of the minority to which they were committed and with it the substance of their own security interest. For the rest, despite much that has been written in praise of Lloyd George's dexterity and statesmanship, they relied amid many postwar preoccupations upon repression and improvisation. A dominion settlement emerged; it did not, however, as might reasonably be, and often is, inferred, represent the fulfilment of a settled British policy. Far from it: members of the Cabinet long continued to contemplate a Home Rule settlement on the basis of the 1920 Act. When they were informed in December 1920 that very little was known about the provisions of the 1920 Act in the area described in that Act, as Southern Ireland, they found themselves in general agreement that steps should be taken to remedy this by giving it the widest possible publicity there.[49] Since the only hope of a settlement with Sinn Fein was to let assuaging oblivion close over the provisions of an Act which had partitioned Ireland, fell far short of dominion status, and indeed conceded rather more modest powers than earlier Home Rule Bills to the parliaments it proposed to constitute, this unconscious essay in irony, while undermining Cabinet credibility, serves more

48. Cab. 23/18, C. 16(19).
49. Cab. 23/23, 81(120), 30 December 1920.

importantly to dispel illusions of calculated Georgian (or other) dominion design. The historical evidence, indeed, suggests that, not for the first or last time in Irish affairs, events shaped policy; not policy the sequence of events. All important in that unfolding story was the fact that the course pursued involved warfare, at once of a seemingly self-defeating kind—the advice tendered by the British Commander-in-Chief in Ireland, Sir Neville Macready, to his political masters having as a recurrent theme: 'Whatever we do we are sure to be wrong'[50]—and of a character that psychologically ran counter to the concept of Commonwealth. Both were by 1920–1 unacceptable to opinion at home where popular British conviction, almost irrespective of party, of the outstanding success, first in peace and then in war, of a Commonwealth deriving from classical liberal approaches to Empire,[51] in fact propelled the man, who had dismissed Asquithian notions of a dominion settlement in Ireland with 'Whoever heard such nonsense?', towards a dominion settlement. It was not Lloyd George who changed the contours of the Irish question, but the widening contours of the Irish question that changed Lloyd George.

In the springtime of 1921 when Lloyd George became so suddenly converted to a dominion status solution, he had reason to be sensitive to dominion views on the Irish question, as also to dominion precedents. There was an Imperial Conference about to foregather in London and its first meeting was held in the Cabinet Room at 10 Downing Street on 20 June.[52] It was there, too, on 14 July 1921 that Lloyd George had his first meeting with de Valera. His secretary had never seen him so excited, 'bringing up all his guns', as she put it, with a big map of the British empire hung up on the wall, 'great blotches of red all over it'. When de Valera came in, Lloyd George pointed with studied deliberation to the chairs around the table at which the dominion leaders sat at the Imperial

50. Quoted in C. Townshend, *The British Campaign in Ireland 1919–1921*, p. 178.

51. Austen Chamberlain's (leader of the Unionist Party during Bonar Law's illness) sharing of it was of particular importance in the course of the Irish negotiations.

52. The conference continued in session till 5 August 1921. Had it still been in session in December the climax of Anglo–Irish negotiations might have been otherwise in character, if not in substance.

Conference—there were Hughes and Massey from Australia and New Zealand; there was Meighen, the representative of English and French united in one dominion; there was Smuts symbolizing the reconciliation of Boer and Briton within the Union. Lloyd George then looked long and fixedly at the remaining chair. De Valera remained silent, so Lloyd George had to tell him the chair was for Ireland. 'All we ask you to do is to take your place in this sisterhood of free nations'.[53] By December, after protracted negotiations, invitation had been superseded by insistence, backed by the threat of force, on free association.

With the dominion settlement of 1921, Unionism in England, though not in Ulster, had lost its *raison d'être*. Conservatism re-emerged as ex-Unionists ensured that Lloyd George never should. Even so, it now appears that Lloyd George, as Liberal leader of a predominantly Unionist Cabinet and sensitive to the Unionist majority in Parliament, overestimated the rigidity of their views on Union—or, alternatively, underestimated his own freedom of manoeuvre in negotiation. He was not only a prisoner, as he was apt himself to say, of the Coalition, but also in some measure, as were many of his colleagues, constrained by memories of the passionate prewar Anglo–Irish past.

In respect of substance, the 1920-Anglo–Irish Settlement had one aspect, so evident as to be deserving of comment, only because in subsequent years it was apt to be glossed over. It was that no reduction in the number of parties involved was achieved as a result of it. They remained as before, their conceptual approaches fundamentally unchanged, though now there were two sovereign states and a subordinate government, where there had been a sovereign state, a national movement and a minority resistant to it. The imperial government retained unimpaired in all respects its sovereignty in one part of Ireland. With demission of power to an Irish state there had not, therefore, come demission of all its Irish

53. The arrangements for the meeting are recorded in extracts from Miss Stevenson's diary reprinted in Lord Beaverbrook, *The Decline and Fall of Lloyd George* (London, 1963), pp. 85–6. The account of the interview, at which Miss Stevenson was not present, is much later recollected by President de Valera. He seemed retrospectively well pleased at not having asked the question expected of him!

responsibility—but, on the contrary, the contingent possibility of its again becoming exacting in yet another triangular context.

In terms of negotiating procedures and priorities the Treaty has two points of interest. To those who entertained the concept of Ireland as a nation, there ought not to have been, as there was not, a third party to negotiations for an Anglo–Irish settlement. For them third-party presence would have been a liability, and as such was to be avoided, as a matter of tactics. 'Nothing,' de Valera told General Smuts on 6 July 1921, 'could come from a conference of the three parties.' The two principals should discuss their differences, including Ulster, and then treat with the minority. In a sense he had his way. The Ulstermen were off-stage during the negotiations that led to the Treaty, but as they already had in substance what they wanted their presence might only have served to reopen negotiations on what they had obtained. From the Irish point of view, therefore, the negotiating advantages of the absence of a third party, in this context the Ulster Unionists, was counterbalanced by the practical disadvantage of their having obtained prior settlement of their claims.

De Valera's misgivings about triangular exchanges were shared to the full by Gandhi, though the Gandhian and Valeran notions of the third party—that the party that was *de trop*—differed, the British filling that unenviable role in the first instance, the Ulstermen in the second. The difference was accounted for by the fact that, whereas de Valera thought of an Anglo–Irish settlement as something to be negotiated overall between Britain and Ireland, Gandhi believed that the British should first quit India, leaving it to the Congress, the League, the Princes and representatives of other minorities to make a settlement thereafter.

Behind such differences in tactical approaches, however, and in part explaining them, was the fundamental difference in the position of the imperial power in Ireland and in India. In the latter, as distinct from the former, it was their declared, though far from universally credited, intent to go. What had to be decided was the nature and timing of their departure—both important matters certainly, but not quite on the same plane of importance as intent. On timing, Gandhi's view ran counter to that of successive British governments, which was that the British should defer departure until agreement had been reached between parties, communities and classes in India. In the thirties, when the diehards in opposition to the Government of India Bill, itself essentially a temporizing device behind its impressive federal façade, apparently saw little inconsistency in championing the cause of the minorities, the illiterate masses and the outcastes, while at the same time seeking to muster 'a solid phalanx of Rolls Royce rajahs'[54] as a barrier, first to the advance and then to the entrenchment of a Congress raj, attitudes uninhibitedly taken up by, but by no means confined exclusively to, the extreme right, seemed to indicate, and not only to Gandhi, that an interpretation might be placed on British responsibilities, which would afford reason for them to stay for ever. In the Congress–British dialectic of the early war years a situation thus developed in which Gandhi became the more insistent that the departure of the British, the third party, was an essential condition precedent to settlement with the second; whereas in the predominant British view agreement within India remained a condition of Indian political advance—the Secretary of State, Lord Zetland, in February 1940 advising his Cabinet colleagues, 'we must insist on an agreement of all the parties concerned as an essential condition of progress'[55] of which he [Lord Zetland] in constitutional terms declared himself to be in favour. It was, however, a condition which rendered such progress unlikely, since it made any advance on the part of the majority dependent upon the concurrence, not only of the Muslims, but of other and smaller minorities as well. Moreover, not quite all members of the Cabinet entertained the Secretary of State's notion of the conciliatory role properly to be played by the third party. On the contrary, the First Lord of the Admiralty commented that he 'did not share the anxiety to encourage unity between the Hindu and Moslem communities', their communal feud being 'a bulwark of British rule in India.'[56]

Some two years later the First Lord, now Prime Minister and at the pinnacle of his power and prestige, in an extempore outburst startled a distinguished Indian representative to the War Cabinet, Ramaswami Mudaliar, coming to London hopefully to hear about

54. The phrase is used by R.J. Moore, in *The Crisis of Indian Unity 1917–1940*, p. 137.
55. Cab. 65/5 30 [(40) 4 2 February] 1940.
56. Ibid.

'progress', by telling him that he (Churchill) was not in the mood to conciliate Indian nationalism, but rather to tell the world of the benefits of imperial rule.[57] For eighty years, he continued, while America had a civil war, Russia its revolutions, China had been torn to pieces, India, thanks to British rule, had uninterrupted peace and even now, he concluded in a splendid climax, 'an Indian maid with bangles on can travel from Travancore to Punjab all alone without fear of molestation . . . in this country today . . . our Wrens and Waafs cannot go two miles with the same feeling of safety'. The Viceroy found Mudaliar's report of the conversation 'most entertaining'. He could afford to. Delhi was seven thousand miles from Downing Street—and even so his successor, Wavell, had cause to develop sensitivity to Churchillian reverberations resounding over the wires from the remote source of imperial authority. Close at hand, in the War Cabinet, the prospect of them, so L.S. Amery as Secretary of State allowed, sufficed to discourage all large-scale discussion of India's future.

When set out in more temperate terms the essence of the matter, as seen by the third party from Whitehall, differed in one important respect, that of intention to go, as Churchill himself was soon perforce to acknowledge, but not greatly in regard to the role of the communal factor in determining the time of departure. Rather was it the difficulty of determining what Indian government or governments would be capable of taking over power when it was transferred. In February that year, however, C.R. Attlee recommended the sending out to India of some person of high standing to negotiate a settlement. He claimed that there was precedent for such action in Lord Durham's mission to Canada.[58] Cripps was chosen or chose himself—it is not quite clear which—to fill that role and he took with him to India two months later a draft declaration which indicated, first, that the War Cabinet was working within a Commonwealth concept and, secondly, and not only to Congress, that by conceding the right of non-accession and the formation, should provinces seizing advantage of that right

---

57. *India: The Transfer of Power 1942–47*, vol. III, no. 2. By contrast with Churchill, Amery felt himself to be a man of liberal views on Indian policy. Not many in India shared that opinion.

58. Ibid., vol. I, no. 60.

so desire, of a separate Union, they were opening the way to partition before the transfer of power. R.A. Butler remarked upon the impression created by the declaration, 'the unity of India—the goal of British policy hitherto—must be set aside',[59] while Field Marshal Smuts, in whose memory I am honoured to give this lecture, the theme of which I venture to believe would have been of much interest to him, mindful of earlier events which fell within the astonishing range of his experience, immediately seized upon the significance of what was apparently about to be conceded. 'Express opening left for partition', he cabled Churchill, 'may be taken as a British invitation or incitement to partition. . . . It may be argued that Irish tactics of partition is [sic] once more followed. . . .' and he expressed his misgivings lest this should prejudice prospects of settlement with the majority.[60] For once he was vouchsafed no reply. But Churchill found further occasion to remind another dominion war-leader, Mackenzie King of Canada, that the question to be resolved was not one between the British government and India 'but between different sects or nations in India itself . . . : the Moslems, a hundred millions, declare they will insist upon Pakistan, i.e. a sort of Ulster in the North.'[61] There was in any case no reassurance to be given to Smuts since, if British governments continued, as they did, to abide by the view that agreement between the first and second parties was a condition precedent to their own departure, they could not, if indeed they were to go, continue to exclude the one condition, partition, on which the second, minority party, expressed willingness to come to an agreement with the first party. That was the third party's dilemma—none the less so for being of their own making. Their freedom of action was restricted by the commitments into which their predecessors had entered and themselves endorsed. In view of those commitments they felt they could not honourably, had they wished— which they did not—and all other considerations aside, contemplate a transfer of power to the majority without minority concurrence.

On the failure of the Cripps mission Churchill was well content to let the problem rest precisely at that point—and when in 1944 the Viceroy proposed a less passive role, the Prime Minister

59. Ibid., no. 255.
60. Ibid., no. 244.
61. Ibid., no. 346.

delivered the magisterial rebuke: 'These very large problems require to be considered at leisure and best of all in victorious peace.'[62] Peace came and Churchill went. What further action within possible limits was to be taken? The British raj was running down; the higher echelons of its services were disillusioned and dispirited—this was a recurrent theme of Wavell's reports as Viceroy—the time had come when it was in British interests, over and above being in conformity with Britain's long-declared intent, to go. The Australian, Richard Casey, for a time Governor of Bengal, with a fresh eye on the scene, was an early advocate of departure in accord with a fixed timetable such as was subsequently adopted by Attlee's Labour administration. Transfer power to one successor, he urged, but if that is not possible, then to two. The advice he tendered stemmed from a conviction that

the demands of Hindus and Muslims have now crystallized into irreconcilability—an All-India unitary government on the one hand and the two-nation theory on the other—centripetal, and centrifugal. . . . I fail to see how we can influence the outcome one way or the other . . . . We can give the Indians independence but we cannot give them unity. I would believe that we have to be completely neutral as between All-India on the one hand and Hindustan and Pakistan on the other.[63]

'Neutral'—the very word used to describe the position of the imperial government on the selfsame issue by Lloyd George to the Irish delegates in 1921.

But in the event it was questionably so. First the Cabinet mission sent to India by the Labour government, in a statement of 16 May 1946, commented upon and expressly rejected the proposal which the League had submitted to them for 'a separate and fully independent sovereign state of Pakistan.'[64] This elicited its inevitable sharp reaction from the League and its leader. Muslims had no intention, so the League declared, of substituting Caste Hindu for British domination. Any attempt to impose majority rule, threatened Jinnah in March 1947, while the leaders of post-colonial Asia were foregathering at the Asian Relations Conference in Delhi, would

62. Ibid., vol. V, no. 111.
63. Ibid, no. 91.
64. Reprinted in Mansergh (ed.) *Documents and Speeches on British Commonwealth Affairs*, vol. II, pp. 644–52.

lead to the bloodiest civil war in the history of the continent. It was a possibility few at the Conference were disposed to discount. With seemingly no peaceful alternative to partition thus remaining, the prospect of it had perforce to be faced and a territorial basis for partition to be determined. Here the League's own arguments for the partition of India, on the grounds of the existence within it of two nations, were turned against it by Lord Mountbatten, the last Viceroy, with the consequence that the Pakistan of Jinnah's initial territorial claims, namely of the whole of Muslim-majority provinces, the majority of whose Muslims opted for Pakistan—a curious contention this—was excluded and in its place there was to be a Pakistan with frontiers in the Punjab and Bengal to be determined by boundary commissions in the light of the 'nationhood' of the population. This meant a Pakistan confined to Muslim-majority areas, or what a Governor of the Punjab had indeed earlier described as 'true' as distinct from 'crude' Pakistan,[65] but what Jinnah had hitherto discounted as 'truncated' or 'moth-eaten' Pakistan, but which none the less, if only by reason of the conceptual realization of aim which it represented, he was in no position to reject.

Partition in India even though on the basis of delimitation by district was bound to, and did, bring into existence new minorities. By some, such minorities had been thought of as assurances of good behaviour. If there are to be separate Muslim states, Chaudhri Khaliq-uz-zaman, the local Muslim League leader, had earlier told the Governor of the United Provinces, they must have plenty of Hindus in them to provide an insurance against the Muslims of Oudh being maltreated by the majority community there.[66] In cruder terms the minorities were spoken of as hostages: in the crudest the phrase was murder for murder. Out of this sentiment of 'hostages and retaliation' which he thought 'barbarous' there flowed in Azad's opinion, 'the rivers of blood' that followed upon partition.[67]

Important in the contriving of the Indian settlement was accord in the last phase between the first and third parties, i.e. the Congress

65. *India: The Transfer of Power 1942–47*, vol. VI, nos. 29 and 51.
66. Ibid., no. 327.
67. A.K. Azad, *India Wins Freedom*, p. 198. See also, p. 210.

and the British—an accord which reflected something more than mutual understanding at the highest level during the period of the Mountbatten Viceroyalty, though it may be that even the staunchest of Congress leaders were that much the more ready to hold the cup of conciliation to the lips of high station. Its all-important outcome was the recognition, painful on the part of Congress, regretful on the part of the British Cabinet and Viceroy, of the absence by that time of a practical alternative to the partitioning of India. The consequence was partition effected with the assent of the majority party, Gandhi on a day of silence indicating his acquiescence,[68] Vallabhbhai Patel allowing 'whether we liked it or not, there were two nations in India', Maulana Azad being left alone in counselling deferment in the hope, albeit forlorn, of unity;[69] as well as of the minority party, Jinnah being committed by the concept he had advanced and the tactics he had otherwise so successfully pursued, to accept the truncated Pakistan he had a year previously deemed non-viable. The basis for the transfer of power once again was dominion status, but by free choice of those to whom power was being transferred, coupled with a sense on the British side of satisfying realization of their view of a right post-imperial relationship.

The role of the third party in Ireland and in India indicates near-identity in the issues demanding policy decisions of it and some marked discrepancies in its making of them. Thus, in respect of Ireland the tactical decision was taken to make a settlement with the minority before making one with the majority; in India the settlement was made with majority and minority leaders simul-taneously, i.e. an overall settlement as against one in two stages. In Ireland the boundaries of the area to be excluded were determined in accord with the wishes of the minority, the possibility of reference to a Boundary Commission (which met but proved abortive) being extended later; in India by boundary commissions making recommendations in the light of the 'national' allegiance of the inhabitants by district, and not by province as desired by the minority, at the time of transfer. In both cases the settlement

68. A. Campbell-Johnson, *Mission with Mountbatten* (London, 1951), p. 101.

69. A.K. Azad, *India Wins Freedom*, pp. 183–90.

was in principal part, or wholly, on a dominion basis; but in the one case acceptance was obtained under threat of renewal of military action, in the other by free volition of the parties concerned.

In all of these matters it may at first sight appear that the imperial government adopted different courses, in the second, Indian, case because of awareness of the unsatisfactory nature or vulnerability to criticism, as reflected in Smuts's comments in 1942, of that pursued in the first, the Irish. No doubt there was the element of experience gained, or lessons learned. But more important were the constraints of past commitments or political circumstances determining the outcome, chief among them being the fact that in India the British government ·was itself pledged to withdraw, whereas in Ireland it had such intent only in a qualified Home Rule form, and with one-party backing. Yet what was most important applied to both, it was a lack of commitment to majority rule, counterbalancing in its binding force the commitments to minorities.

In this lecture I have sought to approach large and debatable historical questions not, as is traditional, in terms of unity forfeited or federation failed—and even federations that failed appear to have an irresistible fascination for many imperial or Commonwealth historians almost as though they carried an in-built presumption or even entitlement to success—but rather in the conceptual contexts in which partition was effected. In those contexts, there is a sufficiency of features in Irish and Indian experience to suggest that in a triangular situation with partition coincidental in time with a transfer of power, there is something in the nature of a partitioning paradigm, with the strategy and tactics of each party in each case in significant, though not uniform, measure conditioned by it. This would seem to suggest that conventional assessments of the interplay of men and events, and of the extent to which there was freedom of manoeuvre as the time neared, may need downward adjustment. By contrast, such comparative analysis suggests that the importance of concepts in the determining or predetermining of policy needs to be revised sharply upwards. There were in varying degrees conceptual imperatives for all of the parties concerned in Ireland and in India, which, once formulated and receiving popular sanction, imposed rigorous constraints upon the freedom of action even of the most powerful of political leaders. This was especially true of majority parties with their twin objectives of independence and unity and who, in India as in Ireland, when the moment of choice came opted for independence. Yet the outlook of both was conditioned by their sense that partition was not a political device but a moral wrong, to Redmond a 'blasphemy'; to Gandhi a 'sin'.[70] Were concessions to be made, recognition to be given to what was iniquitous?—for twentieth-century nationalism thought in such terms where the eighteenth-century enlightenment, affronted by the cynicism of a great power partition, condemned a lapse below what was permissible by civilized standards of international behaviour. But the determining influence of concept applies no less forcibly to minorities who rightly, or mistakenly, are persuaded that their very survival is threatened by subjection to what Jinnah termed the will of a 'brute' majority, not of their own, but of those they deem to be an alien people, and their only safeguard to be found in the uncompromising affirmation and reaffirmation of their separate identity.

How and why such concepts of community or nation came to be expressed and popularly endorsed in the forms in which they were, thus becomes something of enhanced historical importance and something also which may be illumined by comparative analysis over and above study in isolation. Did they spring spontaneously from the authentic aspirations of peoples? Or were they in the first instance, at any rate in their more forceful formulations, tactical devices, of which later their devisers became prisoners?[71] That is one question that arises, and to answer it requires a study of both policy motivation at a high level and also case studies in the evolution of regional and local opinion, especially in rural Ireland and in the million villages of the Indian subcontinent, where causes once adopted might be held to with a tenacity little understood by sophisticated dwellers of the capitals. Another question is the nature of the influence, whether inevitably by reason of the circumstances, or deliberately, exercised by the imperial power either over a long period in the bringing into being a situation, in which partition

---

70. *India: The Transfer of Power 1942–47*, vol. VII, no. 47.

71. See Anil Seal's comment on Jinnah 'hoist with his own petard of Pakistan' in *Locality, Province and Nation: Essays in Indian Politics 1870–1914*, ed. J. Gallagher, G. Johnson and A. Seal (Cambridge, 1973), p. 24.

becomes the only road out or, in a later phase, in determining how and to whom power should be demitted on its withdrawal. In our own age in a Rhodesian setting, imperial policy was formulated in terms of no independence before majority rule, NIB-MAR. But in Ireland and in India the formulation of policy was otherwise—it was in effect NIBMIR, no independence before minority rule or, to be exact, self-rule was assured. Did the difference reflect only differences in circumstances? Or was there also in the light of intervening Commonwealth experience a change of mind?

Behind these particular questions lie others of wider relevance and likely to arise in all areas where majority rule, developing minority nationalism, or the purposes of devolution are living issues. They relate to the nature of nationhood itself and allow of specific formulation. Is there, in respect of nationhood, such a thing as a geographical imperative? How is a second nation within what has been a single state to be identified? How is the authenticity of its nationhood to be established? Can the third party in this analytical enquiry, the imperial power, by its policies and actions, nourish a second nation into existence? Can the first party, the Nationalist majority, by understanding and restraint—or for that matter by force—conjure or frighten it out of existence? Or does its life come from within? Contention and polemics have been a setting in which such questions, understandably emotional in their context, have been approached. But analysis, sparing in judgement, may also have a contribution of its own to make. After all for many men and women it has been a matter of life and death that the answers to all such questions should be as nearly right as lies in human power to give them. While it has been the case that from most partitions the 'untold' sufferings which an Austrian Empress forecast[72] of one of them have followed, yet there have been

---

72. Diderot in St Petersburg in November 1773 in his *Entretiens avec Catherine II* shared Maria Theresa's forebodings, observing that '*nous ne doutons pas que le partage de ce mouton ne devienne un jour la source d'une longue querelle entre les trois loups . . .*' ['we do not doubt that the division of this sheep may one day become the source of a long quarrel between the three wolves. . .'—Ed.] but mindful no doubt of his imperial patroness, went on to express the reassuring view that it was Austria that would pay the price. *Oeuvres politiques*, ed. Paul Vernière (Paris, 1963), pp. 261–2.

perceptible differences in degree and statesmen may do well to study the signposts leading to partition, and the actual timing and process of past partitions, the better to mitigate the consequences of such as may not by understanding or foresight be averted. More particularly in that category of partition of which this lecture treats, it seems that the time of choice comes early, while two communities stand side by side and, despite illusions that continue to be entertained, is likely to be past, short of the use of force, once they stand face to face.

# 2

# The Cripps Mission to India,
# March–April 1942*

At the outbreak of the Second World War the provisions of the Government of India Act, 1935, relating to the provinces of British India had taken effect, elections had been held, and as a result there were Congress ministries in several provinces. But the conditions prescribed by the Act for parallel advance at the centre had not been fulfilled, with the result that the Viceroy remained at the head of government, responsible indeed through the Secretary of State for India to the British Parliament, but not responsible to any Indian assembly. In September 1939, the Viceroy acted, therefore, in accord with the existing constitutional system in declaring, on instructions from London and without consulting with Indian political leaders, that India was at war though whether his action,

'On 22 March Cripps left for India and a new chapter opened.
The Cripps Mission coincided in time with the crisis of the War in South-East Asia. Singapore had fallen on 15 February, Rangoon on 8 March, the North-Eastern Provinces of British India were threatened with actual invasion and the whole country was overshadowed by the possibility of it. These dangers were reflected in the reports of Governors to the Viceroy (e.g. nos. 322 and 651) and were a constant preoccupation of the Government of India and the War Cabinet in London. Nor did they provide only the background to the Cripps Mission; they played at one remove a central part in his discussions with Indian leaders on responsibility for defence.' N. Mansergh and E.W.R. Lumby (eds.), *India: The Transfer of Power 1942–47* (London, HMSO, 1970–83), vol. 1, p. xiii.

even taking into account dominant British views at the time, was also in accord with the dictates of political wisdom is altogether more debatable. Certainly the commitment of India to war without reference to Indian leaders, not least by underlining the disparities in status between India and the dominions, so evidently free to decide whether or not to go to war, caused the deepest resentment, especially in Congress India.

India unfree, rejoined the Congress, could not fight for freedom. In December 1939 the Congress provincial ministries resigned on the issue of non-cooperation in the war, while the Muslim League, rejoicing in their departure, moved on towards the so-called Pakistan resolution at Lahore in March 1940. In August that same year, the Viceroy communicated what is generally known as the August Offer, in which the position of the British government on two main points was made clear. The first was in respect of minorities where the statement declared that the British government could not contemplate the transfer of their existing responsibilities to any system of government whose authority was directly denied 'by large and powerful elements in India's national life', and the second that when the appropriate time came after the war, the British government would do what it could, consistent with its existing obligations, to bring into being a representative constituent body in India to frame India's new constitution in accord with dominion precedent and opening the way to the attainment by India 'of that free and equal partnership in the British Commonwealth which remains the proclaimed and accepted goal of the Imperial Crown and of the British Parliament'.[1]

The August Offer, giving qualified encouragement to Muslim separatism as implicit in the concept of Pakistan and being for that reason in itself unacceptable to the Congress, was rejected by them out of hand because what it offered was relegated to the comparatively remote future, conditional, and hedged about *inter alia* with allusions to the British Commonwealth, membership of which in its contemporary dominion form was thought to fall significantly short of the *Purna Swaraj*, or full independence, demanded by the Congress. The Offer, and the reaction to it, in brief suggested that there would be no meeting of minds between the British

1. United Kingdom, *Parliamentary Papers*, 1940, Cmd. 6219.

government and the Congress on the constitutional question, least of all in a Dominion-Commonwealth setting.

Such in outline was the nature of the Indian deadlock when the Japanese struck at Pearl Harbour. The attack sharply accentuated the already very real importance of India to Britain and the allied cause and accordingly it was not surprising that there was an attempt to break the deadlock. The purpose of this essay is not to describe that attempt in the round but to consider only the Commonwealth context to that attempt in the light of the recently published British official records, partly because of its own intrinsic interest and partly because of the light it may throw upon British thinking about the Commonwealth at that time, including India's possible place in it. To avoid risk of historical distortion it should be understood that there is no implied question that the aspect on which attention is focused was necessarily the most important of the enterprise.

The official record relevant to this purpose begins on 19 December 1941 after Churchill had left for Washington—which may itself have had its significance—when Ernest Bevin at a meeting of the War Cabinet spoke of anxiety about the situation in India in respect both of defence and of the constitutional position and thought it might be desirable to have a general discussion of it at the earliest opportunity.[2] On 1 January 1942 there followed a move from another quarter. On that day a group of distinguished Indian moderates, led by Sir Tej Bahadur Sapru sent an appeal to Churchill to break the constitutional deadlock in India by 'some bold stroke' of 'farsighted statesmanship'. What they asked for especially was a declaration from London that India should no longer be treated as a dependency, but that henceforth its constitutional position and powers should be identical with those of the other units of the British Commonwealth. On 7 January, Churchill, in Washington, warned his colleagues by telegram of the danger of raising the constitutional issue when the enemy was on the frontier.[3] The Indian liberals, he remarked, not without justice, 'though plausible

2. *Constitutional Relations between Britain and India: The Transfer of Power 1942–47.* I. *The Cripps Mission.* Edited by N. Mansergh and E.W.R. Lumby (London, 1970). All subsequent references are to documents in this volume.

3. Ibid., no. 6.

have never been able to deliver the goods', and as a result constitutional change meant inevitably the approach of the Congress to power. 'The Indian troops are fighting splendidly, but it must be remembered that their allegiance is to the King Emperor, and that the rule of the Congress and the Hindoo Priesthood machine would never be tolerated by a fighting race.' Less romanticized but equally clear opposition to any fresh initiative came from the Viceroy on 21 January: '. . . we should stand firm', he wrote,[4] 'and make no further move', his chief argument against such a move being that India was 'hopelessly, and I suspect irremediably split by racial and religious divisions which . . . become more acute as any real transfer of power by us draws nearer.' The Secretary of State concurred. In a paper submitted to the War Cabinet on 28 January he analysed the Indian political scene in these words:

The political deadlock in India today is concerned, ostensibly, with the transfer of power from British to Indian hands. In reality it is mainly concerned with the far more difficult issue of what Indian hands, what Indian Government or Governments, are capable of taking over without bringing about general anarchy or even civil war.[5]

Dominion status in Statute of Westminster terms remained the British goal, but to give effect to it there must be, in the British view, a measure of agreement in India about the succession to power which was altogether lacking.

It was at this juncture when inaction was commended as the higher wisdom, that the lessons of Canadian and Commonwealth experiences were deployed to question the premises on which such conclusions rested. It was Clement Attlee, the Lord Privy Seal, who appealed to them. On 24 January 1942 he wrote to L.S. Amery at the India Office, in manuscript, saying: 'It is worth considering whether someone should not be charged with a mission to try to bring the [Indian] political leaders together.'[6] On 2 February he followed this up in a memorandum[7] submitted to the War Cabinet: 'While I have little or no faith in the value of "gestures" ', he wrote, 'I do consider that now is the time for an act of statesmanship. To

4. Ibid., no. 23.
5. Ibid., no. 43.
6. Ibid., no. 35.
7. Ibid., no. 60.

mark time is to lose India.' There were, he thought, two practical alternatives. The first was to entrust some person of high standing with wide powers to negotiate a settlement, and the second to bring the Indians over to London to discuss a settlement there. He favoured the former. 'There is', he said, 'precedent for such action. Lord Durham saved Canada to the British Empire. We need a man to do in India what Durham did in Canada.'

For many years in lectures I had remarked upon the similarities between the Durham and Cripps Missions both in respect of the undertakings in themselves and, more especially, of the personalities of the two missionaries. Both were radical in their politics and uncomfortable as colleagues; and their respective prime ministers accordingly were well pleased to see them depart to distant places upon doubtful enterprises. But it had not occurred to me, though on reflection it is obvious enough, that the second mission derived conceptually directly from the first. Few things, indeed, more strikingly illustrate the depth of the dominion tradition or the pull of Commonwealth in the thinking of British statesmen than that what Durham did in Canada should serve, just over a century later, as a prototype for what Cripps might do in India.

The official records do not reveal the personal discussions that must have proceeded between 24 January when Attlee first proposed that a mission be sent and 9 March when the Cabinet was apparently in general agreement that Cripps should go. Cripps himself had returned from the embassy at Moscow only on 23 January. What the War Cabinet conclusions of 9 March record is the prime minister's view that in the circumstances 'the right course was to accept the very generous offer made by the Lord Privy Seal to visit India and discuss matters with the leaders of the main Indian political parties.'[8] What was, however, abundantly clear was that Cripps was going, not only wearing the mantle of Durham, but carrying with him a draft declaration for discussion with the Indian leaders, which contemplated, albeit after the war, a dominion

---

Mansergh comments that this is a judgement which little accords with the opinions of some younger historians, to which he was not among the rush of converts.

8. Ibid., no. 282.

settlement for India. In that sense also this was, therefore, a Commonwealth mission.

The draft declaration had been the subject of intensive consideration by the India Committee of the Cabinet and the War Cabinet itself. It started from the hopeful premise that the declaration should be a very short, simple document, drawn in perfectly explicit language, and not open to argument, and was at one point associated, not least in the mind of the prime minister, with the idea of a tremendous Churchillian broadcast to the Indian people expounding its purposes as then conceived.[9] The prospect so disturbed the Viceroy that he submitted his resignation.[10] The idea of the broadcast lapsed, but debate upon the terms of the declaration was intensified. One matter at issue was very relevant to the theme of this essay. It concerned the entitlement of the future Indian union, which it was bound to bring into existence, to secede from the Commonwealth. In an earlier version[11] of the draft the sentence on this point read, quite explicitly: 'The object is the creation of a new Indian Union which shall constitute a Dominion, equal in every respect to the United Kingdom and the other Dominions of the empire, and free to remain in or to separate itself from the equal partnership of the British Commonwealth of Nations.' Amery was concerned *inter alia* to add to this the substance at least of the Balfourian phrase, 'united by a common allegiance to the Crown',[12] commenting to Attlee: 'It is surely conceding enough to Congress to admit the fact that the future India can walk out of the Empire. . . .' Others, including the Permanent Under-Secretary at the India Office, were alarmed at the explicit concession of the right of secession.[13] Amery, who was convinced that a dominion 'may walk out of the Empire without let or hindrance' if substantially united, thought it might well not be wise to phrase the fact.[14] On 6 March he reassured the Viceroy by saying that the phrase would almost certainly be modified or omitted,[15] and the Dominion

9. Ibid., no. 191.
10. Ibid., no. 290.
11. Ibid., no. 194.
12. See ibid., nos. 195 and 200.
13. Ibid., no. 202.
14. Ibid., no. 208.
15. Ibid., no. 249. See also no. 251, para. 2.

High Commissioners at their meeting with the Secretary of State for Dominion Affairs were reported to the Cabinet Committee on India on 7 March as not liking the formula on secession.[16] Later on the same day, the War Cabinet approved a revised draft substituting for the sentence earlier quoted another reading: 'The object is the creation of a new Indian Union which shall constitute a Dominion, associated with the United Kingdom and the other Dominions by a common allegiance to the Crown, but equal to them in every respect, in no way subordinate in any aspect of its domestic or external affairs.'[17] There was, however, also by way of compensation, added to the section on the treaty to be negotiated between H.M. government and the contemplated constitution-making body, an assurance that the treaty would not impose any restriction on the Indian union's power to decide its relationship with the Commonwealth. At his press conference in Delhi on 29 March, Cripps was asked whether the new union could secede and replied categorically that it would be absolutely free to decide its future relationship with the other member-states of the Commonwealth.[18]

Dominion governments were sent the text of the draft declaration. Smuts seized upon the significance of the opening left for partition and feared lest it might be regarded as a British application of Irish tactics to India. Curtin had little to say, but Mackenzie King telegraphed to Churchill on 6 March[19] a hearty welcome on behalf of the Canadian government to the proposals in the draft declaration for 'the earliest possible realization of complete self-government in India.' 'We believe', he wrote, 'that a fully self-governing India has a great part to play in free and equal association with the other Nations of the British Commonwealth . . .' and he reiterated an earlier suggestion that Canada would be glad to make an early appointment of a High Commissioner for Canada in India 'if it was thought that such action on our part would help to signalize India's emergence as an equal member of the Commonwealth.' On 15 March the Canadian Prime Minister with mounting enthusiasm followed this up with a strictly personal and private telegram to Churchill suggesting that it might contribute to the

16. Ibid., no. 262.
17. Ibid., no. 265.
18. Ibid., no. 440.
19. Ibid., no. 258.

success of Cripps' mission 'were Cripps to be fortified,by an expression from each of the self-governing Dominions of their readiness to cooperate at the time of the peace negotiations in ensuring immediate recognition of India's status as one of equality with the other self-governing parts of the British Commonwealth of Nations.' He alluded yet again to the Canadian offer to the exchange of High Commissioners with India; reminded Churchill of the role taken by Canada in respect of peace negotiations in 1919 and its contribution to the attainment of equality of status; suggested 'that strong assurances to India on the part of Canada as to the helpful role we would be prepared to take on her behalf, might not be without some real effect at this time'; and indicated that should Churchill feel that an association of the dominions with the British government 'in Cripps' present mission to India would be at all helpful', he would be ready to lend his good offices.[20]

Alas, they were not in demand.[21] Churchill asserted in his reply, as he had already done to Roosevelt, that the question which had to be solved was not one between the British government and India but between different sects or nations in India. He proceeded to underline this by specific references to the Muslims, the Princes, and the 'Hindu Untouchables', concluding sharply: 'I should strongly recommend your awaiting developments till we see how the Cripps Mission goes.'[22] It was left to Amery to send some soothing comments about King's 'most generous and helpful telegram'.[23]

Perhaps one other point deserves comment in the specifically Commonwealth context. It is Indian misgivings about dominion status. Rajagopalachari mentioned to Cripps at his interview with him that he thought that the word 'Dominion' was better discarded and that the words 'Free Member State' might be substituted with advantage and later was on record as saying that the omission of the word 'Dominion Status' might be one amendment helpful to

20. Ibid., no. 330.
21. Was Mackenzie King diplomatically dissembling, naïvely unaware, or wholly uninformed by Vincent Massey of Churchill's ambivalent attitude to the Cripps Mission? The Canadian records may provide the material for an answer.
22. *Cripps Mission*, no. 346.
23. Ibid., no. 338.
24. Ibid., nos. 412 and 428.

the prospect of Congress acceptance.[24] More significantly Cripps noted that the first point made by Jawaharlal Nehru and Maulana Azad, the Congress president, in his interview with them was about the use of the word 'Dominion'. He explained why it had been used—chiefly to silence possible objections in the House of Commons or from the dominions themselves—and made it clear that it was a question of terminology not substance. They attached psychological importance to it.[25] After the mission had failed, Gandhi alleged in an article in *Horizon* that Cripps should have known that Congress would not look at dominion status, even though it carried the right of immediate secession. Jinnah, by expected contrast, showed himself to be concerned only with clarification of the possibility of a second dominion being set up.[26]

The draft declaration which Cripps brought with him to India in the early spring of 1942 had much to offer on the longer term, little of substance on the shorter, where Cripps, unlike Durham, was deliberately left with negligible freedom of manoeuvre. That essentially was why his mission failed. Even the longer term and Dominion-Commonwealth prospect was conditional upon an allied victory, which looked to many Indian eyes by no means certain, with Singapore having surrendered on 15 February and Rangoon having fallen on 8 March, the day before the War Cabinet decided upon the Cripps Mission. Were the signatories to the post-dated cheque upon a failing bank, of the reputedly Gandhian imagery, likely to be in a position to honour their signatures? Gandhi, whatever the phraseology he may or may not have employed, evidently had his doubts and the mere existence of them was bound to diminish the attraction of proposals which had so little to offer immediately. But when the mission had ended and could be viewed in retrospect, it became increasingly apparent that it had set, among other things, a Commonwealth seal upon the transfer of power in India. Even dominion status was briefly to serve its purpose, while the broader notion of free membership of a Commonwealth was at the least to contribute to the building of a new relationship over a generation.

25. Ibid., no. 435.
26. Ibid., no. 380.

# 3

# The Last Days of British Rule in India
## Some Personal Impressions

'The Kings of the Earth are gathered and gone by together', but to us, thinking upon our own mortality, the hour in which they and their empires pass away has always an irresistible fascination. Succeeding generations turn with undiminishing interest to read the *Travels* in which Arthur Young records his impressions of France in the last years of the Ancient Régime. It matters little, as we turn those pages, whether we feel that the old order merited the fate which was so soon to engulf it, or whether we feel that in the floodgates of violence and bloodshed some of the bonds that held human society together were to be broken beyond repair. It is the moment that lends all its significance to the scene. Because they lived and moved on the eve of a great revolution, we are concerned to discover the thoughts, however trivial, of noble and peasant as all unknowing they moved on their way to play a part in one of the great dramas of history.

No one with a sense of historical perspective would suggest that the ending of British rule in India and the coming of the French Revolution were events of comparable magnitude. Yet it may be that the manner in which the Indian Empire passed away somewhat obscured the momentous consequences of its passing. Of that it is not possible to judge yet. But whatever the final verdict, it is certain that in after generations men will be eager to learn something of the thoughts and actions, whether English or Indian, of those who played a part in the last days of British rule. The extraordinary,

fantastic episode in human history, by which the imagination of
Macaulay was so deeply stirred, has reached the end that he foresaw.
The rule of a small island in the Atlantic over a vast subcontinent
in the Indian Ocean for more than one hundred and fifty years,
something so surprising in character that even familiarity cannot
reduce it to the commonplace, has reached its inevitable close. How
Arthur Young, inquisitive and purposeful, would have enjoyed
noting conditions, impressions, and conversations in the years when
the bonds were loosening.

One day after my arrival in New Delhi in March 1947, the last
Viceroy came to take up his exacting task. The atmosphere in the
capital was that of a political hot-house. Rumours, some well-
founded, others fantastic, circulated everywhere. Everyone was
waiting—waiting for the closing scenes, impatient for the opening
of a new chapter. Some were filled with curiosity, some with hope,
most with a blend of hope and fear in which, at that time, fear
predominated. To paint a picture of this stormy sunset scene would
require an intimate knowledge of India, to which I can lay no
claim. But it is my hope, that even the rather random impressions
of a visitor to India at that critical time may have their own interest
and, incidentally, may throw some light on the future of Anglo-
Indian relations.

Events in India moved quickly in the early months of 1947.[1]
On 22 January the Constituent Assembly, whose proceedings were
boycotted by the Muslim League, unanimously passed a resolution
declaring 'a firm and solemn resolve to proclaim India as an independent, sovereign republic'. On 17 February, Liaquat Ali Khan,
Finance Member in the Interim Government, stated categorically
at Aligarh that only the establishment of an independent Muslim
state, Pakistan, would satisfy Muslim sentiment. Three days later,
on 20 February, Attlee announced the definite intention of His
Majesty's Government 'to take the necessary steps to effect the
transference of power into Indian hands by a date not later than
June 1948'. The players in the last act had taken up their positions,
and still more than a little incredulous, India prepared for the end
of the British Raj.

1. For a full account, see H.V. Hodson's article in the *Annual Register*,
1947 (London, Longmans Green, 1948), p. 145.

It might have been supposed that the arrival in March of the last Viceroy of India would create intense popular interest in the capital. But it was not so. Outside political circles the attitude was one of apathy mingled with mild antipathy. With a certain malicious pleasure an Indian lady told me that on earlier occasions bribes had been paid out to collect cheering crowds to hail each Viceroy's arrival. But whatever the reason, this time there were no commentators, little excitement and a good deal of indifference in the welcome. Lord Mountbatten's popularity was not inherited; it was personally acquired.

Lord Wavell's farewell broadcast, so sincere, so obviously candid, was something by which Indians were moved. But those in touch with affairs were all agreed that the time had come for change. Lord Wavell was said to be tired; to be weighed down by a feeling of frustration; his outlook to be too inflexible. Although he had been Viceroy for a comparatively short time if one thinks in terms of years only, he had been there in a political sense through a long, exacting period. Even his virtues at this juncture weighed against him. When the problem had demanded immediate practical action, as in the days of the Bengal famine, and had been less exclusively political, his contribution was acknowledged to have been great; but now that the only question was the best way in which power could be quickly transferred, he was not felt to have the right touch. Some Indian critics maintained that in recent months negotiation was slow because he had leaned too heavily on his professional advisers. At Cabinet meetings his strong but silent personality was unequal to the very formidable task of bridging the gulf between the representatives of the two major communities. Here Lord Mountbatten's diplomacy and understanding brought about a quick change for the better. His chairmanship of the meetings of the short-lived Interim Government was recognized at once to be masterly. Under his happy influence this Interim Government, for the first time, began to bear some resemblance to a Cabinet as it is understood in a Parliamentary democracy. Lord Mountbatten diplomatically guided where Lord Wavell correctly presided.

Attlee's declaration of 20 February had transformed the political atmosphere in India and made change in the highest office seem natural and appropriate. However criticized at home, the impact of this statement of policy on India was wholly beneficial. At no time during my stay did I hear any criticism of its substance, though one or two of the Muslim leaders argued that the period allowed before the final withdrawal of the British Raj might with advantage to them have been rather longer. It gave them insufficient time to lay the foundations of a new State. Since in fact this period was foreshortened by nearly a year, their observations underline the difficulties confronting Pakistan in the early months of its existence. The Europeans joined in acclaiming Attlee's wise and prudent decision. Nothing indeed was more surprising than the support which the policy of the Labour Government in this respect received from all classes of the British community, who were certainly not otherwise predominantly Labour in sympathy. Responsibility without power is not an enviable situation, and had the transfer been long protracted, that is the fate which would certainly have overtaken the army and administration.

The Indian scene in the spring of 1947 was clouded by the extreme tension between the two major communities. It was a matter of no little surprise that a situation could simmer for so long and yet not boil over. No subject could be discussed; no serious consideration given to the future of India, to the direction of her internal or foreign policy when independence was won; no study of her future relationship with Britain and the Commonwealth undertaken, without bringing out at once this one great unresolved problem. All were preoccupied with the balance of communal forces within India. During the period of the Asian Conference the Congress Party, by the array of eminent intellectual figures it could muster, was able to present an impressive front. It was made clear that on the intellectual side the advantage lay with it; and it was clear as well that so far as finance and industrial resources were concerned, its position was overwhelmingly strong. When to those assets was added its great advantage in numbers, it was not surprising that the Congress leaders, particularly those of the second rank, disregarding the restraint and dignity of Pandit Nehru, allowed a note of arrogance to intrude, in which they benefited neither themselves nor their cause.

Ardent members of the Congress and of the League both spoke freely about the possibility of civil war. At times they shrank from so awful an eventuality, but at times, too, the question that seemed uppermost in their minds was not whether civil war would come but who would win it. Many of the younger generation, notably the younger intellectuals, were resigned to the settlement of the issue by the sword. Better a country united by force than the vivisection of Mother India, was the thought, sometimes candidly expressed by young Hindus. Warning of the long, incalculable consequences of civil war, illustrated by what had happened in Ireland on a comparatively small scale a quarter of a century ago, was something which the younger generation were not prepared to heed. If they learn, they will learn only by experience. It was in Bombay, far removed from the probable scene of conflict, that the most intolerant views found expression. There, too, was to be found some impatience with Mahatma Gandhi's faith in non-violence. By not a few wealthy Hindus it was felt that Gandhi's doctrine had served its day. Warm though the tributes might be to the unique contribution which Gandhi had made to the Indian national movement, it was felt the time had now come when he should stand aside. There was no longer, so it was argued, any alternative to fighting it out because by this means alone could the partition of India be averted. Something of the single-minded passion which prompted such conclusions came to the surface when a Hindu Congress businessman denounced in the most bitter terms the presence of the 'Third Party' in India; a 'Third Party' by whose intervention and by whose intrigues every reasonable hope of a peaceful settlement had been destroyed. Asked to identify the 'Third Party', he replied in surprise, 'The Muslims, naturally.'

The feeling on the part of the Congress supporters that they had the men, the money, and the industrial resources constituted an ever-present incentive to settlement by the sword. It was in the light of this clear predominance in power that there was endless discussion of the role the Army might play. The possibility of a military *coup d'état* was by no means excluded among the well informed. It was, however, the belief of experienced soldiers that, in fact, the Indian Army was a unity. It could not be split up into its component communal parts, and thereby provide the nucleus of both a Hindu and a Muslim fighting force. The units were so intermingled that to carry out such a division effectively was utterly impracticable. At this time the continued immunity of the Army to communal sentiment remained the one great reassuring factor which seemed at the least to rule out the possibility of civil war on an organized scale.

Turbulence and disorder seemed certain. On this score no one was prepared to discount the fears so widely entertained. That India was psychologically both prepared and fearful of civil war was not in doubt, and it was only the military considerations referred to above and the safety valve created by vast size and indifferent communications that provided counterbalancing factors. Incidents in the Punjab were a daily occurrence, though the Government of India censors played down their number and concealed the identity of the perpetrators. But knowledge existed and speculation was rampant. Terrible, but characteristic, was the story of the women in a village in the Gurgaon district not far from Delhi who, rather than fall into the hands of their assailants by whom their menfolk had been killed or overcome, threw themselves down the community well. Of the ninety, all were drowned save three who survived only because the water was not high enough. But these incidents, frightful as they were, were quite insufficient to check the hand of the fanatics. And there was a widespread feeling, which in the light of after-events must honestly be recorded, that in the Punjab the Sikhs were spoiling for a fight, and whatever happened elsewhere, there serious trouble was hardly to be avoided. Where ultimate responsibility lay was a question on which opinion was sharply divided.

The reactions arising from the growing communal tension were too many to recount. But one or two ordinary, personal experiences may convey an impression of the atmosphere for those not in India at that time. I was taken one evening to hear Mahatma Gandhi speak at his prayer meeting in Bhangi Colony in Old Delhi by a Congressman of the older generation. Throughout the drive there the taxi-driver, a Sikh, continued to express his fears lest we should not be back before the curfew, though in fact it was still quite early afternoon, and the curfew was not at that time imposed till seven o'clock. These misgivings communicated themselves to some extent to my companion, who knew, as we all did, that Gandhi's last three prayer meetings had been broken up by Hindu protests at readings from the Koran, on the ground that it was by the teachings of the Koran that Muslim intolerance was fostered and sanctioned. On this particular evening there was a fairly large crowd and after being introduced to the visitors, Gandhi came out to address the meeting. Those who had protested on the preceding evenings, made statements in which they said that while they thought their protests justified they would, out of respect for Gandhi, withdraw. This was conciliatory enough but my companion was not prepared to stay. The sense of strain, of tension not very far from breaking point, communicated itself to him, purposeful and determined though he was. Nothing in fact did happen that evening.

In the cities Muslims and Hindus were keeping strictly to their own quarters. In many areas it was literally as much as life was worth for Hindus to go to a Muslim quarter or for Muslims to go to a Hindu area. This meant in many cases that neither was prepared to cross the street. In Bombay, the banks depended upon Parsee messengers who could go into all quarters without danger. It was the same factor and not large-scale conversions to Christianity, that accounted for the wearing of so many crosses—a device which did not carry immunity for long.

Another result of the same tensions was seen in the pronounced, if in the circumstances surprising, popularity of Europeans and particularly of British people in these last days of imperial rule. It was perhaps fears of the future that were finding an outlet in an emotional friendship for the Raj which was leaving. In Bombay there were many stories of prominent Congress businessmen inviting English residents to propose them for membership of clubs, which would have been inconceivable a year or so earlier. In areas where rioting had been continuous and even while rioting was going on, care was taken to ensure that the lives and property of English people remained untouched. For more concrete consider-ations British troops were welcomed wherever they went, and in Calcutta it was said that any Tommy taking up his position outside an Indian merchant's house was certain to be offered a handsome bribe to stay where he was and not to move on next door! But it would be as much a mistake to take these tributes over-seriously as to discount them altogether. They were, however, sufficiently wide-spread for Gandhi at one of his evening prayer meetings to warn people against indulgence in unworthy thoughts of asking the British to remain so that their lives and property might be kept safe. It was a fear, in the circumstances a very natural fear, for the safety of personal property after the British withdrawal that contributed most to the prevailing state of mind. The anxieties, particularly of businessmen, were many and widespread. Several admitted that their highest hope, like that of the Abbé Sieyès in the French Revolution, was to survive the storm which all foresaw. When keeping safe the property of a firm was a main objective, business was inevitably slowed down, and the conviction spread that the course of wisdom was to limit commitments to an absolute minimum. Long-term contracts were entered into with readiness only with some of the States, particularly Hyderabad, where to judge by conversations in Bombay business circles, planning for the future was continuing on a considerable scale, irrespective of conditions elsewhere in India.

Within the Congress itself there was much discussion on whether the Congress Party should continue to exist after British rule had ended, or alternatively, at what stage the Congress would split into its component parts. There was no doubt that the younger Congress men, some of them terribly conscious of the wretched poverty of the Indian masses, were extremely restive under the higher command of a party which was so largely financed and therefore controlled by Hindu big business. Many of them sponsored the view that the final struggle might be diverted into a class struggle, in which the Muslim, being generally the poorer element, would link up with the Hindu Socialists. It was reluctantly recognized, however, that this Socialist programme could have no decisive appeal until communal passions had abated. But, on the other hand, the concentration of enormous wealth in a few hands, which is so remarkable a feature of Indian economy, seems to make it inevitable, even allowing for the dead weight of inertia, that at some not too distant stage a social revolution must come. There the Congress Socialists seem right, but their calculation of the day when it will come may prove wide of the mark. In the Interim Government and in the Congress Party there was no more impressive figure than Sardar Vallabhbhai Patel, whose realism and ruthless sense of purpose made him a formidable defender of the *status quo*. Nothing was more remarkable in the spring of 1947 than the steady rise in his reputation among both friends and opponents. By his speeches he made it clear that he knew precisely what he wanted when India was free—and it was not a social revolution.

The activities and the interests of the Congress leaders were diverse; those of the Muslim League were concentrated wholly on the creation of a Muslim State. It was at once their strength and their weakness that they had to concentrate on one single aim. If Pakistan did not come into existence, all their wider plans were by that very failure rendered meaningless. And yet if Pakistan did come into existence, all these questions hitherto disregarded had to be disposed of urgently. Jinnah, as constant in saying 'no', with a resolution as unyielding as that of Lord Craigavon, was reaping the reward of a man of single-minded vision. It was clear beyond question by March 1947 that he would get Pakistan, since he was absolutely determined to get it, and he had sufficient cards in his hand to make any alternative unworkable. This indeed was reluctantly recognized in private conversation by Congress men, and the practical issue was in fact, if not in name, whether Jinnah would get Pakistan 'viable' or 'truncated'. In March 1947 the latter seemed much the more likely. To that extent, therefore, there was more agreement on the fundamentals of the solution that, however reluctantly, had to be accepted, before Lord Mountbatten began his talks than was recognized outside India. Earlier and seemingly fruitless discussion had in fact narrowed the issue, and in so doing prepared politically conscious India for the partition of the subcontinent.

Though it was tacitly acknowledged by Congress that the detachment of Pakistan was inevitable, the leaders of the Muslim League were devoting less thought than was altogether prudent to the future constitution, administration, and policy of the new State. To this Liaquat Ali Khan was an honourable exception; at least in some fields of internal policy. At a time when his budget proposals were still a source of friction in the Interim Government and a source of embarrassment to the right wing of Congress, he made it abundantly clear that his aim was the creation of a better balanced social system. Recognizing that in India there is not only an appalling contrast between wealth and poverty, but also, if incidentally, that wealth is concentrated, even in the predominantly Muslim areas, mostly in the hands of Hindu merchants, he had no difficulty in deciding that it was right and just that it should be redistributed. If it is true that the Hindus comprise the wealthier part of the city, it is equally true, argued Liaquat Ali Khan, that in any redistribution of wealth in India as a whole, the Hindus will benefit most, just because there are more of them. Among the rank and file of the League, as distinct from Jinnah, these indications of a progressive policy were highly popular, for while the Indian Muslim has a firm belief in private property, he does not believe in a wide gulf between the rich and the poor.

Though Pakistan would be poorer in resources than the Union of India, there was no lack of confidence about its capacity to pay its way. It was acknowledged that much of the wealth in Pakistan would be in the hands of the Hindus, but it was felt that Muslims in their own State, enjoying a fair deal and more opportunities, would increasingly enter into commerce and industry. Provided there was peace in India as a whole the Muslim leaders had no doubt that financial stability in Pakistan would be maintained. Some of the provinces are wealthy in resources and it is a food producing area.

A far more pressing problem than that of social policy or even financial stability, was the question of the administrative organization of the embryo state of Pakistan. What the Muslim leaders had in mind at that time was a close federation between East and West Pakistan with a capital in each but a unified system of government, of social services, and of taxation. By some it was thought possible that one capital would be administrative and the other parliamentary, but Jinnah by temperament and conviction inclined towards a strong centralized system. But little or no progress had been made with plans for organizing the life of the new State. The principle of Pakistan had first to be acknowledged; then the boundary had to be decided, and not till June 1948 would the new State be formally established. It was only when agreement was reached and the time-table telescoped that the full consequences of the lack of detailed preliminary planning became evident.

In March 1947 the League was satisfactorily holding its position, emphatic in its insistence that there had never been one India, that unity was the creation of the British Raj, and that if Hindu rule were to be forced upon them a civil war more terrible than any in the history of Asia would ensue. To avoid war, not only must partition be accepted in principle, but also power must be handed over to two separate authorities equally. The onus was firmly placed on the British government. They must decide, and in so doing they must recognize that there must be two Constituent Assemblies, one to draft a constitution for Hindustan, one for Pakistan. It was by this insistence on the transfer of power to two recognized successor States and by their unquestioned resolution to risk all in civil war rather than accept the Hindu Raj, that the League made any other settlement seem impracticable even to the most bitter opponents of its pretensions.

Because of its geographical position, the future relationship of Pakistan with the British Commonwealth was recognized to be a matter of cardinal importance. The view that prevailed among the leaders of the League may be summarized as follows. In the world today association, or close cooperation with a great power is a virtual necessity. There are only three great powers. The Soviet Union is an uncertain factor and her materialism is repugnant to Muslims. We have seen a certain amount of the United States in recent years. Their soldiers came to India and they went away again. We do not dislike them, we just feel that we have nothing in common. Therefore we are likely to think first of Britain as an associate since we know her. Once Pakistan is established, arrangements can be made to cover all security questions on a broad reciprocal basis.

The younger Muslims perhaps entertained some reservations in respect of their leaders' views about Russia. They seemed to feel that the Soviet Union was a difficult but not impossible associate in certain circumstances. Some were mildly impressed by the fact that the Soviet Asian Republics' delegations to the Asian Conference contained Muslims, some part of whose assertions about religious liberty in the Soviet Union may have been true. It was possible, too, that either deliberately or subconsciously some Muslims, sensing the relative weakness of Pakistan and the vulnerability of the Arab League States, who are its natural allies, felt that the possibility of a *rapprochement* with the USSR was a not ineffective, if dangerous, bargaining counter not to be too lightly cast aside.

The attitude towards Britain varied less than one might have expected between the two communities. The Hindus were on the whole more conscious alike of Britain's misdeeds in the past and of the positive, if limited, contribution which she might make in the future. Neither seemed profoundly concerned about Britain's place in the world of great powers and one heard little of the discussion, all too familiar elsewhere, about Britain's strength in relation to the USSR and the United States. Despite the Constituent Assembly's resolution of 22 January in favour of a sovereign, independent republic, there seemed to be a surprisingly large crop of *arrière-pensées* about it. There was a good deal of emphasis on the fact that anyway there was no free choice, because clearly India could not be a member of a Commonwealth in which South Africa was a partner. Symptomatic of these feelings were the large notices in the leading hotel in Bombay saying 'No South Africans admitted here'. On the other hand a treaty relationship not only with Britain but also with Australia, New Zealand, and Canada was widely contemplated. A very particular interest was taken in recent constitutional developments in Éire, and the merits of external association were receiving detailed consideration. The Committee drafting the new constitution had devoted the most careful study to the Irish Constitution of 1937. On the broad question of relationship with the Commonwealth it seemed that the sensitiveness of the Congress leaders to attacks from the left, whether nationalist or socialist, might be a decisive factor in favour of independent republican status. Certainly it made dominion status politically unattractive.

In contrast to the League, Congress was confident that the Union of India would be sufficiently strong to stand on its own feet, and so far as a treaty was concerned felt that Britain might well be allowed to make the pace. It had not occurred to Congress, but it had occurred to the League, that the commitments which Britain and the rest of the Commonwealth might be asked to undertake in a divided India would be disproportionate to the political and strategic advantages which she might thereby acquire.

The British community in India faced bravely the 'sad sundown' of the British Raj. In the capital, families of officials were packing up; many reluctantly returning to Labour Britain, with whose political and social outlook they were not at all in sympathy. There was a round of farewell parties, and, though in many cases the men were expected to remain for six or nine months longer, their families were going home as berths became available. And this inevitably had a very disintegrating effect outside official circles. In Bombay it was marked. Only in Calcutta did it seem the firm intention of the business community to stay put. It was the assumption there that while the first three to five years might be a difficult period, normal trading conditions would return at the end of them. It was particularly noticeable in these last days of British rule that the morale of the ICS as an administrative service was undermined. Whatever views might be entertained in London, it was perfectly clear that machinery no longer existed in India by which any policy other than that adopted by the United Kingdom government could be carried out.

The departure of the British community must profoundly affect the future of the Christian Churches in India. Some believe that, except in south India, where their roots have struck deep, the Churches have been fatally compromised by their association with an alien ruling class. Remembering that there are some eight or nine million Christians in India, it was surprising how far the Episcopalian Church, at least, had remained Anglicized. Here there is a sharp contrast with conditions in China. In India it remained till 1947 almost unknown for an English suffragan to serve under an Indian bishop. In the capital, and in the great cities the Church remains overwhelmingly European, and may well have to fight for survival. But in the villages the prospect seems much more hopeful. In general, the most probable outcome is that the Church will be confronted within the next two or three years after the ending of British rule by a testing, critical period, and if, as there is every reason to suppose, it survives, then it should have great opportunities for service in the future. While most recent converts are drawn from the two extremes of the social scale, the great majority come from the depressed classes. To them, to the outcast and the downtrodden, its message of hope will always remain.

If, and when, the Residency Churches are wholly Indianized the memorials which cluster so thickly upon their walls will presumably one day be removed. Many of these memorials are in the most elaborate Victorian style, but on them is recorded information of much historical interest. By the porch in the Cathedral at Bombay my eye chanced to rest on one tablet erected to the memory of the crew of 'the East India Company's frigate *Cleopatra*, lost in a storm off the coast of Malabar 1853.' Beside it was another memorial to a young lieutenant in the Royal Engineers, who, working on the fortifications at Fort Bombay through the noonday heat with 'a characteristic devotion to duty', had 'died of sunstroke'.

What strikes the traveller in India most is its dreadful poverty. In the great overpopulated cities it is always evident, but in the myriads of villages of the central plains it is overwhelming. Many Indian nationalists suggest that British rule has been responsible; that by paying too much attention to big business, because that was the only way in which Indian opinion might indirectly be influenced and Indian economy controlled, it allowed the wealth of the country to be accumulated in a few hands. It is also argued more realistically that by a reluctance to interfere with local customs, many survived under British rule which are a burden and a drag on economic development. Others again acknowledge that, while British rule had brought great benefits to India up to about the close of the last century, 'then something had gone out of us'. Is this true? Remembering at once the vast size of India and its ever growing population, the initial surprise is that the administration of this subcontinent could have been carried out at all with the limited, and in the last years, dwindling resources at the disposal of the British Raj. That in itself has been no mean achievement. On the other hand an Indian government with far greater resources, particularly in manpower, at its disposal clearly could embark on a positive economic policy of the kind from which we shrank. It is not, perhaps, a case of 'something going out of us' but a case in which the negative functions of administration could be, and were admirably, enforced with the resources at the disposal of a foreign ruler, but that the positive planning on social and economic lines, which was the next stage, was beyond our power. Britain's mission, so it had always been conceived, was to pacify India; to unite it; to introduce law and order in a subcontinent where hitherto they had never been respected. When all that had been accomplished the sense of mission weakened. Never had it been conceived as Britain's task to introduce a more just social system, to embark upon the perilous enterprise of reforming an eastern society on an advanced western model. To have attempted this would have demanded faith and a burning conviction in the excellence of the western social system in its industrial age. But such faith did not exist, could not exist. What did remain was the Englishman's profound belief in the 'government of men by themselves'. That belief was all too often blurred by preoccupation with considerations of power or economic advantage, or even of security, and the principal criticism to be made of the last years of British rule in India is, that it was not always true to itself, true to its own most cherished principles. It is on almost every count a profound misfortune that the transfer of power did not take place a generation earlier.

However high its intentions, however excellent its administration, however just in its dealing with the ruled, the government of one country by another exacts no small price from the rulers. They are cut off from the movement of thought and opinion in their own land, and only too often from free, fertilizing interchange of ideas with the inhabitants of the country they rule. So long as their principal task is the maintenance of law and order, the administration of justice, their loss in freshness of outlook is not apparent. But once the discharge of more creative responsibilities is demanded, it becomes so. In respect of the Indian Civil Service this did not escape the discerning eye of James Bryce on his brief visit to India some sixty years ago. 'The Civil Service', he wrote,

somewhat disappoints me. There is a high average of ability among the service men in the upper posts—'tis these chiefly I have seen—but a good deal of uniformity, and a want of striking, even marked, individualities. They are intelligent, very hard working, with apparently a high sense of public duty and a desire to promote the welfare of the people of India. But they seem rather wanting in imagination and sympathy, less inspired by the extraordinary and unprecedented phenomena of the country than might have been expected, with little intellectual initiative; too conventionally English in their ways of life and thoughts to rise to the position. . . . They are more out of the stream of the world's thought and movement than one was prepared to find. Society is monotonous; it is in some places more military than civil, in some more civil than military; it has nowhere the variety and sense of intellectual activity which one feels in England . . . .[2]

All that could have been written with at least equal truth of the Europeans in the largely Indianized Service in 1947. By then the lack of contact with opinion at home had been accentuated, largely because for the past twenty years, while opinion was moving to the left in Britain, recruits with left-wing opinions did not for the most part come forward as candidates for the Indian Civil Service. The predominant outlook was that of an earlier age hardened in its ways of thought by antagonism to the rising tide of nationalism in India and of socialism in Britain.

Many Congressmen, particularly the young left-wing group, feel that they have quick and easy remedies for the poverty of India. On them Gandhi's dislike of industrialism has made no

2. Letter to his Mother, 20 November 1888; quoted in H.A.L. Fisher, *James Bryce* (London, Macmillan, 1937), vol. I, pp. 259–60.

impression. Their thoughts run along the lines of social, democratic planning now fashionable in Western Europe. Often they seem almost oblivious both of the way of life in India's unnumbered villages, and of her predominantly agricultural economy. Here they had much to learn, both from Gandhi and Nehru. It is only necessary to go for a short tour in central India; to visit some of the farms, for ever being subdivided, and watch methods of agriculture, which must have been practised for at least 2,000 years, to recognize that the solution is not so easy as all that. The small farms; the thoroughly wasteful methods of cultivation—I remember watching eight oxen yoked together tramping round and round threshing corn—the lack of proper water supplies, and above all the innumerable herds of useless cattle, impress on one's mind a picture of how very, very much there is to be done before the means of subsistence can keep pace with the rise in population. It is generally calculated that there are about 150 million head of cattle in India and I can well believe that that is an underestimate. Few sights are so utterly depressing as these herds of ill-bred, ill-nourished, ill-watered oxen dragging their weary way in the noonday heat through the parched fields of the United Provinces. Because none can be slaughtered by Hindus, many of the heifer calves never give any milk and the only profit derived from them is the shoes made from their hides when at last they die. In the meantime they hasten the process of soil erosion which in some places reaches terrifying proportions.

It is easy for anyone visiting India at this particular time to be unduly depressed. It is true that in the period of marking time, corruption and a degree of administrative disintegration were noticeable. But new forces of great vitality, with idealism and determination to compensate for lack of wide experience, were waiting to take over. Moreover, it is a naïve western reaction to imagine that because corruption is widespread the administration will necessarily break down altogether, or indeed to think that life itself is dependent on the working of an administrative machine. Even when there is fairly large-scale disorder, life in large parts of India remains comparatively unaffected, provided—and this is all important—that food can be moved from surplus areas to overpopulated famine areas. Fear of complete breakdown may be discounted.

In India it is a case of nothing being quite so good or quite so bad as it seems at first sight.

So small a proportion of India's vast population is politically conscious that, to an extent greater than westerners find it easy to believe, the future of the subcontinent is likely to depend on the quality of the leaders which she brings forth. In 1947 the scene was dominated by Gandhi, Nehru and Jinnah, with Vallabhbhai Patel and Liaquat Ali Khan exerting ever increasing influence. The Sikhs lacked effective leadership; that was their tragedy. In this, the last year of his life, Gandhi's influence was transcendent. By the people of India he was treated with the awe given to the great prophets and religious teachers of the past. Indeed he was already numbered with them. It was his preaching of the doctrine of non-violence more than any other single factor that stood between India and bloodshed on a frightful scale. To a European the happiest verdict on Gandhi may seem to have been that of W. Casey, who has written that 'among statesmen he is a saint; among saints he is a statesman'. But to simple and sincere Indians he was just a saint. As his inclinations seemed to lead him to withdraw more and more from the narrow political issues of the hour and to devote his efforts to the noble work of pacification, so his reputation grew, even if some of his early and more militant followers wavered in their allegiance. Bitterly opposed to the 'vivisection of Mother India', he remained the great protector of those who demanded it. It was this that the Hindu extremists could not forgive. Recently returned from his exacting and successful mission to the troubled area of Bihar, he was received at the Asian Conference with reverent and profound respect. Leaning on his pillows, with Nehru holding the microphone before him, Gandhi spoke to the assembled delegates less of the practical problems of the new Asia than of her age-old spiritual heritage. 'We do not' he said, referring to the disturbances in India,

know how to keep the peace within ourselves. We think we must resort to the law of the jungle. It is an experience which I would not like you to carry to your respective countries. We want to be our own masters. Man is supposed to be master of his own destiny, but it is only partly true. He can make his own destiny only in so far as he is allowed by the Great Power which overrides all our intentions and plans. . . . I call that Great

Power not by the name of Allah, not by the name of Khuda or God, but by the name of Truth. For me Truth is God and truth overrides all our plans. . . . A great Englishman taught me to believe that God is unknowable. But he is knowable if only to the extent that our limited intellect allows.

The deep impression which he made upon the delegates, most of whom were not destined to hear him again, is something not easily described.

It was Lord Halifax 'the Trimmer' who said that the dependence of a great man upon a greater was a thing not to be readily understood by ordinary men. While Nehru was always the devoted disciple of Gandhi, there was in the relationship no hint of dependence. Nehru, endowed with all the charm of a gifted and popular aristocrat, is the leader born. He has the assurance of one accustomed to command, coupled with some impatience at the criticisms of colleagues. Equally at ease in addressing vast popular meetings and small gatherings of learned men, his eloquence is easy, often inspiring, with a capacity for rising to the great occasions, and fluent—perhaps too fluent. Somewhat incalculable he remains, but his stature has grown steadily with his responsibilities. Of the wide range of his interests and his intellectual ability there is no doubt. Perhaps he insists a little too much that he is a man of action, for one is left with the impression of a dual personality, and with the feeling that he himself has not quite succeeded in resolving this dualism to his own satisfaction. He has a very profound sense of history, though he is not a historian and does not apply critical historical standards. He delves into the past for inspiration and for ideas, but always applying the practical standards of a statesman. His principal criticism[3] of the emperor Akbar is directed to his failure to remedy India's powerlessness at sea. With all his prestige as the Grand Moghul, with his genius for invention, with all his might on land, Akbar left his dominions defenceless against the Portuguese who were masters of the sea. India's greatness in earlier ages had been partly at least due to her control of the sea-routes, and Nehru's awareness, through his study of history, of the impact of sea-power on her destiny in the past will assuredly influence his naval policy in the future. He is also profoundly convinced of the 'spiritualism' of the East which he contrasts

3. *The Discovery of India* (Calcutta, The Signet Press, 1946), p. 221.

obliquely with the materialism of the West. In religion as in politics, finalities do not appeal to him. It may be that the wide range of mind and of his cultural and political interests will prove a source of weakness at critical moments, though undoubtedly it adds to the charm of his personality and fits him to play the role in international affairs to which he aspires and which he might fill with high distinction.

Like other Indian leaders Nehru's life has been spent in a struggle to end British rule in India. At times he is bitter. A man who has spent so many years of his life in prison would require a remarkable degree of detachment to feel otherwise. Of India he thinks emotionally and the outlet for his emotion has been nationalism. 'Nationalism', he has written, 'was and is inevitable in the India of my day: it is a natural and healthy growth. For any subject country national freedom must be the first and dominant urge, for India with her intense sense of individuality and past heritage it was doubly so.'[4] Further, his experience has moulded his outlook as well as those of the other Congress leaders. That is something never to be overlooked. It is a fact which must influence India's future relationship with the Commonwealth. Vision on both sides is needed to transcend the memories of the past, and coupled with it a new realistic approach to the problems of the future. If this will not always be easy, at least it will be helped by the fact that under difficult circumstances the parting was both peaceful and friendly. For that, a high tribute may fairly be paid to the wisdom and understanding of English statesmanship—and of her last Viceroy—at a most critical hour.

For many years to come Englishmen and Indians will think very differently of British rule in India—not merely of the great dividing issues which clouded its closing days, but also of smaller, apparently less significant, factors. Has India, to take one example, even yet come to regard New Delhi, so spaciously and delightfully planned, as its own? I think not. I remember—if I may recall a personal incident, because it brings out something on which we should do well to ponder—driving with one of the Congress leaders up the long vista to the Secretariat and Legislative Assembly and his asking me what I thought of Sir Herbert Baker's masterpiece.

4. Ibid., p. 33.

Never having quite made up my mind about it, I merely remarked that I thought the vista very fine. My companion commented, slowly as though he were seeing it for the first time, 'Yes, it is a fine vista.' There was a longish pause and then he went on as though I were no longer there: 'but the buildings; they are imposed!' How many things that have been done in India, excellent in themselves, must seem to Indians to have been imposed. That is something for Englishmen to remember and for Indians to forget.

# 4

# The Asian Conference, 1947

In the affairs of men and nations there come moments when the many are instinctively conscious that they are passing across one of the great watersheds in human history. Sometimes contemporary opinion is mistaken, sometimes its vision is clouded by sentiment, but more often the cool judgement of the historian confirms the instinctive impression of the multitude. All over Europe men hailed the falling of the Bastille—an event of little importance in itself[1]— as the herald of a new age. In that they were not mistaken. But little indeed they foresaw of what the age would bring; little they understood the nature of the forces that were released when high upon the pikestaff was hoisted de Launay's bleeding head.

Some such impressions must have passed through the minds of many who attended the first Inter-Asian Conference in New Delhi in 1947. The conference was not an affair of great moment, but the time of its assembly was. The representatives of a continent then gathered together to welcome, a trifle self-consciously, the dawn of a new era in their long-exploited age-old continent. The Japanese had been decisively defeated by the Allied Powers; but the ending of a short-lived Japanese domination in Eastern Asia had little psychological significance in comparison with that created by the impending withdrawal of the West. It was by the death-bed

1. Louis Madelin in his history of *The French Revolution* (Eng. trans., London, Heinemann, 1916), p. 78, recalls that the prisoners released from the Bastille on 14 July 1789 were four coiners, two madmen, and a sadistic debauchee.

of the Indian empire that delegates hailed the birth of the new order in Asia. When Britain voluntarily laid down her sceptre, what places remained for the lesser imperialisms of France and the Netherlands? It was with the peoples of Asia alone that the future of Asia at long last lay, and eager, clamorous, rejoicing, filled with a great ambition and high ideals, they came forward to claim their own.

As a political event the Asian Conference was of secondary importance; as the symbol of the emergence of a new order it is likely to live in Asian history. And if its idealism wavered in the face of primeval passions loosed from restraint as the bonds of authority were temporarily relaxed; if its high hopes were tarnished by hitherto unsuspected national tensions; if its sense of direction was blurred by not always purposeful discussion, these are things that should not be allowed to conceal the fact that the conference chanced to be held at a psychologically decisive moment in the history of the continent. The ideas which found expression at it; the motives which inspired it; the trends of thought which emerged from it, conflicting and imprecise in some respects though they may have been, are, and are likely to remain, relevant not only to any consideration of Britain's future role in Asia but far more to any consideration of the pattern of future relations between East and West.

The Asian Conference had a character of its own. In part it was a visible, dramatic evidence of the awakening of a continent and of India's significant contribution to it; and in part it was a quasi-academic discussion of social, cultural, and political problems in Asia. There was among the leaders of the Indian Congress Party a sincere conviction that the hour had struck when India should take the initiative in Asian affairs. On the eve of independence she had a decisive contribution to make, a new role to play; and the interests of India and of South-East Asia at least demanded that she should play it. In December 1946, Nehru had expressed in the Constituent Assembly his hope that:

the new constitution for India will lead India to real freedom, that it will lead also to the freedom of other countries of Asia because, however unworthy, we have become—let us recognize it—leaders of the freedom movement of Asia, and whatever we do we should think of ourselves in these larger terms.

And leadership, with the responsibilities it brings, had come at a decisive, historic moment. In his opening speech to the conference in the Purana Qila, Nehru threw this into bold relief:

Standing on this watershed which divides two epochs of human history we can look back on our long past and look forward to the future. . . . Asia after a long period of quiescence has suddenly become important again in world affairs.

This feeling that the moment was historic was no doubt reinforced by the calculation that the time happened also to be propitious for India to lay a claim to leadership in the new Asia. China, rent by civil war, scarcely seemed in a position to dispute such a pretension, and nationalist sentiment running high in South-East Asia certainly favoured in principle the creation of a continental or more probably regional bloc under the leadership of a soon-to-be independent India. Indian leadership wisely exercised might well prove a powerful stabilizing force. Although at the very beginning of the conference Nehru explicitly denied that there was any ground for the fears expressed, particularly in the United States, that the conference heralded the birth of a pan-Asian movement, later discussions showed that many delegates were temperamentally prepared to think along such lines. The proposal that a permanent Asian organization might be set up in Delhi at the end of the deliberations of the conference reinforced the feeling that Congress India would welcome some formal recognition of its leadership in Asia. These ulterior aims were fiercely denounced in the *Dawn*, the Muslim newspaper, which spoke of the conference as the 'Asian fraud' perpetrated by Nehru 'the Hindu imperialist'. And, in consequence, rightly or wrongly, delegates from other Asian states came to regard the establishment of a permanent interim organization in Delhi as the criterion by which to measure the achievement of the Congress Party at the conference.

In fact, the Asian Conference, which lasted from 23 March to 2 April 1947, was as much the product of chance as of design. The Indian Council of World Affairs, which convened it, had in the first instance contemplated a regional conference for the South-East Asia area alone, and it was only when all the implications of such a regional conference were examined that it was felt that the time and the political conditions prevailing in Asia made the summoning of a continental conference the more appropriate course. Though the conference was in fact called by India there was much truth in Nehru's assertion that 'the idea of such a conference arose simultaneously in many minds and in many countries of Asia' because there was 'a widespread awareness that the time had come for us, peoples of Asia, to meet together, to hold together and to advance together.'

The conference was nominally a cultural conference. It was so designated partly to deflect criticism, partly to escape from certain practical political difficulties, but it was clear from the first that the discussions could not be confined to the cultural plane. Indeed, what the leaders in most Asian countries wanted was a conference which would fully and frankly discuss the political implications of the postwar world in their continental context. That being so, the cultural camouflage was something of a liability because it meant in practice that the politico-economic field was surveyed not as a whole but only in those parts which could, in some way or other, be linked with culture. That was why—to refer at this stage to one striking omission—there was virtually no consideration of strategic problems and their bearing on the new political order.

In his speech at the opening plenary session, from which a quotation has already been made, Nehru made much of the fact that 'one of the notable consequences of European domination of Asia has been the isolation of the countries of Asia from one another.' Before the British came, India had always had contacts and intercourse with neighbouring countries, but for the last two centuries she had been almost completely isolated from the rest of Asia, with her 'chief window on the outer world looking out to the sea route which led to England.' This sense of an enforced separation one from another in the past certainly enhanced in the eyes of the delegates the significance of the reunion. It was explained by Dr Sjahrir that so large an Indonesian delegation had been nominated just because in the past Indonesians had had so little opportunity of meeting fellow Asians. Of the delegates to the conference only a small minority, even of those from neighbouring countries, had visited India before. Inevitably, this first meeting of so many of the leaders of opinion in Asia invested the conference with a character and a potential importance which Nehru had in mind in claiming that 'when the history of our present times is written, this Conference may well stand out as the landmark which divides the past of Asia from the future.'

The conference was reasonably representative of the new forces in Asia. Geographically its character may be judged by the list of national representatives who attended (see Table 4.1). The total number of delegates was about 190 and the number of observers about 50. To these should be added distinguished visitors, mostly Indians or foreign diplomats accredited to the Government of India, who brought the total attendance up to nearly 400. The number of countries represented was 31 if the Soviet Asian republics are listed separately. The republics whose delegates were actually present for the deliberations of the conference were: Armenia, Kazakhstan, Tajikistan, Georgia, Uzbekistan, and Azerbaijan. The delegates

Table 4.1. Countries Represented at the Inter-Asian Conference, 1947

| Country | Delegates | Observers |
|---|---|---|
| Afghanistan | 5 | 1 |
| Arab League | - | 1 |
| Bhutan | - | 2 |
| Burma | 17 | 5 |
| Ceylon | 16 | 3 |
| China | 8 | 1 |
| Egypt | 3 | 1 |
| India | 52 | 6 |
| Indo-China | 7 | - |
| Indonesia | 8 | 8 |
| Iran | 3 | 2 |
| Korea | 5 | - |
| Malaya | 12 | - |
| Mongolia | 3 | 1 |
| Nepal | 5 | 2 |
| Palestine | 9 | 1 |
| Philippines | 6 | - |
| Siam | 2 | 2 |
| Soviet Republic | 14 | 2 |
| Tibet | 8 | 1 |
| Turkey | - | 1 |
| Australia | - | 2 |
| United Kingdom | - | 2 |
| United States | - | 3 |

One observer for the United Nations was also present.

from the two remaining Soviet Asian republics, Turkmenistan and Kirghizia, arrived characteristically enough in New Delhi after the conference had ended. Owing to travel and other difficulties, the delegations from Korea and Outer Mongolia arrived very late in the proceedings, and Dr Sjahrir reached New Delhi only a few days before their close, delayed by critical negotiations with the Dutch in Indonesia. The West Asian countries were but thinly represented.

Politically representative of the dominant trends and aspirations in Asia, the conference was not well balanced on particular regional or national questions. The delegations varied in quality as well as in numbers. For the most part they contained a strong official element, and when this was the case they were in a position to speak on political questions with a certain authority. The Chinese delegation, for example, was led by Cheng Yin-fun, a member of the Central Committee of the Kuomintang, and included the Vice-Minister of Education, and Professor Wen Yuan-ning whose contributions to the discussion were always purposeful. George Yeh of the Chinese Foreign Office was present as an observer.[2] Communist China was unrepresented. The delegates from Indonesia, who received so sympathetic a welcome, and the young, realistic team from Burma were representative of locally dominant political opinion. On the other hand, the delegation from Malaya did not fairly reflect the balance of opinion there.

The Indian delegation was by far the largest. Of its 52 members, 39 were Hindus, 7 Muslims and the remainder Sikhs, Parsees and Christians. The boycott of the conference by the Muslim League meant that the Muslim members of the delegation were either Congressmen or politically detached. As a result the delegation was politically unrepresentative of India as a whole, but it is perhaps not unfair to say that intellectually it was representative enough. Throughout the discussions this large Indian delegation played a predominant part. Since it reflected many conflicting political and more especially economic views, a coherent, considered statement of the Indian outlook was not placed before the conference. On the contrary, there was a refreshing variety of opinion which incidentally prevented the conference from feeling swamped by the Indian contribution to its deliberations.

2. Later, first Chinese Ambassador to the Republic of Burma.

The inherent dualism of the conference emerged in the speeches made at the opening plenary sessions. Its cultural purpose was insistently proclaimed, but it was the political and economic future of Asia that delegates had come to discuss, and they were not to be deflected from their purpose. The very atmosphere was permeated with political ideas and speculation. Those opening sessions, held in the Purana Qila, attended by vast crowds, heightened an agreeable feeling of history-in-the-making. At such a moment, culture could be no more than the modest handmaid of politics.

It was in the discussion groups that the work of the conference was done; it was from their deliberations that the trend of opinion among the Asian peoples emerged. To give a comprehensive summary of their discussions is not the purpose of this essay,[3] and it may be indeed that an impressionist record of their salient features is the more enlightening for a western reader.

The discussion groups covered five principal topics:

1. National movements for freedom.
2. Migration and racial problems.
3. Economic development and social services.
4. Cultural problems.
5. Women's problems.

Except for the first, these subjects could usefully have been treated in a non-political context, but the border-line was narrow and easily crossed. The Indian delegation and the delegations from South-East Asia played by far the most prominent part in the discussions, which as a result tended to circle round the problems of this area.

The general starting-point for the discussions was that the day had now come for the ending of imperialist exploitation and foreign rule in Asia. This assertion commanded so enthusiastic and general an assent that there was little or no examination of its political implications. Interest, therefore, tended to shift to the economic side. It was felt that economic development in Asian countries lagged behind even their political development; it was essential that living standards for the masses of the people should be raised, and the only way in which this could be done was by creating in

3. A full record is to be found in *Asian Relations* (Asian Relations Organization, New Delhi, 1948).

each state a planned economy. None of the states in the south-east margin of Asia felt that they could aim at national self-sufficiency. The objective must, therefore, be a planned economy over the area as a whole. This was impossible while the colonial powers were in control, but might, it was felt, soon become practicable.

Since the smaller countries could not hope to carry through this industrialization with their own resources, they favoured strongly a South-East Asian or even a continental bloc. Both the delegates from Ceylon and those from other countries, including India, expressed great misgivings about dollar imperialism, saying that they did not wish to shake off a political master only to be subjected to an economic master. Ceylon, Burma, Indonesia and Malaya, however, expressed equal mistrust of Indian and Chinese penetration and this subject, once raised, was a recurrent feature of the conference. No sooner was western exploitation denounced than fears emerged of a more stringent Indian and Chinese economic stranglehold once it had gone.

When opinion within the group appeared to be crystallizing in favour of the South-East Asian or even an Asian bloc, a leading Indian delegate intervened. Industrialization, he said, was the only means of raising the standard of living. For that, India and other countries must have a planned economy, but it was madness to think in terms of an economic bloc in Asia. Such a concept was neither desirable nor practicable; it would lead to conflict with the West, it would mean 'putting a rope around our own neck'. There was no reality in this sharp division between continents and, waving his hand in the direction of the Soviet and Palestinian delegates, he asked, 'To which continent do these gentlemen belong? Are they Asians or Europeans?' But he agreed that the Asian countries should have nothing further to do economically either with the imperialism 'that was retreating' or with the imperialism 'that was advancing behind dollar loans.' From this last point, the Chinese implicitly dissented. Provided that the loans were negotiated on satisfactory terms and did not give a foreign country any economic stranglehold, they maintained, there was no valid objection to them.

The same point of view emerged from the discussions on the racial question. There was a pronounced sentimental feeling for Asian unity, but once the general principles, on which it was easy to reach agreement, were disposed of, there emerged more and more clearly great mistrust of Indian and Chinese expansion in South-East Asia. It was in the final discussion on the racial question that a formal resolution was proposed by an Azerbaijan delegate, to the effect that no Asian country should permit discrimination on grounds of race. This resolution, which evoked much sympathy, was debarred on procedural grounds.

It is worth recording also that the group on racial problems felt that each country had a right and must necessarily retain the right of determining its own immigration policy. This view, which was accepted in the light of the formidable threat which the teeming millions of India and China constituted for the smaller South-East Asian countries, carried implications for the 'White Australia' policy which did not fail to elicit comment in the press. In a sense the views recorded by the group undoubtedly provided a not ineffective answer to Asians who challenge this policy on grounds of equity. On the other hand, it is clear that the conference itself had not in mind exclusion on a strictly racial basis.

The most significant of the discussion groups was the most political, that on national movements. Here it was generally accepted that the first essential step was the liquidation of imperial regimes in Asia, and autonomy for all dependent peoples. Some of the delegates spoke in extreme terms of the life blood having been sucked from their peoples by European exploitation, but on the whole their eyes were focused on the future rather than on the past. It was assumed that the day of western imperialism was over, and the delegates entertained in the Viceroy's House felt they were witnessing the last departing gleams of its sunset splendour, not only in New Delhi, but throughout a continent. The days of domination were drawing quickly to their close; the last page in the lamentable history of exploitation of the East by the West was being written and the sentiments of the hour were voiced by the Indian poetess, Sarojini Naidu: 'Fellow-Asians, my comrades and my kinsmen arise: remember the end of darkness is near. Together, men and women, let us march towards the dawn.'

In facing up to practical issues, the delicate question arose whether or not active assistance should be given by the more powerful Asian states to their smaller neighbours 'struggling to be free'. The possibility was frankly considered. Many of the delegates from South-East Asia, including the not very representative delegation from Malaya, argued the case for common action. This was fully endorsed by the delegates from Indonesia and Vietnam, who appealed to the greater Asian powers to give more than mere moral or sentimental support.

These outspoken appeals for intervention called forth a rejoinder from Nehru. He urged the delegates not to tread the dangerous path of recommending armed assistance to national movements. The situation in Indo-China was most complicated. It was the path of wisdom to try to narrow the area of conflict, not to enlarge it. Though every delegate should know that freedom movements in South-East Asia would have the whole-hearted moral sympathy of India, it was altogether unrealistic to expect active intervention.

A suggestion was also made that a neutrality bloc should be formed in the continent as a whole, or alternatively, in South-East Asia. This proposal clearly contemplated that the participating countries should not only refrain from taking an active part in any war irrespective of the cause of its outbreak, but should also deny to all belligerents a supply of raw materials. These views, which seemed to command wide sympathy, were hardly consistent with the acceptance of United Nations obligations, though it was interesting to observe that a neutrality bloc was advocated at one and the same time as fuller United Nations representation for Asian countries.

The conference was debarred from passing resolutions, and therefore, although the general sense of the Conference emerged clearly enough on a great many questions, it was not recorded in precise and practical form. There was revealed, however, a tolerably wide area of agreement amongst Asian peoples and a desire to act in concert. The one positive conclusion was the decision to hold a similar conference in two years' time in China and in the meantime to set up a Provincial Council on which all Asian states would be represented, under the presidency of Nehru, with a view to creating some permanent machinery for the summoning of continental or of regional conferences. What form the permanent organization should take remained undecided. Nehru remarked that as President of the Provisional Council he would have nothing to guide him but the 'memories of a thousand years'. It is clear, however, that its work must depend largely on the vitality of the various national organizations for its effectiveness. The Provisional Council, recognizing this, recommended as a first step that institutes devoted wholly to Asian studies should be set up in each country.

The most significant thing about these practical conclusions was that the second conference should be held in China. This was the question about which delegates were much concerned, particularly in the concluding days of the conference, and the decision reached was an undoubted disappointment to the Indian representatives. They had hoped that a strong and lasting organization might be established, and for that a permanent centre was a well-nigh indispensable condition.

The countries attending the conference fell very roughly into five groups: India, China, South-East Asia, with which Siam may be included, the West Asian states, the USSR. There were, of course, many cross-currents and on certain subjects there were even sharp divisions of opinion within individual delegations, but by and large this was the pattern that emerged.

It was the aim of India to acquire implicitly some form of leadership in Asia. Sympathetic though many might be to the fulfilment of her legitimate aspirations there was something curiously unpropitious, even ominous, in the news of a boycott by the Muslim League as the conference assembled. At the first plenary meeting, further indication of the prevailing tension was given by an announcement of the curfew hours in New Delhi. Throughout the proceedings, somewhat fulsome references to the work of the conference in the Congress papers were matched by bitter attacks in the League press. In these attacks Nehru was not spared and in the *Dawn*'s final commentary on the conference a vicious onslaught was made on him.

Skilfully he has worked himself into some sort of all-Asian leadership. That is just what this ambitious Hindu leader had intended—to thrust himself upon the Asian nations as their leader and through his attainment of that prestige and eminence to further the expansionist designs of Indian Hinduism.

These were reminders that behind the conference, though casting only passing shadows on its deliberations, lay the dark, smouldering passions of communalism. Some six months later, among historic ruins in the Purana Qila, where the plenary sessions had been held, were herded together some 50,000 wretched, fearful Muslim refugees seeking sanctuary from the fury which had devastated the Punjab, and was now let loose in all its horror in the capital of India.

During the Asian Conference many responsible Indians frankly recognized the possibility of civil war. A few entertained fears of the emergence of a militarist Hindu state. Both had some influence on the opinions of delegates. If India were to fall the victim of civil war, then she was not likely to prove an effective leader of the Asian nations. Moreover, might not internal dissension bring in its train the possibility of ultimate intervention from outside in Indian affairs? That such questions were asked was in one sense more important than their actual justification. They go far to explain why the Chinese view that Delhi should not be the permanent meeting place for continental conferences was acceded to unanimously. On this point the Chinese representatives, anxious to ensure that China's claims to political and cultural leadership in Asia were not overlooked, had reason to be well satisfied. Her delegation, representative only of Nationalist China, was more experienced in international conferences than any other, and intervened rarely but usually with effect.

The South-East Asia group, anxious to assert itself, took advantage of the conference to confirm the newly acquired status of its several members. To them the concept of a continental bloc—the slogan 'Asia for the Asians'—made a great appeal. They were conscious, however, that individually they were not strong enough to stand on their own feet either economically or politically, and whilst anxious to throw off foreign rule, they were filled with mistrust of the naturally expansive tendencies of both China and India. As a form of safeguard it was implicitly understood, though rarely explicitly stated, that these countries would probably retain a treaty link with their former European rulers.

There was a particularly close bond of sympathy between the Indonesian and Vietnam delegates. Both, in common with the Malayans, were keenly interested in the possibility of strong moral support amounting to positive assistance from their great neighbours. The undoubtedly powerful sentimental appeal of these small states might have produced more concrete results had the situation been less confused. In this respect Vietnam suffered particularly. Indo-China was represented not only by the Republican delegates from Vietnam but also by French-approved delegates from the other territories. It was some little time before the conference as a whole was able to identify these rival representatives and to distinguish clearly between their respective claims.

The delegates from West Asia chose to play a comparatively minor, non-committal role. Thinly represented in any event, these states clearly stood outside the main field of discussion, though the Jewish delegates from Palestine made a good impression by their contribution to the talks on agricultural reconstruction. The representatives of the Muslim states acquired no one-sided picture of Indian politics.

The Soviet representatives made a rather mixed impression. It will be recalled that the republics represented were Armenia, Kazakhstan, Tadjikistan, Georgia, Uzbekistan and Azerbaijan. To what extent they are culturally autonomous was left a matter of speculation, though their representatives lost few opportunities of emphasizing their distinctive regional contributions to the life of the Soviet Union. In the earlier stages the continued iteration by the delegates of the transformation effected in Soviet Asia by the Revolution of 1917 rather wearied their audience. The delegate from Kazakhstan—to take one example—said that the Revolution had brought freedom to the people of Kazakhstan, guaranteeing human rights and making possible a great national regeneration. The Tsarists had done everything to check industrialization, but now Kazakhstan enjoyed one of the most advanced industrial economies in the world. Before 1917, 98 per cent of her people had been illiterate; now they were 100 per cent literate. Where formerly there had been no institutes for higher studies there were now twenty-three such academies. In time the repetition of this theme with minor variations by the Soviet representatives made its impression and this, perhaps, was reinforced by a film show which included, amongst more cultural subjects, a full-length colour newsreel of the victory march in the Red Square on May Day 1946.

Apart from publicizing the achievements of the USSR in every field, the Soviet delegates were concerned to defeat any move towards the emergence of a continental bloc. Though the tenor of their speeches was anti-imperialist they did not seem to have any specific target, and they were not anti-British in tone.

English was the official language of the Conference and the majority of the delegates, including virtually all those from South-East Asia, were able to speak it fluently. Some of the delegates from West Asia and all the delegates from the Soviet Asian republics required interpreters. The practice both in plenary session and in discussion groups was for speakers to speak in their own language, with the interpreter immediately following with an English translation. Proceedings were not slowed down as much as might be expected, partly because several of the delegates who required interpreters were able to understand English even though they could not speak it. Indeed one of the outstanding impressions left by the conference was that English is by general consent the only possible lingua franca of Asia. It was a Soviet delegate from Georgia who observed that there existed in the world already two forms of English, one spoken in Britain, the other in the United States. 'The need was for a third, Asian English, better than either of the existing forms of this impossible language.'

The conference threw up many personalities who seem destined to play a prominent part in Asian affairs in the coming years. Some of these personalities, such as Dr Sjahrir, whose quiet good sense much impressed the assembled delegates, were already well known to a wider world. Others who made their mark in the conference were Wen Yuan-ning and George Yeh from China; Justice Kyaw Myint, the leader of the Burman delegation, a most resolute chairman, who later in the year presided at the trial of U Saw in Rangoon, Dr Abu Hanifah, leader of the Indonesian delegation and Akvlediani from Georgia; Dr Hossein Sadighi from Iran who recalled the higher things of the mind in fine, mellifluous phrases, and was clearly marked out from the first as the chosen spokesman for the great ceremonial occasions; the Honourable S.W.R.D. Bandaranaike from Ceylon, later a member of the first Dominion Government of the island, and the Tibetan representatives, who were the most colourful figures in a conference that was by no means lacking in colour. Of one of them there is a story that deserves to be told. Educated at Rugby, he preserved throughout the conference an air of courteous, gentlemanly detachment from the seething, restless crowds of delegates from less happy lands. There was a never-to-be forgotten moment in the economic discussion group where the validity of advanced left-wing socialist doctrine had hitherto passed unquestioned, when he walked slowly up to the dispatch box in Tibetan costume, carrying an incongruous Homburg in his hand, to answer inquiries about the sordid question of economic conditions in Tibet. After some desultory remarks he was asked, 'Who owns the land in Tibet?' 'The nobles, of course' was the reply. The Soviet interpreters worked overtime, the young Indian delegates jumped to their feet, clamouring for further elucidations, but with a dignity of which Dr Arnold would have been proud, the Tibetan spokesman declined to answer; and picking up his Homburg walked with cool, unhurried steps back to his seat. By word and action he had explained, with an effectiveness that left no room for argument, that there were still large parts of Asia to which contemporary social and economic thinking is utterly and absolutely irrelevant.

In the Indian delegation were many already well known: N.M. Joshi, the veteran labour leader, who presided over the group on labour problems; Krishna Menon, later Indian High Commissioner in London; Vijayalakshmi Pandit, sister of Nehru and later first Indian Ambassador to Moscow; Sardar Panikkar, Dewan of Bikaner and later first Indian Ambassador to China; and above all, Nehru. The conference in a real sense was Nehru's conference. None could fail to be flattered by the time he devoted to its deliberations. He was present not only in the plenary sessions but also at many of the discussion groups. He lunched at Constitution House where the conference was held; he personally showed delegates round the Constituent Assembly. The more cynical might talk of 'Nehru fiddling while India burned', but among delegates as a whole his already high reputation was enhanced. His interventions in the discussions were uniformly helpful; his speeches in the plenary sessions were remarkable both for their fluency and for their consciousness of high responsibility at this critical hour in Asian history. When dangerous courses were advocated he threw his great influence on the side of statesmanlike moderation. Throughout, his personality and charm showed to great advantage, though a certain restlessness carried with it the suggestion of a man who was running the risk of overstraining himself by the weight and variety of the responsibilities he undertook. It passed through some minds that this Kashmiri aristocrat might be destined to fill the role of Kerensky in an Indian revolution, perhaps because he gave the impression of being a man of many gifts who lacked the single-minded, narrow strength of purpose which in the past has often carried leaders safely through a revolutionary epoch.

Mahatma Gandhi, who attended the last two sessions of the conference, was received with the reverential awe that is so rarely accorded to a prophet in his own country. Hailed as 'the beloved teacher', 'the saviour of India', 'the father of a continent', his message was a spiritual message and he recalled with pride that all the great religions of the world had come from Asia. Non-violence and love, he said, were the virtues which the past had to teach the West. In India, too, these lessons had still to be learned.

Nehru was justified in saying that the most important thing about the Asian Conference was that it was held. That in itself made it the herald of a new era in Asia. Its more detailed significance is difficult to assess, partly because the conference, possessing no mandatory authority, reflected tendencies not yet clearly defined, rather than carefully considered opinions on future policy. However, certain practical, if intangible consequences seem clear. By recording a unanimous view that imperial rule in Asia should end, the conference probably hastened the day of its ending. But even in the anxiety to rid Asia of colonialism the predominant impression was one of moderation, and delegates were as much concerned to consolidate the ground which had already been won as to remove the last vestiges of imperial rule. Here it was perhaps influenced by the desire to reinsure against any revival of imperial pretensions and in that respect there seems little doubt that the conference did succeed in creating a spirit which would make it dangerous, if not impossible, for any imperial power to try to regain what had been lost. Within the new Asia, the first stage may be merely mistrust on the part of the smaller powers of the greater, but the next, unless wiser counsels prevail, may well be a struggle for leadership between the three Great Powers on the Asian mainland, India, China, and the Soviet Union, in which Japan might eventually play no insignificant part. An awareness of these still distant dangers underlies the contribution which the Asian Relations Organization may take to the future peace and prosperity of the continent. By bringing divisions to the surface, by encouraging a frank discussion of them, a great deal may be done to lessen or even remove their harmful consequences.

The conference was primarily concerned with continental problems, but it was well understood that these could be viewed only in a wider context. Those states who had recently or were about to become autonomous were particularly concerned to play a part in world affairs, and the instrument that lay ready to hand was the United Nations Organization. For the time being these new recruits to the number of sovereign states think in terms of the opportunities which the United Nations Organization may afford for putting their case before the world, and not of the obligations which membership will entail. But allowing for this understandable and probably short-lived reaction, the advantages of bringing these new states into the arena of world politics are great. They have a distinctive contribution to make and their influence is likely to be pacific. From what was said at the conference and from subsequent events, it is clear they are resolved for as long as possible to 'paddle their own canoe', and not to become tied to either of the Great Power blocs.

Though there were many criticisms of the rule of the European powers in Asia, the political doctrines and political practice of the western world, and particularly of Britain, were not disregarded. At the conference, English, as has already been noted, was the recognized language; parliamentary democracy was acknowledged as the highest form of political life by all the South-East Asian countries, and the goal of a planned social democracy was accepted almost without dissent as the end for which all should strive. Future conferences will show whether the rival system outlined with such consistency by the delegates from the Soviet Asian republics has won over many adherents.

The effectiveness of the Asian Relations Organization, in the long run, will clearly depend on the vigour of the national organizations which will work for it. The decision to hold the 1949 Conference in China, carrying as it did the implication of a peripatetic organization with no fixed headquarters—for this, geography made New Delhi the ideal site—has in effect vested final responsibility in the respective national organizations. This might prove to be a fatal source of weakness should the spontaneous enthusiasm which called the 1947 Conference into existence fade away. That is the risk involved in the decision to emasculate the central organization, but it may reasonably be hoped that it will be avoided. For if the welcome of the outside world to the Asian Relations Organization must for some time remain a trifle cautious, it should be none the less sincere, for it is only just to recognize that the organization has great potentialities for promoting peace and goodwill in the most heavily populated regions of the earth. At this stage its work is not to be judged by concrete results alone. It was Cromwell who said that no man goes so far as he who knows not where he is going. The first Asian Conference did not know precisely where it was going; still less did it reach any particular destination, but it would not for these reasons alone be wise to conclude that it may not go a long way. And whatever the fate of the organization it has founded, the conference did at a decisive moment in Asian history provide a platform for ideas and aspirations, many of which in the fullness of time will bear their fruit, sweet or bitter as it may be. It is these ideas and these aspirations which the western world, and most of all the British Commonwealth, cannot afford to disregard.

# 5

## Mountbatten: Noted Impact as India's Last Viceroy

On 18 December 1946, Britain's Labour Prime Minister, Clement Attlee, invited Lord Mountbatten to succeed Lord Wavell as Viceroy of India. Mountbatten accepted on condition that an early time-limit was set to British rule, that he was to have plenipotentiary powers, and that he was to be the last viceroy.

In late March 1947, Mountbatten arrived in Delhi to take up his appointment. His impact was remarkable, as I can testify, being in the Indian capital at that time as an observer at the Asian Relations Conference which had been called by Nehru to symbolize the re-emergence of an independent Asia.

### GLITTERING FIGURE

Mountbatten's impact was made by force of personality—he was indeed a glittering figure—and he was possessed of coolness as well as courage as was memorably shown later when, on hearing news of Gandhi's assassination, Mountbatten quietened a clamorous crowd by saying that the assassin was a Hindu fanatic without knowing if this was so, but aware that any hesitation on his part would have led to a massacre of Muslims.

But in 1947, most important was Mountbatten's resolve to transfer power at the earliest possible moment coupled with his understanding of the mood of the new India and the new Asia, which enabled him to establish easy, friendly relations with the Indian National Congress leaders of that historic time, Gandhi,

Nehru, Patel.° His one failure—with the Muslims' leader, Jinnah—
was perhaps inevitable. Mountbatten wished to transfer power
quickly to a united India; Jinnah was resolved that the British
should divide before they quit. On this issue, the Congress leaders
and Mountbatten were in accord, but when it was evident to both
that there was to be partition—and the Congress leaders were
explicit in their rejection of use of force—Mountbatten turned
Jinnah's two-nations argument against him with rigorous logic,
contending that if indeed there were two nations, then the frontier
between them would have to cut across the two key provinces of
the Punjab and Bengal on the basis of communal allegiance. Jinnah
complained bitterly that, as a result, he was being left with a moth-
eaten truncated Pakistan.

At midnight on 14/15 August 1947, India, in Nehru's words,
held her tryst with destiny. Mountbatten was acclaimed in the
crowded streets of the capital on Independence Day, while India's
first independent government invited him to stay on as first
Governor-General.

In Karachi, however, the atmosphere was first cool and then
hostile.

Nor was Mountbatten a friend to Indian princely pretensions.
He told the princes very plainly that it was their duty to cooperate
with the new order.

Mountbatten strongly supported the accommodation of India
as a republic within the Commonwealth, such as was achieved in
1949 almost coincidentally with Ireland's departure as a republic
from it. That settlement owed much to Irish precedents, of which
Mountbatten was fully aware and, had the settlement come earlier,
it would, I have reason to believe, have commended itself to
President de Valera.

'[He] lost no time in having a series of meetings with Indian leaders at
which he sought to get to know them and to elicit their views on major
issues. The records of them constitute one of the more remarkable examples
in modern times of history in the making, conveying, as they do, something
of the immediacy of moments when the fulfilment of purpose was
conditioned by the resolution of complex problems and over-shadowed
by uncertain and dangerous prospects, civil war, to which there were not
infrequent allusions, the most menacing among them. (N. Mansergh and
P. Moon (eds.), *India: The Transfer of Power 1942–47*, HMSO, 1981, vol. x,
p. xiii).

Mountbatten had his critics of his Indian policies. They were chiefly of the Right where some thought of him as a sort of Philippe Égalité in naval uniform, while those of cautious temperament felt that he moved too fast to Indian independence.

But Mountbatten's reputation will long be cherished by those who believed in the independence of that great nation, whose people not only continued to hold Mountbatten in highest esteem but took him to their hearts. What terrible irony is there in the reported manner of the death of one who was instrumental in bringing about the greatest act of national decolonization in the twentieth century.

# 6

# The Implications of Éire's Relationship with the British Commonwealth of Nations[*]

It is not my intention to review the course of Anglo-Irish relations but to examine in some detail the implications of the political and constitutional relationship between Éire on the one hand and the United Kingdom and the British Commonwealth of Nations on

[*]This lecture, which popularizes de Valera's pioneering concept of external association, was written after the author's return from the 1947 Asian Relations Conference in Delhi. It was delivered in Chatham House to a large audience, including cabinet ministers, government officials and diplomats. Mansergh recalls:

Since the Cabinet papers for this period have become available, I have discovered that at the suggestion of Stafford Cripps this paper was sent to Attlee, who referred it to a committee who were examining Commonwealth relations. The Canadians became interested and something of this kind did emerge. India became as a republic a full member state, with an acknowledgement of the King as the symbol of the free association and as such Head of the Commonwealth—a further acknowledgement to Mr de Valera for his pioneering of the way would not have been unfitting. My lecture was referred to in the *Sunday Independent* and prompted questions to John A. Costello when he went to Ottawa—or so the Canadians tell me—on the question of whether the External Relations Act should be repealed or not. The repeal took effect in April 1949, at which date the Indian republican membership which exists to this day was established. *Nationalism and Independence—Selected Irish Papers* (Cork University Press, 1997), p. 252.

the other in the years of Irish membership of or association with it. That these implications have been of far-reaching importance for Éire itself and for the development of the Commonwealth as a whole is evident and certain, but over and above that they have or have had a particular relevance in a wider field. In Asia, and in many parts of Africa, the British Commonwealth will be confronted with nationally self-conscious peoples balancing in their minds the relative advantages of equal partnership within the Commonwealth and independent existence outside it. Many factors will determine their choice and among them the psychological factor will be by no means least. However different in form, the problem that now confronts British statesmanship is the same in essentials as that which confronted it in Ireland a quarter of a century ago. The problem, broadly stated, is that of associating a people with a cultural tradition of its own and an intensely national outlook with a group of states whose existence depends upon the reconciliation of individual interests with those of the community as a whole. In 1921 the problem was solved by the grant of dominion status to the Irish Free State. Was this the right solution? Can dominions be made artificially as well as grow naturally? Has the wisdom of the solution been justified in the sequel? Did it display the right psychological approach? These are questions that seem to deserve critical examination. Like India, Ireland is a mother country with a cultural tradition that may be traced back to the earliest centuries of the Christian era, and for that reason, if for no other, recent experience of Anglo–Irish relations is likely to provide a source from which many lessons may be learnt. Of that, those who determine the destinies of India, of Pakistan, of Burma and of the other countries in South-East Asia, are well aware. The possibility of finding a solution to the Dutch–Indonesian problem in some form of 'external association' on the Irish model was examined in the past year and it was also considered perhaps too casually, as a possible foundation for our future relations with Burma. In both instances, political tensions made progress difficult. But the lasting impression left from these somewhat desultory discussions is that there is a real need for some considered assessment of the concept of 'external association'; of its history in the general context of Anglo–Irish relations, and of the lessons to be drawn from it for application in other fields.

It was on 30 July 1921 that Lloyd George invited de Valera to come to a peace conference in order to 'ascertain how the association of Ireland with the community of nations known as the British Empire can best be reconciled with Irish nationalist aspirations.' That, concisely stated, was the problem on which the prolonged, tense treaty negotiations turned. To Lloyd George's question there were in fact answers given. The first was that given by the Irish delegation briefed as they had been before leaving for London by the Dáil, the Cabinet and its President, de Valera. It was external association. Opposed to it was the British answer, dominion status.

The phrase 'external association' was interpreted by the Irish delegates as meaning absolute sovereignty in all internal affairs for an Ireland associated with the British Commonwealth for purposes of external concern. The significant points in the draft treaty which the Irish delegation took with them to London were: (i) that Ireland be recognized as a sovereign independent state; (ii) that Britain renounce all claim to govern or legislate for Ireland; (iii) that Ireland agree to become an external associate of the Commonwealth on the understanding that in this capacity her status should not be less than that of the 'sovereign partner States of the Commonwealth'. It followed logically from this concept of external association that while Irish citizens and citizens of the British Commonwealth might and should enjoy reciprocal rights, the idea of a common citizenship had to be discarded. In broader terms, under the original tentative pre-treaty drafts for external association and in the variant put forward by de Valera and the dissident republicans in Document No. 2 after the treaty had been signed, Ireland would have been a republic not within the Empire but associated with it. Throughout—and this is important—the emphasis was placed upon Ireland's internal sovereignty, upon which no restriction formal or informal was to be tolerated, to so great an extent that the Irish delegation to the conference were instructed, if compromise they must, to compromise on external affairs. After the issue had been decided Document No. 2, which constituted de Valera's considered alternative to the treaty settlement, explicitly recorded that the matters of common concern should include defence, peace and war and all matters considered as being of common concern among the members of the British Commonwealth. Throughout, one is left with the impression that agreement in the field of external affairs presented comparatively little difficulty in 1921 provided no concessions of substance or form were asked for the internal field.[1]

It was precisely on the question of the symbols of sovereignty in Ireland that the United Kingdom delegation were least prepared to compromise. Mindful of the problem of Northern Ireland and for more general reasons of policy and sentiment, they were insistent that the bond of unity represented by a common loyalty to the Crown should be recognized and that in conformity with existing practice in the dominions, the King be the head of the state, acting through a Governor-General appointed by him, and that an oath of allegiance to the King, in recognition of his position, be taken by the members of the Irish Parliament. Here the doctrinaire republicans remained adamant; it was an issue on which they were prepared to make no concession. To them as indeed to the United Kingdom delegates, the form and symbols of the state were fundamental. The Irish delegation, led by Michael Collins and Arthur Griffith, influenced more by practical considerations than theoretical conceptions, decided on the other hand that dominion status offered a reasonable compromise solution and signed the treaty. Civil war in Ireland was the sequel.

The treaty which was signed in December 1921 gave dominion status to the Irish Free State which comprised twenty-six of the thirty-two counties of Ireland. The new state was to have the same constitutional status in the British Commonwealth as 'the Dominion of Canada, the Commonwealth of Australia, the Dominion of New Zealand and the Union of South Africa'; more particularly the status of the Irish Free State was defined as being that of the Dominion of Canada, and 'the law, practice and constitutional usage governing the relationship of the Crown and of the Imperial Parliament to the Dominion of Canada shall govern their relationship to the Irish Free State.' This intimate association of the Irish Free State with the other dominions was intended to ensure that Ireland should evolve in status step by step with the oversea dominions: that she should feel her position guaranteed by the mere

1. See Frank Pakenham, *Peace by Ordeal* (London, 1935), ch. IV, where a full and authoritative account of the Irish proposals is given. See also D. Macardle, *The Irish Republic* (London, 1937), pp. 600–12, 653–64.

fact that it rested on the same constitutional foundation as theirs; and finally in this way the danger of defining dominion status, of which Lloyd George was so rightly conscious, was wholly avoided. Dominion status was therefore conferred on a country which had not evolved towards it but reached it in one revolutionary step. In 1921, Latham wrote 'the quiet waters of the conventional Commonwealth' were disturbed 'by the immersion of a foreign body.'[2] What have been the consequences?

Between the British view of the treaty and the Irish there has always been a gulf. The signature of the treaty was regarded by Churchill, in words which acquired a fuller meaning in 1940, 'as one of the most questionable and hazardous experiments upon which a great empire in the plenitude of its power has ever embarked.' If one may judge by the comments of the press on 7 December 1921, the popular welcome for the treaty was cordial, all the more cordial because there was in it a sense of relief coupled with a satisfying sense of achievement. The *Daily Telegraph* on 7 December 1921 summed it up in saying 'this event is the greatest that has happened in the internal affairs of the country for generations'. The critics were on the right, the *Morning Post* denouncing the treaty as 'the most disastrous blunder ever committed by a British Government', and their intransigence explains many of the manoeuvres to which Lloyd George felt bound to resort during the negotiations. Not to be overlooked either was the great body of opinion which regarded the whole affair as a tiresome intrusion in the brave, new postwar world. They found their voice in the *Daily Express* which commented: 'Now for business! The settlement of the Irish question throws wide open the door for the entry of the Boom in Trade.'

The Irish reaction is most faithfully reflected in the Dáil debate on the Treaty. There the settlement was endorsed only by a narrow margin of seven votes and even those who supported the treaty took as their text Parnell's saying that 'no man can set a boundary to the march of a nation.' In other words the pro-treaty party defended the treaty as one step forward on the road to independence, while their opponents denounced it as a step sideways leading them on to a road along which they had neither the wish nor the right to travel. And to their denunciation was added the

2. *Survey of British Commonwealth Affairs*, vol. 1 (London, 1937), p. 513.

condemnation of the dead—of the martyrs of 1916. Nothing throws into clearer relief the width of the gulf that separated English and Irish opinion at that time than the fact that Document No. 2 was put forward by de Valera as a compromise solution embodying every concession which republican opinion was prepared to make. The reaction to it in Britain is well known, but less well known is the fact that to this day doctrinaire republicans in Ireland taunt de Valera with having gone too far and abandoned his principles in a vain search for compromise. No one on the Irish side, except perhaps Arthur Griffith, regarded the treaty as an ideal settlement, though the majority believed it was to be preferred to any practicable alternative. In such circumstances its prospects of survival were clearly slight.

Looking back over the years one reflection can scarcely be avoided. Dominion status despite its flexibility was not the most obvious answer to Lloyd George's question. What place was there for an inflamed self-assertive Irish nationalism in full and equal partnership with a British Commonwealth composed as it then was of states peopled for the most part by immigrants from the British Isles? Ireland herself was a mother country and for that reason, if for no other, felt she had little in common either psychologically or culturally with the oversea dominions. The very flexibility of dominion status, which was the pride of the statesmen of the Commonwealth, evoked only misgiving in Irish minds. They craved, whether wisely or not is beside the point, for precise, logical definitions. They thought not in terms of evolution but of revolution. While the majority were probably not convinced republicans, they certainly felt no natural, spontaneous loyalty to the Crown. Later de Valera referred to the King as 'an alien king' because if given a free choice the people of Ireland would not 'elect him'. The Balfour Declaration of 1926 by its emphasis on the Crown as the symbol of unity of the Commonwealth enhanced its importance as a factor in determining the attitude of Ireland to the Commonwealth.

The treaty was a great step forward for the Irish Free State. There Griffith was right. Even de Valera admitted, some ten years later, that progress under it had been rapid and substantial. But it must also be recognized that it was a step forward along a road different from that along which the Irish Nationalists had hoped to travel. The result of this incompatibility between status and ideology in fact on the one hand meant that Ireland never psychologically regarded herself as a dominion and on the other hand, it introduced into the circle of the dominions a state which shared the ideals and the outlook of the oversea partners but remained unreconciled to the particular constitutional system which they had evolved. The sequel was very much as might have been expected. In the great period of the Commonwealth evolution between 1926 and 1931 Ireland played her full part. At the Imperial Conferences of 1926 and 1930 her representatives were in the forefront of every move to secure equality not only of status, but also of function. She strengthened greatly the fissiparous tendencies within the Commonwealth, though it is probable that the impact of the Irish Free State on the Commonwealth served for the most part to hasten a development which Canadian and South African opinion would in any event have demanded; this is a subject which deserves far more detailed study than it has so far received. One result of forcing the Irish Free State into the same pattern as the oversea dominions was to change the pattern. So long as it was a case of 'pulling asunder the old colonial empire', to use McGilligan's phrase, there was a community of purpose with the oversea dominions, but when that task was completed it was inevitable that their evolution and that of the Free State should tend to diverge.

The divergence became apparent as soon as de Valera assumed office in 1932. For the next six years in the constitutional field the symbols of Commonwealth unity were one by one removed. The first to go was the oath—that oath which Lord Birkenhead is reputed to have described as 'the greatest piece of prevarication in history', because there were embodied in it so many nice inflexions of meaning in a vain attempt to reconcile all parties to its adoption. It was denounced by de Valera as 'an intolerable burden', 'a relic of medievalism imposed from outside under the threat of immediate and terrible war'. There followed the appeal to the Privy Council, the functions and then the office of Governor-General. In defence of this unilateral abrogation of the treaty, de Valera maintained that Commonwealth symbolism had been imposed under duress. That there was incompatibility between Lloyd George's pressure, to use no stronger word, to secure the acceptance of dominion status in 1921 and the Balfour Declaration of five years later with its description of the members of the Commonwealth as autonomous communities 'freely associated as members of the British Commonwealth' is hardly to be denied. But whatever the merits of the dispute, by 1937 the wheel had come almost in full circle; de Valera drafted a new constitution, had it accepted by a plebiscite, and with the sanction of popular approval established a system of government in Ireland conforming in all essentials to the external association which had been rejected in 1921. Under this constitution the Governor-General was replaced by an elected President, the oath of allegiance by an oath of loyalty to the state; its enactment was preceded by legislation which repudiated common citizenship and replaced it by the concept of reciprocal citizenship. Only one thing, however, the constitution did not do. It did not declare that the state was a republic.

Why was Ireland (Éire) declared in the Constitution of 1937 to be 'a sovereign, independent democratic State' without an explicit affirmation that it was a republic? The answer is threefold. Britain might have retaliated in the economic field at a time when Irish trade was still suffering from the economic war; more important, sentiment in Northern Ireland would have been further alienated with the result that the already slender prospects of bringing about the reunion of Ireland would have disappeared for generations; and finally, de Valera's own predilections, which were not made known till 1946. For nine years the state remained without a name but in that year this regrettable lacuna was remedied when de Valera rather casually, in answer to a question in the Dáil, stated that she was in fact a republic, and had been one since the Constitution of 1937 was enacted. To the question as to why no formal designation had then been made, de Valera replied that while this state is 'a sovereign independent republic unfortunately it did not cover the whole of Ireland and for that reason I did not introduce into the Constitution the name of Poblacht na h'Éireann because that was a name which was sacred.'

What was the attitude of the republic to the Commonwealth and to the symbol of its unity, the Crown? In September 1947, de Valera for his part defined the position. 'As a matter of our external policy', he said,

we are associated with the States of the British Commonwealth of Nations. We are not members of it. We are associates of the States of the

Commonwealth; but if they regard the existence of the King as a necessary link, if they consider that it is the bond they have, then we have not got that bond. . . . We are externally associated with the States of the British Commonwealth.

This view was at first accepted without substantial modification by the inter-party government which came to power the following year. MacBride, the Minister for External Affairs, stated categorically in August 1948 that Éire was not a member of the Commonwealth. The relationship was described by him and reaffirmed by the Taoiseach, Costello, as being one of friendly association for purposes of common concern.

The Irish interpretation of her constitutional development has always conflicted with that of the United Kingdom government and of the other governments of the Commonwealth. In 1937 the United Kingdom government with the assent of the governments of the oversea dominions stated that they regarded the new constitution 'as not effecting a fundamental alteration in the position of the Irish Free State.' This statement had unquestionable tactical merits. It averted a final severance; it left the next move to de Valera and he did not make it for nine years. To maintain a bridge between the two countries was no mean achievement, and it was one evidently welcomed by de Valera, for when asked to record his views about the United Kingdom government's statement he replied 'No comment.'

On a long-term view the wisdom of the policy of continuing to regard Éire as a dominion seems much more questionable. The statement of 1937 in the form in which it was made carried certain implications, the more far-reaching because the opinion then expressed is still understood to be the official view of His Majesty's government. It follows from it that Éire remains a dominion within the Commonwealth even though her constitution is that of a republic, though the Crown has no place either in her executive or in her legislative organs of government, and, most important, even though in the view of her own government she owes no allegiance to the Crown, and is not a full partner in the Commonwealth but a sovereign state outside it associated with it for certain purposes. The statement introduced superficially a new element of flexibility into Commonwealth relations, but fundamentally did it not betray a disturbing rigidity of outlook? For if in fact, de Valera's sustained and unremitting efforts to uproot the treaty settlement had effected no fundamental alteration in the position of the Irish Free State, then, after due allowance has been made for the changes in status embodied in the Statute of Westminster, the stand of the British negotiators against external association in 1921 was, at the least, short-sighted. Were not the United Kingdom government papering over political inconsistency by verbal consistency? Were they not saying, in effect, we will continue to recognize Éire as a dominion even though Éire herself does not consider she is a dominion and even though she does not pay allegiance to the Crown which was regarded by the Balfour Declaration as the symbol of the free association of the Commonwealth because it is tactically a good thing to do and because the admission of the existence of a new form of relationship within the Commonwealth might have all sorts of embarrassing repercussions? While the policy of maintaining a bridge was sound the method adopted seems in retrospect unfortunate.

It is true that it can be, and was, argued, for example by K.C. Wheare, that Éire owed allegiance to the common Crown because the Constitution of 1937 provides that

for the purpose of the exercise of any executive function of the State in or in connection with its external relations, the Government may . . . avail of or adopt any organ, instrument or method of procedure used or adopted for the like purpose by the members of any group or league of nations with which the State is or becomes associated for the purpose of international cooperation in matters of common concern.[3]

This skilfully drafted permissive clause sanctions the procedure already adopted in the External Relations Act of 1936, which authorizes the use of the Crown in the form of the King's signature for the purpose of appointing diplomatic and consular representatives to be accredited to foreign countries. The practical difficulties in war time were circumvented by the appointment of Chargés d'Affaires, and this use of the King's signature remained thereafter as the one formal indication of the association between Éire and the Commonwealth. To say with Wheare that it meant that Éire owes allegiance to the common Crown seems unwarranted except

3. *The Statute of Westminster and Dominion Status* (Oxford, 1938), pp. 272–3.

in a nice legalistic sense, and his view was not accepted by the Éire government. The link was one, as de Valera emphasized time and again, that remained so long as it was useful and convenient. 'The day', he said in 1946, 'we find that inconvenient we can get rid of it very simply by arranging to have other methods in the accrediting of our representatives abroad.' The fall of his government two years later hastened its approach.

It is more profitable, in trying to form some final opinion of the advantages and disadvantages of external association to leave on one side theoretic considerations and to examine its working in the field of foreign affairs both in peace and in war.

In the field of political realities, it may appear that external association proved a very negative concept. That was not and need not, in my opinion, be the case. One reason for it, so far as Ireland is concerned, may be that the imposition of dominion status provoked a greater self-assertive desire for independent action in the foreign field than might otherwise have been the case. From 1921 to 1936 the place of the Crown in the constitution was felt by the majority to be a symbol of subjection. Though it meant nothing of the kind in actual practice, the existence of the Crown in the constitution carried, above all for the Fianna Fáil Party, this implication. To offset it Cosgrave and still more de Valera were in turn at great pains to emphasize the importance of the League of Nations over against that of the Commonwealth. The Irish point of view has consistently been that intra-Commonwealth disputes are international disputes and, therefore, should not be reserved, but referred, to the international tribunal. In the broader fields of foreign policy, a distinctive line has been pursued so far as circumstances allowed, but the emphasis on the League resulted in the middle 1930s in a coincidence in outlook between British and Irish representatives at Geneva. To take the outstanding example, despite the very close links between Ireland and Italy, de Valera advocated a strong League policy and supported sanctions in the Abyssinian dispute as he had done in the earlier Sino–Japanese dispute. He felt profoundly that here the League had its last chance of effective self-assertion. But he had to face considerable opposition at home particularly when the policy of sanctions against Italy brought him face to face with Catholic sentiment and with an anti-British sentiment to which the thought of such intimate cooperation with Britain in the international field was anathema. To a protagonist of this school of thought de Valera retorted in the Dáil, 'if your worst enemy happens to be going to heaven by the same road as you are, you do not for that reason turn around and go in the opposite direction.' But once the League had failed to save Abyssinia, de Valera made no secret of the fact that he believed, also, that the experiment in international government, which it had embodied, had broken down and must be abandoned. From then onward he was convinced that another European war was coming and publicly stated that the only course to be adopted by Éire was neutrality.

To de Valera, and indeed to the great majority of Irishmen, neutrality appeared as a final vindication of sovereign status. It was final, convincing evidence of freedom and in that sense it was a psychological necessity. But there are two things to be noted about the policy of neutrality. The first is that it was a policy not deriving exclusively from the concept of external association. As the debate in the South African House of Commons in September 1939 made so abundantly clear, the decision between peace and war rested with each dominion Parliament. If Éire be regarded as a dominion, there was no difference in principle between a South African Parliament deciding by a small majority against neutrality and the Dáil deciding virtually unanimously in favour of it. However important the consequences in practice, the neutrality of Éire did not mark a final break with dominion status. Here again there is something in the argument that because Éire remained a dominion in name, her determination to pursue her own course was thereby reinforced. But this is not to be pressed too far. Neutrality was not so much the product of external considerations as of internal conditions. De Valera gave the most convincing summary of them immediately after the American entry into the war, a moment when the foundations of Irish policy were challenged. After describing Ireland's position as that of a 'friendly neutral', he added,

from the moment that the war began there was for us only one policy possible—neutrality. Our circumstances, our history, the incompleteness of our national territory from the partition of our country made any other policy impracticable. Any other policy would have divided our people, and for a divided nation to fling itself into war would be to commit suicide.

By this policy of neutrality Éire's detachment from the other nations of the Commonwealth during one of the most critical periods in their history was underlined, but the character of her association with it was not fundamentally altered, though the normal and elaborate machinery of intra-Commonwealth consult-ation was presumably suspended so far as she was concerned and her policy made inevitable her exclusion from the Commonwealth Prime Ministers' Conferences of 1944 and 1946, and she was not invited in 1948.

About Éire's neutrality there was an element of misunder-standing on both sides—and by misunderstanding I mean a genuine failure to understand. In Britain it was recognized that Éire had a right to exercise a free choice on the vital issue of peace and war, but it was felt by some that in the case of war against aggression, naked and unashamed, there was a certain moral obligation for all members of the Commonwealth to act in concert. It was felt in such circumstances that the unity of the Commonwealth should transcend individual or sectional interests. Membership of the Commonwealth carries with it obligations as well as benefits, and in a war for survival the obligations could not be lightly overlooked. These feelings though they received expression from persons in official positions were given no official endorsement. To this wise restraint de Valera inserted a diplomatic tribute in his reply to the American note of 1944 requesting the removal of the Axis legations from Dublin. He observed then, 'It is perhaps not known to the American Government that the feelings of the Irish people towards Britain have undergone a considerable change, precisely because Britain has not attempted to violate our neutrality.' Britain, he remarked on another occasion, had behaved 'not unworthily'. All is well that ends well, but undoubtedly Éire's confused consti-tutional relations with the Commonwealth were responsible for a good deal of the misunderstanding that existed in both Britain and Ireland; an influential section of opinion approached neutrality from different points of view because each started from different premises. The United Kingdom government had stated that Éire remained a dominion; Éire maintained that she was not a dominion but a sovereign state externally associated with the Commonwealth. Because she was externally associated, her moral obligations—she had no treaty obligations after the return of the ports in 1938—

were, so it was argued, comparable not with those of the oversea dominions, but with those of Holland or Belgium, Norway or Sweden, or Portugal or indeed the United States. None of these countries had in fact entered the war unless and until they had been attacked. Therefore, why should Éire enter the war unless she were attacked? The Commonwealth, it was concluded, had no justifiable cause for complaint. This line of argument implied that association unlike dominion status carried no obligations in a war against aggression, without its exponents fully realizing that they were, by implication, fixing upon external association so negative an interpretation. Was there then no difference between a foreign state and an associated state?

To condemn neutrality as unrealistic was an altogether different matter. The Irish correspondent of the *Round Table*,[4] writing after the Munich crisis, remarked, 'One has only to look at the map to realize that Ireland could not remain neutral in a major war in which Great Britain was engaged.' But de Valera calculated otherwise and partly by diplomatic skill and, still more, thanks primarily to Ireland's position on the map, was enabled to pursue his chosen policy, without deviation and not without dignity, until the end of the war.

Now that the tensions—let us admit them—and the growing cooperation—let us not overlook it—of the war years are a matter of the past, it is well to consider what lessons are to be drawn in the field of Commonwealth relations. One lesson, I think, is that calling a country a dominion, which does not aspire to be a dominion, is liable at critical moments to promote not understanding, but misunderstanding. Another is that external association on the lines originally contemplated by the Irish delegates in 1921 is likely to provide a more satisfactory basis for common action in external affairs between two countries, who share a wide community of interest but different political concepts, than dominion status, based as it is on unwritten conventions. External association came into being as an alternative to dominion status because it allowed of a form of government more acceptable to Irish opinion, but, at the same time, envisaged cooperation between Ireland and the Commonwealth in matters of common concern. This cooperation might

4. The *Round Table* No.113, December 1938, p. 34.

well have been based on certain minimal Commonwealth obligations freely undertaken by both parties. Its foundation would, therefore, have been more rigid, because defined, than the unwritten conventional basis of Commonwealth cooperation. Definition incurs some risks, but I submit they are not so great as the risk of conventions, which may be misunderstood or which may prove unacceptable. In the case of Éire, so intimate in many respects is the association with Britain and the Commonwealth, both socially and economically, that cooperation is a necessity, but in other places where these non-political bonds are less strong, the soundness and the suitability of the constitutional foundation may well prove of the most vital importance.

In thinking of external association it is easy, in the light of Irish experience, to put too much emphasis on the adjective, too little on the noun. But the essential foundation for this concept is the desire on the part of two or more countries to be associated. If one turns one's eyes away from the frigid, constitutional field, one finds indeed that relations between Britain and Ireland are in many respects more intimate than between any other of the partners of the Commonwealth. In the economic field the trade figures over the past twenty years bear the most striking testimony to the mutual interdependence of the two countries and, more recently, no one will have missed the significance of Éire's cooperation in the Marshall Plan. There is a profound truth in Lemass's remark on his visit to Paris to the effect that 'We have an interest in preserving the exchange value of British money', though he added character- istically and reasonably that any plan which emerged from the Paris Conference must be designed to benefit all countries equally, and concluded that provided that was done 'Éire was ready to cooperate in any measures to protect sterling and to develop the resources of the sterling area.' Behind Lemass's statement lies the fact that the Irish sterling balance totals now some £400,000,000, while on the other hand her balance of trade with the dollar area is exceedingly unfavourable. In the first five months of 1947, Éire's imports from North America are calculated to have amounted to some £8,500,000 and her exports to only £117,000 and only a small part of this gap will be bridged by invisible exports.[5] Éire's

5. *The Economist*, 4 October 1947.

interest, therefore, in reducing dollar expenditure and increasing trade within the sterling area is almost as great as Britain's It is in this context that the recent trade agreement between Britain and Ireland should be viewed. Its conclusion will strengthen the balance of payments position of the sterling area as a whole, particularly by effecting substantial reductions in dollar requirements. More important still, the machinery which has been set up in the form of a standing committee of officials to keep trade relations between Britain and Ireland under review will enable all proposals for increasing trade to be considered sympathetically and practically 'within the limits of the economic policy of each country.' The possibilities of developing trade to mutual advantage have been underestimated in recent years, and the agreement affords welcome evidence that they are no longer to be neglected even if not yet to be fully exploited. The export of coal, agricultural machinery and fertilizers from Britain, coupled with the proposed upward revision of prices for Irish agricultural products, should lead to a substantial increase in the exports of Éire's products to Britain. Certainly that has been the consistent policy of Costello's inter-party government since its accession to office. Close and continuing economic cooperation between the two countries at home and in the broader field of the European recovery plan is likely to have far-reaching and beneficial consequences.

But while the economic interdependence between Britain and Ireland must be duly underlined, more fundamental still is the scale of social intercourse between the two countries. Even during the war years there was a continuing flow of Irishmen into the United Kingdom. The number of volunteers from Éire serving in the forces was certainly not less than 50,000 and the number of workers in war factories somewhere between 120,000 and 150,000. These are almost all men and women of the younger generation; and the fact of their having lived in England, in many cases having settled here permanently or married English wives, should have a lasting and beneficial effect on Anglo–Irish relations. Of the reactions to some of the recent English settlers in Ireland it is difficult to feel so confident. If in the political field the area of cooperation between Britain and Ireland is narrower than between Britain and the other dominions and, in de Valera's view is likely to remain so, so long as partition exists, the field of common interest is at least as wide. This is a point to be borne in mind because, if my line of thought is justified, the more important conclusions to be drawn from this review of Éire's relationship with the Commonwealth apply with most force not to Anglo–Irish relations, but to future relations with former non-self-governing territories in the East. The smaller the area of common interest in the social and economic field, the greater the importance of establishing a right relationship in external policy, in which I am including the all-important and related fields of foreign affairs and defence.

External association is in a sense a via media between dominion status and treaty relationship, but it is a mistake to think of it as a colourless compromise. Rightly regarded, it is the positive answer to a certain set of circumstances. Its foundation should be the desire of two or more independent countries to form a close and lasting association. In that, it is similar to dominion status, but distinct from a treaty relationship which is normally founded on a short-term coincidence of interest in a limited and particular field. On the other hand, as distinct from dominion status, it rests, not upon a sense of underlying unity in history, development and tradition, symbolized by allegiance to a common Crown, but upon a sense of partnership between two peoples with different histories and different loyalties but sharing common interests, common aims in world politics and, above all, a common sense of values. Viewed in this context it is at once apparent that the lessons to be drawn from Éire's relationship with the Commonwealth are instructive but limited. External association has never been put into practice because the United Kingdom and the oversea dominions have never recognized that it exists. To them Éire remains a dominion. And external association is naturally dependent for its proper working upon all parties to it recognizing it as the foundation of their relationship. Equally on the other side, the value of Irish experience is limited by the isolationist policy pursued for many years though not recently by the Éire government. External association, rightly viewed, is an instrument for cooperation between independent states, not a means of bringing about an ever greater degree of detachment.

From this survey of Ireland's relationship with the Commonwealth certain conclusions emerge which suggest that the wisdom of British policy in the strictly political field was not matched by an equal understanding in the constitutional field. Politically the resolute determination of the United Kingdom to treat each question on its merits as it arose, to avert a final breach in the face of considerable provocation, to escape from formulae, and to eschew finalities seems in retrospect to have been more than justified. For that policy the war provided the supreme test and it is greatly to the credit of the United Kingdom government that it refused to be deflected from its chosen path during those critical years. The marked improvement in Anglo-Irish relations which we see today is the fruit of this policy of wise restraint. It represents a considerable political achievement towards which in recent years Lord Rugby, the first United Kingdom Representative to Ireland, has made no small contribution.

On the constitutional side, the conclusions are more negative. The initial mistake was made in 1921; it was persisted in in 1937, and only today are Anglo-Irish relations escaping from its consequences. That mistake was the application of dominion status to the Irish Free State. Because of it the constitutional ties with the Commonwealth acted as an irritant in relations with the United Kingdom and more and more, as years went by, were a barrier to the partnership which community of interest demanded. The removal of the symbols of this status by de Valera was—it is paradoxical but true—an essential preliminary to full and cordial cooperation with the countries of the Commonwealth. From that point of view it is open to question, particularly in the light of recent debates in the Dáil, whether the one remaining constitutional link embodied in the External Relations Act any longer possesses practical advantages outweighing its psychological disadvantages.

Unfortunate also in some respects have been the consequences of the initial constitutional mistake for the Commonwealth as a whole. Irish policy in the past twenty-five years has been directed not deliberately but inevitably towards a loosening of the fabric of Commonwealth cooperation. Every step she has taken to emphasize her national as against her dominion status has stimulated one or more of the oversea dominions to follow in the same path. The emphasis she has placed on the theoretic conception of absolute national sovereignty has deflected the thought of the Commonwealth away from its natural line of development. By making the Irish Free State conform to a constitutional relationship inappropriate to her circumstances and outlook, the character of the relationship itself has been modified. Many Irishmen, profoundly concerned to maintain the strength and unity of a Commonwealth in the postwar world, acknowledge that almost every step towards the fulfilment of their national aspirations has incidentally involved some weakening of this community of nations. But they maintain they were placed in a position in which no alternative course was open to them just because in 1921 the Irish Free State was forced into a pattern in which she had no natural place. From the point of view of the Commonwealth the lesson to be drawn is the supreme importance of reconciling constitutional forms with political and psychological realities.

It is because external association was\ the constitutional relationship contemplated by Irish republicans in 1921 that it provides so good a starting-point for an examination of what may be the most satisfactory relationship with the newly established nation-states of the East. Today indeed the new relationship between the United Kingdom and Burma in certain essentials corresponds more closely to external association than that with Éire, but possibly it was not so designated because the political background of the governing group of parties in Burma, the Anti-Fascist Peoples Freedom League, made any association with the Commonwealth difficult. Burma, it is stated in the Burma Independence Bill, shall become on 6 January 1948, 'an independent country neither forming part of His Majesty's Dominions nor entitled to His Majesty's protection.' By that decision, Burma is likely in the long run to lose considerably, for while the material foundation remains the same, the sense of intimate and growing partnership may well be lost. No one would wish to question the very real measure of goodwill that exists towards Britain in Burma today, but goodwill tends to be transient. Under the Treaty of Relationship which has now been established, it will find little scope for expression in day-to-day relations over a period of years. Whatever may be the intentions and hopes of the signatories, treaties are usually interpreted in a literal and restrictive sense. They are not a stepping-stone to a closer and more intimate relationship, just because they provide no machinery for making relations more intimate. It is here that the concept of association could have made a valuable and distinctive contribution. Even had it been based upon a treaty whose essentials corresponded in almost every particular to the details of the treaty just signed, association with the Commonwealth would have allowed for a continuing and expanding consultation and cooperation in all matters of common concern. As a direct consequence the area of common interest might have widened as the years went by and the friendship deepened. Therein lies the supreme merit of association as against treaty relationship. It allows, it is designed to allow, for growth.

In 1921 Lloyd George asked the question how best can Ireland's national aspirations be reconciled with the community of nations known as the British Empire. The question to be asked today is, can the interests of India, of Pakistan, and in a rather different context, of Ceylon, be reconciled with those of the community of nations known as the British Commonwealth and if so, how can this best be done? Tomorrow the same question will be asked in Africa and in the West Indies, and they will be profoundly influenced by the Asian precedents, whatever they may be. It is quite certain that in answering this question Irish experience has a significance all its own. So far as India and Pakistan are concerned, the question is answered by dominion status, for Ceylon it is answered by 'fully responsible status within the British Commonwealth of Nations'.[6] For India and Pakistan this is acknowledged to be a temporary expedient. What is the long-term solution? It goes without saying that there will be no lasting relationship unless the peoples of Asia desire it. Whether they will desire it depends now to no small extent on what is offered to them. The statesmen of the British Commonwealth have always maintained that its greatest virtue is flexibility and adaptability to changing circumstances. The boast is justified, but recently—is it since the 1926 declaration?—there has crept in an element of standardization. Dominion status is the goal whatever the background.

A few months ago in New Delhi a distinguished Indian statesman remarked to me that dominion status could not in the long run work in countries like Ireland or like India which were themselves mother countries. In that there is much truth. But an even graver objection exists when in addition there is no common historical

6. *Proposals for conferring on Ceylon fully responsible status within the British Commonwealth of Nations*, Cmd 7257 (London, HMSO 1947).

background. That a final solution will be found to Anglo-Irish relations may be regarded as a reasonable expectation, just because over and above the wide area of common interest there is a common background. Both Britain and Ireland and the oversea dominions are peopled by men of European stock who are the heirs of the Christian civilization of the West. A much more formidable problem arises when one contemplates transplanting a political concept peculiar to this western civilization to the East. It is perfectly true that one of the results, and I believe one of the most beneficial results, of British rule in India has been the spread of ideas of democracy and constitutional government. At the Inter-Asian Conference in New Delhi in the spring of 1947, English was the official language and the delegates from almost all countries, other than the Soviet Asian republics, tacitly assumed in this dawning of liberated and triumphant nationalism that a parliamentary social democracy was the form of government at which all should aim. During its deliberations I thought more than once of Macaulay's words:

The sceptre may pass from us. Victory may be inconstant to our arms. But there are triumphs which are followed by no reverse. There is an Empire exempt from all natural causes of decay. Those triumphs are the pacific triumphs of reason; that Empire is the imperishable Empire of our arts and our morals, our literature and our laws.

Of our language and our laws that still seems true today. Politically it is very important and it encourages the hope of close and lasting cooperation in the future. What form should it take?

Dominion status depends for its working upon a whole set of ideas, a whole range of common associations, containing nice implications only to be readily understood by people whose background and whose training have been very similar. But how can the peoples of the East attach precisely the right weight to all these unwritten conventions and think instinctively along the lines on which we have been accustomed to think in Commonwealth affairs? What is dangerous is not a difference of view within the Commonwealth—that in many respects is healthy—but misunderstanding. The appeal of the Pakistan government to the other Commonwealth governments at the height of the communal warfare in the Punjab is a portent and a warning. It may be, and in many cases will be, that representatives of the eastern states will have difficulty in recognizing precisely what are the obligations or what, for that matter, are the benefits of Commonwealth member-ship. Even a paper so well informed as the *Manchester Guardian* recently remarked that 'as long as India and Pakistan remain Dominions they have the automatic guarantee of the British Alliance.'[7] What does that mean? We know that there is no alliance in any formal sense binding the partners of the Commonwealth. But do the great mass of the Indian people? We know from past experience that in the event of aggression, the member states of the Commonwealth of their own choice will freely unite to resist it, but we know equally that this common action derives from a common outlook and common sense of values and rests on no formal obligation arising automatically when war begins. But it is doubtful if public opinion in an Asian country, or for that matter any country with a different historical background, would rightly understand anything so flexible and so conventional. They might well tend to assume that at the least there existed an overwhelming moral obligation which, in certain not inconceivable circumstances, not all the partners in the Commonwealth would be prepared to admit.

Peter Fraser said recently in a message to the Indian people that dominion status means 'independence plus'. But Indians wondering whether or not their country should continue to have dominion status will want to know plus what? The advantages are solid and substantial, but I think that the Indian mind which, in common with the Irish and French, inclines towards precision, would welcome them more if at least the foundations on which this new relationship may be built could be more closely defined. It was, for example, my impression both in New Delhi and in Karachi that informed public opinion was not favourably impressed by the fact that Commonwealth flexibility today was so great that it allowed the neutrality of one partner in a major war. The prevailing view seemed to be that the right to remain neutral in such circum-stances might well be regarded as an asset for countries in a sheltered geographical position, but for India and Pakistan it was not an asset, but a liability. It subtracted from the strength of the Common-wealth and introduced a disturbing degree of uncertainty. The

7. 11 October 1947.

Irish precedent in effect reinforced the demand for greater definition. Now definition is wholly alien to dominion status: Lloyd
George said in 1921 it would be extremely dangerous to attempt
to define it and that is equally true today. There is left one expedient,
external association, or association as I would prefer to call it,
which would diminish the dangers of definition and which, at the
same time, would maintain partnership. It is here that the most.
valuable lesson of Anglo–Irish relations is to be found. It is not in
external association as it has evolved, but rather in external
association as it was originally conceived. In other words it should
have a foundation of common purpose and mutual obligation stated
and clearly understood by both parties. On that foundation the
association could grow without fear of any fundamental misunderstanding and little by little conventions could be added which
would enrich and deepen the association. As against a treaty, such
as that recently signed with Burma, it would, as I have already
emphasized, have the great advantages of allowing for growth. We
should not have to treat one another as foreign countries. That in
itself would be an immeasurable gain. As against dominion status,
external association, by defining the foundations to the extent that
seems desirable in each individual case, removes many potential
causes of misunderstanding and, incidentally, the slightest suggestion
of subordination. Otherwise thorny questions of allegiance and of
the place of the Crown would be settled on their merits by mutual
agreement and it must be frankly recognized that the concept of a
common Crown as a symbol of unity might or might not prove
acceptable. 'If no place can be found in a British Commonwealth
for republics', wrote Berriedale Keith in 1938, 'then the enduring
character of the Commonwealth may well be doubted.'[8] The new
constitution of India is a republican constitution. If the Union of
India is to remain within the Commonwealth it will remain so as
a republic.

Here the decision of Burma to leave the Commonwealth must
be considered again from a different point of view. The choice
which she made is not one which the members of the Commonwealth can, or should, regard with any complacency. It suggests at
the least that a new approach is required. The problem is perhaps

8. *The Dominions as Sovereign States* (London, 1938), p. ix.

as much psychological as political. It is believed in Burma, as it is believed in every Asian country, that dominion status means subordination. No amount of explanation will remove the conviction that somehow or other, whatever its material advantages, dominion status implies something less than full sovereignty. It is perfectly understandable how this conviction became implanted in the Asian mind. It is only within the last two decades that dominion status has, in fact, carried with it full sovereign status, and many of the political leaders and intellectuals, to whom these things are a matter of direct concern and who influence public opinion, first learned of dominion status in the years when it meant something less than it means today. The very fact that the years that elapsed between the Imperial Conference of 1926 and the outbreak of the Second World War witnessed an intense preoccupation within the Commonwealth with questions of status, of the right to neutrality, of secession, inevitably suggested that the dominions doubted whether they were fully masters of their own destinies. If they were certain, why were they so concerned with these things? The impression then received has not been eradicated and it is my firm conviction that no amount of discussion will eradicate it. The stigma, if that is the right word, is one that cannot be removed by lucid exposition of the facts, or at any rate cannot be removed in this way in time. If, therefore, the only possibility that lies before the Asian peoples contemplating partnership within the Commonwealth is dominion status, the misapprehensions and the psychology that lies behind them may well lead to a decision to go outside the Commonwealth. The emotional background in this way reinforces the political and constitutional considerations, which lead one to suggest that some new form of association, call it external association or any other name you will, is needed. One advantage of external association is that no one in Asia, or in any other continent, has ever supposed that the actions of de Valera are in any way controlled by the British government, or that any subordinate status would ever be acceptable to him. The integrity of his nationalism is above suspicion. By broadening the basis of the Commonwealth in this way, the associated states including Éire need not, unless they so desire, feel outside it, but a natural element within it.

At this stage one important question arises. In a Commonwealth composed of autonomous and sovereign states there can be no distinction in status, but there would be difference in relationship between the states that are dominions and the states that are more formally associated. Both would be full and equal partners, but the origin from which their partnership derived would be different. What would be the relation between them? If the experiment were tried, I believe that in practice this problem would be solved satisfactorily by regarding all partners in the Commonwealth as having equal privileges and equal obligations and using the defined relationship of the associate states as a statement of first principles to which appeal is made only on those rare and critical occasions for which it was designed to provide. In saying this I do not wish to dismiss this difficulty lightly, but I believe it is certainly not insurmountable. An element of constitutional untidiness is a small price to pay for a flexibility in Commonwealth relations which enables peoples of many races and different traditions to cooperate wholeheartedly in the common purposes which the Commonwealth serves in the world.

The implications of Éire's relationship with the Commonwealth have led us, therefore, into new fields. They suggest a Commonwealth of the future in which there are both member states and associate states, the distinction between them being one, not of status, but of history, tradition and cultural background. By such a development the Commonwealth could only be strengthened, for it would mean that political and constitutional realities would once again be brought into harmony. In this great community there would be a natural place for nations peopled by many races and speaking many tongues but all, from their vast store of varied experience, contributing to the common good of the whole and thereby to the peace of the world.

# 7

# Postwar Strains on the British Commonwealth

Has the British Commonwealth of Nations been fundamentally weakened since 1939? Certainly it has suffered contraction of territory through the secession of Burma. Its military position in Asia has been weakened by the transfer of power in India, and its position in the Middle East has been damaged by the withdrawal of troops from Egypt and Palestine. It has sustained heavy loss of economic resources by destruction in war and by expenditure in the waging of war. These are injuries, some of them formidable in character, whose final consequences cannot yet be foretold. But not all are to be taken at their face value. Was not, for example, a discontented India as much a liability as an asset to the Commonwealth in 1939? Moreover, the lasting consequences of wartime changes on the position of the Commonwealth are best judged not by an analysis of economic or territorial loss, but by their impact upon its essential nature. The Commonwealth's contribution, said Field Marshal Smuts, 'in human qualities of balance and moderation, good sense, good humour, and fair play are of a very special character. They are worth more than scores of divisions and without them divisions must ultimately fail.' This may seem paradoxical at a time when thoughts of men are again preoccupied with the analysis of tangible material strength. But it remains true that no assessment of the position of the Commonwealth in the postwar world can neglect these human and political factors, for it is on them, for good or ill, and not upon its organization of power or its capacity to wage war, that the Commonwealth is founded.

The drafters of the historic 1926 *Report on Imperial Relations* implicitly recognized that a Commonwealth whose member states were autonomous communities within the British Empire, equal in status, in no way subordinate one to another in any aspect of their domestic or external affairs, could not be a centralized Commonwealth. Its unique character emerged only with the transfer of power from the centre to the circumference. Thenceforward cooperation has depended not upon the working of central institutions designed to produce it, but directly upon the existence of a common sense of purpose, a common outlook among the member nations. It was because of this fundamental reliance upon an indefinable sense of community that the 1926 Imperial Conference remained of the opinion that

nothing would be gained by attempting to lay down a constitution for the British Empire. Its widely scattered parts have very different characteristics, very different histories, and are at very different stages of evolution; while considered as a whole, it defies classification and bears no resemblance to any other political organization which now exists or has yet been tried.

But if the Commonwealth has had no constitution and no common council with powers sufficient to produce a concerted, still less a common foreign, economic or defence policy, this is not to say that the existing central machinery, mainly advisory in character, has had no important role to play. On the contrary, it was for long the accepted view that the underlying unity of the Commonwealth would be sustained and find expression through frequent meetings of the Imperial Conference. But in fact no Imperial Conference has met since 1937, and the tide of opinion in the dominions is not wholly sympathetic to its revival. Is this to be interpreted as a sign of the weakening of the fundamental Commonwealth link? Some Empire statesmen, notably Menzies, leader of the Opposition in Australia, believe the answer to be in the affirmative. To them, lack of formal consultation at the highest level is the ominous symptom of a drift toward disruption.

This question of cardinal importance, though not susceptible to a categorical, factual answer, may best be approached from a rather different angle. It was the confident belief of the makers of the new Commonwealth that no common cause would suffer through the exercise of full sovereign powers by each of the member states. How far have events justified their confidence? Since the end of the First World War the dominions have played an ever increasing role in foreign affairs. If their separate representation at the League of Nations in 1919 was questioned, none doubted when the United Nations came into being that they were fully sovereign states pursuing their own foreign policies in the light of their own interests. In the original list of signatories to the League Covenant the dominions were grouped together in order of seniority; while in the Charter list this grouping was discarded as if to dispose of any idea that the Commonwealth countries comprised a unit in foreign policy. But what is really important is not the superficial change in practice, but the spirit that lies behind it.

To understand the attitude of the dominions toward separate and collective responsibility in foreign policy, it is useful to remind ourselves of one or two of the stepping-stones on the road to full decentralization. The first and familiar one was the Locarno Pact of 1925 when the United Kingdom undertook responsibilities from which the dominions were specifically stated to be free unless they wished otherwise, which none of them did. Ten years later, as the menace of Nazi aggression loomed ever larger, the attitude of the dominions toward Britain's policy in Europe remained the same in form. There was, on their part, a studious determination to undertake no formal commitments or responsibilities but it was coupled with a growing conviction that in the event of war they would be ranged on the same side as the United Kingdom because their interests as free peoples coincided and because, too, they shared a deep sense of community.

The Imperial Conference of 1937 was the last meeting of the prime ministers of all the dominions (except Éire) before the war. Their attitude toward formal responsibilities in Europe remained unchanged, but as a result of what they heard in London their predisposition toward isolationism was profoundly modified. The new approach may best be summarized in the words of Mackenzie King, who remarked that Canada would take part in any war 'against the forces of evil', not as part of the British Empire, but because the British Empire was ranged on the side of the forces of good. This view of imperial relations, with its implication that the issues on which the Commonwealth was united were issues which transcended specifically Commonwealth interests, was one which still enjoys general acceptance throughout the Commonwealth, finding expression today in a devotion to the ideal of the United Nations that has survived every disappointment. But if in the prewar period dominion opinion distinguished more clearly 'the forces of evil', after 1937 their view of the right policy to be pursued was no different in essentials from that of the United Kingdom. This is a point of some importance. Today the argument is often heard that if the Commonwealth had had a common foreign policy in 1938–9 the war might not have taken place because Hitler, confronted by such an array of force, would have hesitated to attack Poland. This is extremely doubtful, but even more dubious is the assumption that a common foreign policy for the Commonwealth would have differed in any material respect from that of the United Kingdom. There is no indication that any of the dominion prime ministers pressed Chamberlain to take a more resolute line toward Germany in 1937, or later, nor that any of them challenged the wisdom of pursuing a policy of appeasement to all reasonable limits and beyond. On the contrary, it seems that General Hertzog, then Prime Minister of South Africa, greatly encouraged Chamberlain in his chosen course. The signature of the Munich Pact was hailed with general acclaim in all the Commonwealth countries. Taking the picture as a whole, therefore, it is clear that had the Commonwealth pursued a common foreign policy involving specific commitments for all its members, it would have differed in no fundamental respect from that which the United Kingdom pursued upon its own responsibility.

The course of events in 1939 did, however, expose some weaknesses in the machinery for the discussion of foreign policy which have not since been wholly removed. The guarantees given to Greece, Rumania and Poland in the spring of 1939 were not underwritten by any of the dominion governments. About the all-important Polish commitment, which was hurriedly entered into to check an imminent onslaught on that country, the dominions were informed, but not consulted, because time did not allow of that being done. Yet as the sequel showed, the guarantee to Poland involved a decision which was of as great concern to the dominions as to the United Kingdom. This incident, not without parallel, prompted misgivings, particularly in Australia and New Zealand, where it is still felt to have exposed a serious defect in the machinery of intra-Commonwealth consultation. It lies behind the Australian desire to obtain a greater voice at the formative stage in policy and not merely to be confronted with the necessity of dealing with consequences.

The separate responsibility of the dominions in foreign policy has been more widely extended during, and particularly since, the war. One reason for this has been the great expansion in their diplomatic representation overseas. So long as dominion representation was confined to one or two foreign capitals, the dominions were hardly in a position to interpret events independently of the Foreign Office in London. The position, however, is very different now with Canada represented in twenty-four foreign capitals and Australia in ten. The more active dominion participation in foreign policy, coupled with the existence of more effective machinery for putting individual dominion policies into practice and taken in conjunction with the decline in formal cooperation at the centre, has sharpened doubts about the continuing strength of the sense of common purpose. Not merely is there no common foreign policy, but even on important issues like Palestine there are conflicting policies. Nor are the dominions, despite their relatively increased strength, any more prepared than before the war to undertake specific commitments of an exclusively imperial character. Their formal obligations of a general character are undertaken by them as UN members.

All this was convincingly illustrated in the debates on the revision of the Anglo-Egyptian Treaty in 1946. It may well be that the Mediterranean, which in Bismarck's day had been, in his words, 'the spinal cord' of the Empire, is so no longer; none the less, with good reason, Australia, New Zealand and South Africa have displayed a marked interest recently in the balance of power in the Mediterranean area and particularly in the disposal of the former Italian colonies in North Africa. There the troops of all the dominions campaigned in the World War, and there, if anywhere, it might be supposed that they would be prepared to undertake explicit responsibilities. But what happened? As Attlee explained in the debate in the House of Commons, the dominions were consulted about the revision of the Anglo-Egyptian Treaty and, with the stated exception of Canada, they commented upon the proposed policy of the United Kingdom government, which took their comments fully into account. But they did not record any formal views or decisions about the policy to be followed, nor were they asked, nor did they wish, to share the responsibility for it. That rested with the United Kingdom government alone.

Dominion aversion to formal responsibilities is widely misunderstood both as to cause and consequences. But by itself it is liable to give a most misleading picture of the measure of Commonwealth cooperation. It is indicative of an approach, of a political psychology, not of an ultimate objective. It is not because relations within the Commonwealth are so loose, but because they are so intimate that specific commitments, recorded views, and even formal consultation are felt to be so wholly out of place. What happened in 1939 was a most remarkable testimony to the unity of outlook and purpose which informal consultation can achieve in the face of a threat transcending exclusively Commonwealth interests. In the light of that experience the view is strongly and in the opinion of the writer, rightly held that to state the extent of mutual obligation in written or specific form would seriously weaken the connection between the United Kingdom and the older dominions and reduce its value to each one of them. Definition could only restrict the area of cooperation. As things stand, there is no formal obligation on the part of any dominion, except Ceylon, to come to the assistance of the United Kingdom in the event of unprovoked aggression. But no one for a moment doubts that in such circumstances the aggressor would be confronted by a united Commonwealth, as in 1939.

To judge the cohesion of the Commonwealth, however, only by its ability to unite effectively in common resistance to the challenge of a powerful aggressor is not enough. Its effectiveness in day-to-day cooperation, its contribution to the maintenance of peace, must also be taken into full account. And it is here that a new approach to Commonwealth affairs, which bears closely upon the question of its inner cohesion, most clearly emerges. The dominant trend in the later war years was a growth in regional responsibilities. The breakdown in the communications on which the Commonwealth so greatly depends, the isolation of some parts of it—particularly the Pacific Dominions menaced by the Japanese while United Kingdom and many of their own forces were heavily engaged in other theatres—all served to reinforce the conviction that the nations of the Commonwealth must play a greater part in formulating policies of direct regional concern to them. This view was provocatively expressed by Field Marshal Smuts in his self-styled 'explosive speech' to the Empire Parliamentary Association at Westminster in November 1943, when he commented on the difference in approach toward the self-governing and the non-self-governing Empire. The fact that decentralization in the self-governing parts of the Empire went side by side with a high degree of centralization in the dependent Empire seemed to him an anomaly. He felt it could be best corrected by encouraging the dominions to assume greater responsibilities in relation to the colonial territories lying within their area of interest. If for South Africa itself this policy has always presented many difficulties, now enhanced by Malan's* doctrine of 'apartheid', which accentuates the fundamental differences in the approach of the Union of South Africa and of the Colonial Office toward the African peoples, the area of regional interest remains, and must remain, continental. Whether imperialist or nationalist, South Africa thinks in terms of economic expansion to the north just because she is so vitally concerned, in view of her predominantly African population, with economic and political developments in African colonial territories administered by European powers. What happens there must sooner rather than later have its repercussions within her own borders.

In the Pacific Dominions, Field Marshal Smuts' words were assured of a cordial welcome. The Canberra Pact of 1944 expressed the determination of Australia and New Zealand to cooperate not only in defence, but also in all problems of common concern in the southwest Pacific area. It is not too much to say that it embodied a new concept of the Commonwealth, a concept in which the dominions will play a decisive part in the formulation of regional policies, and, as a result, have a much larger voice in the framing of Commonwealth policies as a whole. Evatt's** view is that Australia

*Dr Daniel François Malan, Nationalist Prime Minister of South Africa, 1948–54—Ed.
**H.V. Evatt, Australian Labour Minister of External Affairs, 1941–9 —Ed.

should be the spokesman of the Commonwealth as a whole in the Far Eastern area, just because she is the member of the Commonwealth most interested in the future of that area. The 1947 Commonwealth Conference, held at Canberra to discuss the terms of the Japanese Peace Treaty, represented a notable endorsement of this view, for it was the first time that a Commonwealth conference on an issue of major importance had been held in the capital of one of the Pacific Dominions.

What has happened in the Pacific finds a parallel in North America outside the Commonwealth. By her adherence to the North American Defence Pact in 1940 Canada entered into formal regional commitments on the North American continent, and by the renewal and extension of it in 1947 she made this a permanent feature of her policy. This was partly because, as Mackenzie King explained, with the coming of polar warfare Canada had not, as hitherto, to look only to the east and to the west, but also to the north; and there her interests and those of the United States coincide.

The emphasis placed on these regional interests of the dominions throws into relief the widely dispersed nature of their responsibilities in the postwar world. Even if one thinks only in terms of the older oversea dominions, leaving aside for the moment both Éire and the three new Asian Dominions, it is clear that geography makes impossible any close coordination of detailed policy. There are, and must continue to be, many matters in which a dominion has a particular interest but in which few, if any, of her partners have any direct concern. More important, there are obviously issues which because of their regional character affect the dominions in different ways and therefore make it difficult to secure a coincidence of view. This is an important fact, for it suggests that it is not any weakening of the sense of community but the rapid development of the power and responsibilities of the dominions which accounts for their more independent postwar contributions to world affairs. A comparison between the predominantly one-voiced Commonwealth of prewar years and the many-voiced Commonwealth of today is fatally easy yet profoundly misleading.

There remains the question whether a growing concentration on widely dispersed regional interests, even if it springs, not from any lessening of the sense of community, but from an extension of the power and responsibilities of the dominions, will weaken the

Commonwealth connection. And that brings one back to the natural counterpoise which the central or common institutions of the Commonwealth might be expected to exert. But do they? As has already been noted, no Imperial Conference has been held since 1937, though there have been several conferences of prime ministers. Fundamentally, the Commonwealth depends upon the sharing of common ideals and fundamental common purposes. If they did not exist, the whole system would break down. But on the assumption that they do exist, clearly there must be some machinery through which they may be fertilized and ultimately find expression in action. That machinery is a highly elaborate system of informal inter-government consultation, vastly improved during the war years. By means of it, an opportunity is given for full and frank discussion on any issue in which the various governments are interested. Its apex, once the Imperial Conference, has recently been provided by the more informal Dominion Prime Ministers' Conferences. One was held in the spring of 1944, another in the spring of 1946, and another is due to take place in October 1948. Throughout, the emphasis has been placed on their informal character. The assembled dominion statesmen had come to London in 1946 to have an informal exchange of view; they were not concerned with reaching decisions on particular points, but rather with reviewing the whole field of imperial relations, of foreign policy, and of defence, with a view to formulating their own policy in the light of the discussions in London.

Of the value of these informal discussions there seems no doubt. Mackenzie King, in an address delivered to both Houses of Parliament at Westminster in May 1944, remarked that while the Commonwealth had not a visible war cabinet or council sitting continuously in London, it had

what is much more important, though invisible, a continuing conference of the Cabinets of the Commonwealth. It is a conference of Cabinets which deals from day to day, and, not infrequently, from hour to hour, with policies of common concern. When decisions are taken, they are not the decisions of Prime Ministers, or other individual Ministers, meeting apart from their own colleagues, and away from their own countries. They are decisions reached after mature consideration by all members of the Cabinet of each country, with a full consciousness of their immediate responsibility to their respective Parliaments.

This endorsement of the existing machinery was coupled with a warning against any attempts to improve the machinery of Commonwealth cooperation, in such a way as might appear to limit the freedom of decision of Commonwealth countries, or of forming a separate Commonwealth bloc. 'Let us beware', said Mackenzie King, 'lest in changing the form we lose the substance or for appearance's sake, sacrifice reality.'

Mackenzie King's satisfaction with the existing machinery for Commonwealth cooperation was shared by his colleagues at both the Dominion Prime Ministers' Conferences, but has not passed unquestioned. During the war and since, the opinion has been voiced that, in a world where the Great Powers are becoming greater, the Commonwealth countries simply cannot afford the luxury of uncoordinated foreign policies pursued in the light of their own individual interests. This theme, developed against the broad background of world affairs by Field Marshal Smuts in November 1943, and by Lord Halifax at Toronto in January 1944, was related more specifically to the practical problem of Commonwealth cooperation by Curtin* before his visit to London in 1944 and, more recently, by Menzies.** With his eye always fixed on the Pacific area, Curtin advocated the formation of a Commonwealth Consultative Council, served by a Commonwealth Secretariat drawn from all the member nations of the Commonwealth. His proposals aimed to coordinate the foreign and defence policies of the Commonwealth more closely, so as to enable the dominions to have a say in the formative stage of policy. But to this plea for a superficially modest improvement in machinery, and even more to the spacious pleas of Smuts and Halifax for the grouping of the Commonwealth countries so that together they might form a third Great Power, co-equal with the United States and the USSR, there was a cool response. In Canada, indeed, it was definitely hostile, for the feeling prevailed that any steps toward a more centralized Empire were steps along 'the road to yesterday'. So strongly was this felt that Mackenzie King at Ottawa firmly repudiated the proposals which Lord Halifax had put forward. He

*John Curtin, Prime Minister of Australia, from 1941 until his death in 1945—Ed.

**Sir Robert Menzies, leader of the Australian Opposition Party, 1943-9, Prime Minister of Australia 1949-63—Ed.

argued on the one hand that the formation of a closely integrated Empire bloc would be not an aid but a barrier to the achievement of world peace; on the other, that the competition in power between the great victor states was likely to produce, not peace, but a third world war. Fundamentally, he opposed all measures toward Empire centralization on the ground that they would limit the freedom of action of the dominions.

All this is worth recalling because it is easy to lose sight of political realities in discussing the precise measure of Commonwealth cooperation that is possible or desirable. One of those realities is the fact that any degree of centralization would serve to make the Commonwealth relationship a matter of acute internal controversy both in Canada and in South Africa. After all, however well devised, machinery is of little value unless it is suited to the outlook of those who have to work it. That is why, for the past quarter of a century, the Commonwealth countries have consistently placed their faith in decentralization. It has been their belief that by this policy the broad supranational basis of the Commonwealth may be preserved; the greatest contribution by its member nations to the building up of a world order made possible; and the sense of Commonwealth community deepened by free cooperation for purposes that transcend strictly Commonwealth interests.

This emphasis placed by the older dominions upon the need for decentralization has been accentuated by the entrance into the Commonwealth of the new self-governing dominions in Asia. Their addition to the number of member states has materially strengthened the predominant centrifugal forces, and it is difficult indeed to conceive of a centralized Commonwealth in which they would form an integral part. To what extent in other respects they will tend to modify the character or structure of the Commonwealth can hardly be judged yet. It is, however, likely that these new dominions in Asia will bring to the surface certain constitutional problems.[1] For India and Pakistan, dominion status was used as a device, by which the transfer of power might be quickly effected. But in the longer view, it may well be questioned whether the

---

1. These are considered in detail in my article 'The Implications of Éire's Relations with the British Commonwealth of Nations', *International Affairs*, January 1948, and reproduced in this volume as Chapter 6.

forms of dominion status correspond with the political realities of the relationship that at present exists, and is likely to continue, between the Asian Dominions and the rest of the Commonwealth.

A quarter of a century ago, Lloyd George, confronted with the task of reconciling Irish national aspirations with the unity of the British Empire, decided in favour of dominion status. The history of those intervening twenty-five years has suggested that the decision rigidly adhered to by the United Kingdom government was not the correct one. Like India and Pakistan, Ireland is a mother country which had not evolved toward dominion status, but had reached it in one revolutionary step. The symbolism of dominion status was not congenial to her, for it was a political concept appropriate to circumstances and traditions quite other than those which prevailed in Ireland. Conformity to a dominion pattern, in which there existed no appropriate place for a nationally self-conscious mother country that felt no spontaneous loyalty to the common Crown, has resulted only in straining relations between the United Kingdom and Éire. Of more far-reaching importance, it also modified the whole pattern of the relationship between the overseas dominions and the United Kingdom in a way that may not have been altogether helpful. With these lessons in mind, therefore, we may conclude that, if the Union of India and Pakistan decide to remain within the Commonwealth, some form of association may be adopted, similar to that external association which is now, in fact, the link between Éire and the British Commonwealth. It would correspond most closely to political realities. If so, they will be nations associated with the Commonwealth, not using its symbolism (for that is something that lies outside their national tradition), but sharing in its broad common purposes and participating in that process of discussion through which they are given effect. And whatever may be the precise relationship between the Commonwealth and the new Indian Dominions, the precedent established in the case of Ceylon suggests that both parties will welcome a greater degree of definition than exists between the older member nations of the Commonwealth.

The emergence of the new Indian Dominions in place of an Indian Empire whose external policy was controlled from London underlines the redistribution of power that has taken place within the Commonwealth itself since 1939. The United Kingdom has been relatively weakened both by the losses sustained during the war and by the development of new weapons which make her more vulnerable than ever in her history. On the other hand, the overseas dominions, and particularly Canada and Australia, have been correspondingly strengthened from the impetus given to their industrial development and agricultural production by the pressing needs of the war and postwar years. This redistribution of strength should rightly carry with it a redistribution of responsibilities. Here there has been a time-lag. Both the dominions and the United Kingdom have been preoccupied with their regional responsibilities, and that has led to neglect of some matters of common and urgent concern. The recognized need is now for concerted action, taking into account the strategic resources and position of the member nations, and stimulated either by a Commonwealth Conference or by a series of conferences between the member states interested in particular regions. Malan had proclaimed his preference in principle for such regional conferences within the Commonwealth, and it is easy to see that in practice a series of conferences covering issues of regional concern could serve a most useful purpose, though their full success would seem dependent upon a concluding general conference at which all the member nations are represented. The realities of the postwar position and their implications for the Commonwealth as a whole have still to be assessed. Some such assessment will be the broad responsibility of that Commonwealth Conference now expected to assemble in London in October. It will be given particular urgency by the need to consider in some detail the attitude of the Commonwealth toward Western Union.

When, in 1943, Field Marshal Smuts originally advocated closer association with the democratic states of western Europe, he underlined as a fundamental condition the retention and maintenance of 'our sovereign status'. This emphasis was in full accord with thought in the dominions, which conceive most naturally of a union in western Europe leaving each member state master in its own house. But in actual practice it may well be that, as the number of coordinating authorities in western Europe multiply, what is natural and appropriate within the Commonwealth is not in all respects well suited to this new relationship. Central machinery for cooperation may prove essential when cooperation is in the early, formative stages, as it is today in western Europe. And the reverse holds good too. Just as the informality of the Commonwealth system may as yet have little relevance for Western Union, so too the formal instruments for cooperation in western Europe may have few lessons for the Commonwealth. Developments in the institutional field in western Europe are, therefore, not likely to be paralleled by corresponding developments within the Commonwealth; and this in itself suggests that the Commonwealth system may not be one that can usefully be imitated at this stage in building up a world order. Where fundamental unity of outlook does not exist, but has to be deliberately and carefully created, it would be over-optimistic to suppose that the assistance of well-devised machinery can be dispensed with.

The underlying strength of the Commonwealth is that it is united by a conception of a world order which transcends exclusively Commonwealth interests. It is this, reinforced by a will toward friendly cooperation, that constitutes the most impressive assurance of its present and future cohesion. For whatever the appearances of international conferences may seem to indicate, the Commonwealth countries are probably more closely knit today than at any other time in history. The Communist challenge is something which no dominion is prepared to disregard. Even those groups, like the Nationalists in South Africa and some sections of French Canadian opinion, who questioned whether the war against Hitlerite Germany was not another 'imperialist' war, will have no such doubts about any future war brought about by Communist aggression. Their own interests and their own way of life are too closely and evidently involved. All this is relevant, also, to Éire, which decided to remain neutral in the 1939–45 war, but which now participates as one of the sixteen nations under the European Recovery Programme and has always been profoundly anti-Communist in outlook.

But while common resistance to aggression is indispensable, it is not enough. The Commonwealth countries recognize that the first aim of their policy must be the preservation of peace, and they have welcomed Britain's participation in Western Union because they recognize that the building up of a league of free peoples within the broad framework of the United Nations is the most practical means of attaining it. Inevitably, any union with western Europe which would involve loss of the United Kingdom's freedom of action overseas or leave it unable to fulfil the role outside Europe which it has played in the past, must raise profound misgivings for the dominions.

Yet to regard the crystallization of Britain's dual personality in international affairs as bringing to the surface an acute tension between the rival claims of the overseas dominions and of western Europe is to see the whole in a false perspective. Some immediate difficulties may loom large, but what is fundamental and what makes a solution at once desirable and practical is the fact that the consolidation of western Europe could only safeguard the Commonwealth by building up a barrier against any aggressor on the Continent. Here its interest coincides with that of the United States. This is a final and all-important factor in the position of the Commonwealth today. As a result of the war and of its aftermath, the Commonwealth countries and the United States are more closely linked than ever before. The development has been helped by the existence of a common language, but it is conditioned by more fundamental considerations, and enhanced by the challenge which now confronts both alike.

# Part II. The Commonwealth in Asia

# 8

# The Commonwealth in Asia

'Strong winds are blowing all over Asia', declared Nehru at the opening of the Inter-Asian Conference at New Delhi in 1947 and there were many who believed that the ending of western imperialism should also bring to an end intimate relations with the West. 'Asia for the Asians' was in their eyes synonymous with an exclusive continentalism. Talk of an Asian bloc was fashionable and hopes were expressed that at least South-East and South Asia might become a neutralized region. Yet, however attractive such proposals might seem to peoples long subjected to alien rule, a closer inspection of them brought to view rivalries within Asia which cast serious doubts upon their practicability, as well as the probability of reactions which could be only unhelpful to both West and East. Fundamentally it was the long-term maritime interests of the countries of South and South-East Asia which precluded any such policy of contracting out or of isolation from world affairs. Yet the fact that such thoughts were in men's minds deserves to be recalled in any review of the relations between the new dominions of Asia and the British Commonwealth. For, in thinking of a future association with the Commonwealth, the Indian leaders particularly were concerned lest permanent membership of this hitherto predominantly European group should in itself loosen the newly forged ties with neighbours in Asia. That anxiety was later modified by a growing appreciation of the unexclusive nature of the Commonwealth relationship, and by the practical experience afforded by the New Delhi conferences on Indonesia, where the attitude of the Pacific Dominions made it clear that moderate nationalist forces in Asia could count on support from non-Asian members of the Commonwealth, but it has not been removed. The psychological difficulties which its existence created were reinforced by more concrete considerations. The two principal aims of Indian, and for that matter of Pakistani, external policy were, and continue to be, national freedom for colonial peoples and the ending of racial discrimination. In themselves these aims implied antagonism to European imperialisms. And however clearly Asia might distinguish between Britain's liberal policies, as applied in India and Burma and as epitomized in Attlee's assertion that the Commonwealth desired to have no unwilling members, and the attitudes of the reactionary imperialisms, of the Netherlands and France, it could not be overlooked that Britain's vast colonial Empire in Africa had not reached the goal of self-government and, far more important, that in South Africa, a member of the Commonwealth, racial discrimination was enforced as a matter of political principle. Indeed, in 1947 the fact that South Africa was a member of the Commonwealth seemed to many Congress leaders sufficient reason why India should not be, and if easy justification for negative policies had been wanted, it lay there ready to hand.

In late 1947 and in 1948 there was a gradual and discernible trend in Indian opinion away from isolationism and towards the maintenance of friendly associations which would not commit India to explicit policies but would enhance her influence in world affairs and contribute to international understanding in a wider field. In particular it was increasingly felt that friendly association with the Commonwealth might act as a steadying influence at a time when revolutionary forces within and without were challenging established authority. In February 1949 Nehru spoke of the policy of the Communist Party in India as one of open hostility 'bordering on open revolt'. And, however firmly resolved the Indian government might be to remain aloof from the grouping of the powers, events in South-East Asia and the advance of communism in China suggested that the Commonwealth connection might prove to be at the least a valuable reinsurance. Yet, while a cool appreciation of the international scene might in these ways suggest the wisdom of continued association with the Commonwealth, external factors in themselves were not decisive. Recent history was a barrier which could be surmounted only by imaginative understanding and, above all, by magnanimity in outlook. It was those qualities that were tested to the full by the constitutional problem with which India confronted the Commonwealth—a problem which, while strictly constitutional in form, was in fact symbolic of historical, cultural and racial differences that had to be reconciled before the Commonwealth could be reconstituted on a new and broader foundation.

While the older dominions were largely British and almost wholly European in origin and outlook, India was a mother country with memories and traditions that went back to the dawn of history and with a cultural influence that had at one time or another spread over much of Asia. Could this India, never more mindful of the glories of her past, find a satisfying sense of fulfilment in the membership of a Commonwealth formally united by a symbolism alien to her history? Dominion status as a practical expedient by which a threatened deadlock over the transfer of power in 1947 might be resolved was one thing; as a permanent element in India's constitution, it was quite another. Here was a problem that required both study and reflection on the part of India's leaders; for in their hands lay full freedom to decide. To some the Congress resolution of January 1947, announcing that India would become a sovereign, independent republic, seemed to dispose of it. Admittedly, republican sentiment in India had not acquired the doctrinaire, uncompromising character of Irish republicanism after the Easter Rising of 1916. But in a sense that distinction was irrelevant. Indians felt beyond question that republicanism was the only form of government appropriate to their circumstances. It was also the only form of government which seemed to them to make clear beyond all question or manner of doubt that India was a wholly independent nation. It could be, and was argued, that dominion status, too, conferred full autonomy, but these arguments carried only partial conviction in Asia. Long, and at times somewhat acidulous, prewar discussions about the right of a dominion to secede or to remain neutral in a war in which the United Kingdom was engaged had sown doubts and reservations, not easily to be removed, about the fullness of the autonomy which dominion status conferred.

But was not the question of Indian membership by implication already decided? Between 1926 and 1931 the three conventional characteristics of dominion status were defined as free association, equality, and common allegiance to the Crown. Did not the third of these qualifications exclude an India about to become a republic? Earlier experience was discouraging. In 1921, when Irish republicans had suggested that republican status might be reconciled with membership of the British Commonwealth of Nations by a form of external association which would have acknowledged the King as head of the Association, the answer had been a rigid negative. It is true that the External Relations Act of 1936 and the new Constitution in 1937 had made Éire a republic in fact; but constitutional lawyers justified her continued membership of the Commonwealth on the ground that the King's signature to the letters of accreditation of her ministers overseas implied, none the less, allegiance to the Crown. The argument was legalistic and politically without substance, but the importance attached to it illustrated the central position given to common allegiance as the keystone of the unity of the Commonwealth. Could it be so qualified that a republican India might remain a member of the Commonwealth if she so wished?

Nothing more surely illustrates the pragmatic approach to Commonwealth relations than the fact that these delicate questions were not approached in a hasty, still less in a theorizing or legalistic spirit. On the contrary, long after the question loomed on the horizon, Commonwealth statesmen continued almost to ignore it. The Conference of Commonwealth Prime Ministers in London in October 1948 was a landmark in the history of the Commonwealth because then, for the first time, the three new dominions of Asia were represented. But if this meeting was the outward sign of the new phase in Commonwealth relations, a phase in which non-British and non-European peoples would contribute as equals to the framing of Commonwealth policies, the form of their membership or relationship was not discussed in full sessions at all. On the contrary, this conference concerned itself with severely practical questions of defence, security and economic development, and though discussions about the Irish repeal of the External Relations Act irrupted onto the stage at the time that the prime ministers were meeting in London, the tacit agreement of all parties to leave constitutional questions, affecting the Asian Dominions, on one side remained unaltered. These prudent, Fabian tactics enabled the prime ministers of the Asian Dominions to see at first hand how the Commonwealth worked before taking any final decisions about their own position, for it was rightly felt that only by participation in the councils of the Commonwealth at the highest level might a full understanding of its working be acquired. Since India, Pakistan and Ceylon 'have come into the Commonwealth,' said Liaquat Ali Khan, the Prime Minister of Pakistan, after the conference, 'its complexion has changed—now it is a Commonwealth of free nations who believe in the same way of life and in the same democracy. To my mind, these ideas are even stronger than racial ties.' These were remarkable words, and they reflected a new confidence on the part of the Asian Dominions that they could find an enduring place in the Commonwealth and in so doing could modify its character to suit their particular needs and outlook. There was also evidence of a similar realism in India. In judicious phrases the Congress on 18 December 1948, at Jaipur, gave unmistakable signs of the coming rapprochement between India and the Commonwealth.[1]

The Jaipur Resolution, however, in reflecting a more sympathetic attitude to Commonwealth membership, implicitly posed the problem with which Commonwealth statesmen were squarely confronted in April 1949. It was a republican India that contemplated continued association with the Commonwealth. There was no suggestion from any quarter that India could or should renounce republicanism for membership. The question was, could the two be reconciled? The problem was, however, distinct in one important respect from that which had been raised by Irish nationalists a quarter of a century earlier. Here was a nation, hitherto a member

1. Its Resolution deserves quotation:

In view of the attainment of complete independence and the establishment of a Republic of India which will symbolize that independence and give to India a status among the nations of the world that is her rightful due, her present association with the United Kingdom and the Commonwealth of Nations will necessarily have to change. India, however, desires to maintain all such links with other countries as do not come in the way of her freedom of action and independence, and the Congress would welcome her free association with independent nations of the Commonwealth for their common welfare and the promotion of world peace.

of the Commonwealth, about to become a republic, which expressed a positive wish to cooperate as a full member with the other countries of the Commonwealth. The Indian desire to reconcile republicanism with full membership could be met only by a modification, even if for her case alone, of one of the conventional conditions, common allegiance, of membership as set out in the Balfour Report and restated in the Preamble to the Statute of Westminster.

The prime ministers, including those of the three new dominions in Asia, met again in April 1949 to settle the issue. Agreement was reached in the short period of six days. Making due allowance for the preliminary work done by the emissaries sent from Downing Street to the dominion capitals, this was a very remarkable achievement. The text of the communiqué issued at the conclusion of the Meeting was as follows:

The Government of India have informed the other Governments of the Commonwealth of the intention of the Indian people that under the new constitution which is about to be adopted India shall become a sovereign independent republic. The Government of India have, however, declared and affirmed India's desire to continue her full membership of the Commonwealth of Nations and her acceptance of the King as the symbol of the free association of its independent member nations and as such the Head of the Commonwealth.

The Governments of the other countries of the Commonwealth, the basis of whose membership is not hereby changed, accept and recognize India's continuing membership in accordance with the terms of this declaration.

The settlement reached, it will be noted, was specific, not general, in application. There was no decision that a republic, as such, could be a full member of the Commonwealth. The conference simply recorded that when India, under her new constitution, became a sovereign, independent republic, she would remain, in accordance with her own wishes, a full member of the Commonwealth and would acknowledge the King as a symbol of the free association of its independent member nations, and as such, the Head of the Commonwealth. The Indian Republic, therefore, owes no allegiance to the Crown, and the King has no place in its government. It is in this respect that the settlement involved a notable departure from the doctrine embodied in the Preamble to the Statute of Westminster in which the members of the

Commonwealth were declared to be 'united by a common allegiance to the Crown.' In the external field, the President of India, and not the King, signs the letters of credence for India's representatives abroad, and in this direction, therefore, the solution adopted went further than that embodied by de Valera in the Irish External Relations Act. Republicanism, which in the past both in Ireland and in South Africa had been regarded as synonymous with secession, was thereby accepted as compatible with full membership. It has been maintained that this compatibility extended only to the case of India, and that one exception did not constitute a category and did not modify the general conditions of Commonwealth membership. But it is hardly likely that this restrictive interpretation would withstand any practical challenge. On the contrary, the wider consequence of the Indian settlement was to make republicanism not incompatible with membership of the Commonwealth.

At first sight the Indian constitutional settlement seemed almost metaphysical in its refinement. It had, however, the supreme merit of going a long way towards reconciling constitutional forms with political realities. In the dominions and particularly in the older dominions, which are predominantly British in extraction, loyalty to the Crown had been a unifying force of transcendent value. For them all, the constitutional position remained unchanged. The King remained King of Canada, King of New Zealand, King of Ceylon, just as much as King of the United Kingdom. But the different traditions, the very different history, of India demanded that she should have another symbolism, which, with the agreement of all of her partners, was accepted in April 1949 as compatible with membership of the Commonwealth.

Of the broad political advantages of the solution reached, there was no question. The Commonwealth, as a result of it, became an international democracy in a fuller sense than ever before, and the successful outcome of this historic conference meant that the association of Asian peoples with the older dominions, predominantly European in stock, was to be, not an episode, but an enduring factor in its history.

In India, the Constituent Assembly endorsed the settlement reached in London with only one dissentient voice. No doubt this did not fairly reflect the balance of opinion within India, for the settlement was severely criticized by socialists as well as by communists, both then and later when India's first general election was held in 1951–2. Yet the general satisfaction with the solution reached was unmistakable. By any criterion by which it may be judged, this welcome was striking evidence of the continuing vitality of the Commonwealth idea. Nehru's carefully balanced language does something to explain it. 'We joined the Commonwealth', he told the Constituent Assembly,

obviously because we think it is beneficial to us and to certain causes in the world that we wish to advance. The other countries of the Commonwealth wish us to remain there because they think it is beneficial to them. In the world today, where there are so many disruptive forces at work, where we are often at the verge of war, I think it is not a safe thing to encourage the break-up of any association that one has . . . it is better to keep a cooperative association going which may do good in this world rather than break it.

He admitted that he was 'a bad bargainer', that he was not used 'to the ways of the market-place', and that he had thought it, in London, 'far more precious to come to a decision in friendship and goodwill rather than to gain a word here or there at the cost of ill will.' Here was magnanimity as well as statesmanship, and the prime ministers of the Commonwealth responded to it with imaginative understanding.

Upon Pakistan, which, unlike India, inherited no established administrative system and few trained administrators, the telescoping of the period originally contemplated for the transfer of power, however necessary politically, imposed a severe handicap at the outset of her career as an independent nation. She had, in fact, only a brief period of some three or four months in which to make preliminary plans for the organization of a new state, and at the end of it she was confronted by some of the most terrible and pressing problems with which any country can be overtaken. In such circumstances, relations with the Commonwealth aroused only intermittent public interest. Moreover, in Karachi, as distinct from New Delhi, it was generally assumed in 1947 and even in 1948 that Pakistan would remain within the Commonwealth. In the past there had been easier understanding between Moslem and Briton than between Hindu and Briton, and the traditional friendship of the United Kingdom for the Moslem world reinforced the presumption of close association with what was now to be the largest Moslem state. These arguments of sentiment and tradition were powerfully reinforced by the advantages which Commonwealth membership seemed to hold out to a state in an exposed position geographically, determined to survive despite all of the dangers and difficulties which then confronted her.

It was not till the closing months of 1948 that the cordiality of Pakistan's relations with the older Commonwealth members, and particularly with the United Kingdom, began to decline perceptibly. It is true that the continued, intimate association of Lord Mountbatten with India as its Governor-General evoked from the outset hostile, mistrustful comment from Pakistan. But that in itself was a symptom of a growing feeling that Pakistan was not receiving from her Commonwealth partners the sympathetic consideration that her circumstances warranted. This sense of neglectful indifference became more pronounced when the Commonwealth governments felt themselves compelled to return a negative response to the appeal from Pakistan to arbitrate in Kashmir. Even while many Pakistanis admitted that Commonwealth arbitration in a dispute between two dominions was practicable only when both agreed to such arbitration, it was none the less felt that the studious correctness of the Commonwealth attitude cloaked an indifference to the dangers which threatened the very existence of Pakistan as an independent state.

The reaction in Pakistan to the London Declaration of 1949 was tepid. It was thought that India had gained too much too easily. It was thought that by being difficult, by making demands on the Commonwealth, India had come to occupy an unduly prominent position in it, and misgivings soon gave way to resentment. On 28 April, the day after the communiqué had been issued in London, Liaquat Ali Khan, while praising the flexibility of the Commonwealth system and the spirit which inspired it, was careful to point out that Pakistan had not yet decided whether she would remain in the Commonwealth. The doubts he expressed were restated more sharply later and the leisurely pace of the drafting of the Pakistan Constitution was well calculated to keep the question of Commonwealth membership open for some considerable time. Yet such expressions of dissatisfaction were, it must be emphasized, very closely related at all times to developments in respect of

Kashmir and did not dispel for most Pakistanis their underlying sense of affinity with the Commonwealth.

Too much should not be read into the dissatisfaction of Pakistan. By early 1950 there was evidence that it had been somewhat modified. The Prime Minister's proposed visit to Moscow, warmly welcomed at home when first arranged, was abandoned the more readily because the purpose behind it had already been largely served. Washington, not Moscow, was to be Liaquat Ali Khan's destination. At the same time Britain's increasing, if belated, awareness of the economic problems of Pakistan was indicated by the dispatch of an Industrial Mission in February 1950, and the suggestion of more cordial relations which it implied was reinforced by signs that the employment of British professional personnel was not, after all, likely to terminate quite so soon as had been supposed in the previous year. In a wider context the readiness of Pakistan to resume trade relations with South Africa suggested again a return to a more positive Commonwealth policy. Yet, despite these modifications in policy, it would be very unwise to dismiss Pakistan's critical, restless scrutiny of Commonwealth relations and purposes as a necessarily transient phenomenon. There is little doubt that, if Pakistan were confronted with the choice of being overrun by India or of being absorbed into the Russian sphere of influence, she would almost certainly prefer the latter alternative, whatever risks it might entail. Commonwealth statesmanship, therefore, is likely to be severely tested in the coming months. Fundamentally, the problem derives from tensions in the Indian subcontinent, and the repercussions on the Commonwealth as a whole are indirect. That in itself makes any useful contribution from the Commonwealth outside more difficult.

Yet there are two more encouraging considerations. The first is that the countries of the Commonwealth feel genuine goodwill towards Pakistan and, while always mindful that she is wholly free to make what choice she will, they sincerely hope that she will continue to cooperate in the common purposes of the Commonwealth to the advantage of all of its members. This advantage would, and should, be mutual, and it would appear to the outside observer that Pakistan had much to gain through full membership of the Commonwealth. It is understood, for example, that the United Kingdom government gave vigorous support to Pakistan in the recent dispute with Afghanistan, and support from a great power in such circumstances has its value. The second, and even more important, consideration is that the interests of India and of Pakistan are so closely interwoven as to be inseparable. In all of the discussions at the Bigwin Conference this fundamental community of interest emerged only too plainly. In economics, in defence, in most of the broad political issues which confront them, the interests of India and of Pakistan are not antagonistic but supplementary. It is impossible, for instance, to imagine any successful defence of the Indian subcontinent against a powerful and well-equipped aggressor unless India and Pakistan are prepared to cooperate, not only when attacked, but in planning precautionary defensive measures. At present military discussions between London on the one hand and Pakistan, India and Ceylon on the other are conducted on a bilateral basis, which obviously restricts their value. So long as there is a lack of confidence between India and Pakistan, and so long as the dragging dispute in Kashmir, which is at once its cause and consequence, remains unresolved, it is unrealistic to imagine that any solid advance can be made. All of this makes a settlement in Kashmir a matter of concern to the peoples of South Asia, to the Commonwealth—for its spirit of friendly and trustful cooperation cannot fulfil its purposes while these tensions between members continue—and indeed to the free world as a whole. For, without subscribing to the dramatic forecasts of communist pressure in South-East or South Asia, it is not at all improbable that one result of the success of the Atlantic Pact in securing a breathing space in the West will be an increase of political pressure in the East, and in such circumstances the removal of causes of internal dissension among the free nations of Asia acquires a very real importance.

The relations of Ceylon with the Commonwealth have a less chequered history than those of either India or Pakistan. Ceylon, indeed, is the model Dominion. It graduated from the status of a Crown Colony through internal self-government to full dominion status with some hard bargaining but with a spirit of mutual goodwill and friendship wholly unimpaired. Its membership of the Commonwealth is of advantage to the Commonwealth and to Ceylon itself. For Ceylon occupies a key strategic position in the Indian Ocean. This in itself is both an asset and a danger. Dependent wholly on its own resources, Ceylon would be one of the first objectives of any air or sea power embarking on a career of conquest in that part of the world. The Commonwealth connection and the treaty with the United Kingdom, by which United Kingdom forces retain facilities on the island, are frankly welcomed by its people · as a guarantee of continued security. Within Ceylon communism, though divided, is not a negligible force. There was a serious risk lest intransigent Dutch policies in Indonesia, by playing into the hands of the extreme nationalists with whom communists are so closely identified, might have strengthened the communists' appeal in Ceylon. Here, therefore, the Indonesian settlement removes a possible cause for anxiety. Though the standard of living compares favourably with those on the mainland, its needs, like those of India and Pakistan, are primarily economic. All important for the Asian Dominions is a programme of economic development which will make possible better conditions for the great mass of the people. This is essential on grounds of humanity and of policy alike. The coming of self-government has raised high hopes for improving standards of life, whose disappointment might well have far-reaching repercussions. Political democracy, as it is understood in the West, is on trial in the East, and its fate will depend on the capacity of the governments it produces to satisfy some of the social aspirations of the people and to govern well.

Evatt has remarked instructively that, with the addition of the Asian Dominions, the centre of gravity of the Commonwealth has moved eastward. While his dictum needs to be qualified by the reminder that the main strength of the Commonwealth, militarily and industrially, continues to lie in the North Atlantic area, it is true that, in respect both of the number of the member nations and of population, the centre of gravity of the Commonwealth now lies in the eastern half of the world. That means that it is no longer a British Commonwealth, if the word British is used to designate the composition of its population, for the great majority are now both non-British and non-European. This profound modification in the make-up of the self-governing Commonwealth has added very notably to the range of its outlook. At the Bigwin Conference there were for the first time delegates from independent countries in Asia to formulate the problems of Asia and to make their essential contribution to the discussions on colonialism and racial discrimination. All of this is undoubtedly a great gain. A new vitality, a wider perspective, has been infused into Commonwealth relations. From this the Asian Dominions themselves should benefit. Through their membership of the Commonwealth they have opportunities of influencing world policies in a way which could hardly be open to them outside the Commonwealth. This is all the more true because the trend in Commonwealth affairs in recent years has been towards the assumption of increasing regional responsibilities by all of its members. Commonwealth membership today does not preclude, but positively encourages, close relations with geographical neighbours. On his return from the Prime Ministers' Conference in April 1949, Pandit Nehru stated explicitly that the continued membership of India in the Commonwealth did not mean that she was drifting away from her neighbours in Asia but that through membership it was being made easier for her to develop closer relations with other countries than it otherwise might have been. This is a very important fact. The closer relation of Britain with Europe is likely in the future to be paralleled by the closer association of the Asian Dominions with the countries of South-East Asia and the Middle East. All of this, on the broad view, is greatly to the advantage of the Commonwealth because it means an enlargement of its opportunities for improving and extending relations between East and West.

The membership of the Asian Dominions has brought non-European races into the inner circle of Commonwealth membership. That is a historic development. Yet it may be suggested that, in respect of relations between wholly self-governing members of the Commonwealth, this association of different races will constitute no very formidable problem. It is when different races are living side by side in one community, not when they are cooperating in an external field, that the problem of race relations assumes difficult and dangerous forms. In free cooperation within an association of autonomous nations, racial differences should constitute no barrier to full understanding and intimate friendship. More important, and hitherto insufficiently considered, is the difference in social composition of the new and the older dominions. In the older dominions the middle class, using the term in a broad Aristotelian sense, predominates. In the days when this class was more fashionable than it is today, Aristotle maintained that its predominance was a condition of good and settled government. However that may be, it is a fact that in India, Pakistan and Ceylon the middle classes do not predominate in numbers. The great bulk of the population are impoverished and illiterate peasantry living close to the margin of subsistence, and until their conditions are bettered it is idle to suppose that they will have any particular understanding of the Commonwealth connection or indeed of the causes for which the free peoples of the world stand today. Yet it is an important fact that the middle classes, many of them educated in European countries, do hold power in India and Pakistan as they have never held it in China, where, in recent years, they have been almost ground out of existence. It is the chief concern of this minority, now responsible for the conduct of affairs in the Asian Dominions, to educate its masters, those great electorates on which for the first time lie the dimly understood responsibilities of representative government.

There can be no question that in this respect the conference of foreign ministers of the Commonwealth at Colombo in January 1950 was a step in the right direction. The Commonwealth for the first time had come to Asia. It is true that the educational value of this conference is not to be exaggerated. The communiqués, as always, were discreet and for the most part unenlightening. Yet the actual presence of statesmen from all of the countries of the Commonwealth assembled in conference in one of the Asian Dominions was an event of unmistakable significance which at the least promoted a wider awareness in South Asia of the character and the reality of the Commonwealth association. Nor was it without importance that Asia provided, not only the meeting place, but also, in Nehru, the outstanding personality of the meeting. From this point of view, Bevin's indifferent health, which did not lessen the value of his contributions to the conference itself but which did debar him from outside engagements, helped in itself to discredit Communist propaganda which had been suggesting that for the Asian countries full membership of the Commonwealth was no more than a clever camouflage behind which British imperialism could continue to function almost unimpaired. If there was one thing that was self-evident at Colombo, it was that the conference was not run from London.

The Colombo conference was an indication not merely of the goodwill of the older dominions, but also of their desire to lend what positive assistance they could towards the solving of the most pressing of Asia's problems, the raising of the standard of living of its peoples. But while the positive proposals put forward with this end in view were timely and welcome, it should be clearly understood that the goodwill of the Commonwealth countries in itself cannot accomplish much just because the practical assistance which they can give from their straitened resources is severely limited. Spender, the Australian Minister for External Affairs, spoke the plain truth in New Delhi on 18 January 1950, when he said that the Commonwealth plan for economic development in South-East Asia could succeed only with United States' assistance.

For the Asian peoples one condition of a popular external policy is opposition to colonialism and to the racial discrimination which in the past has often accompanied it. This condition is not always easy to reconcile with the primary concern of the western powers to create effective opposition in Asia to the advance of militant communism. The Asian Dominions do not dispute the need for checking communism, but their hostility to colonialism implies for them a different approach. While, therefore, all at Colombo welcomed the settlement in Indonesia, attitudes towards Indo-China were not to be so easily reconciled. Where the older members of the Commonwealth detected in Emperor Bao Dai a possible bulwark against communism in South-East Asia, the new Dominions were more mindful of his imperialist backing. It was their fear that, if the Emperor were diplomatically supported by the western powers, the communists might well be the principal gainers because they would be able to argue that the western powers showed by their reactions that they sought through dependent puppet regimes to restore what they could of the old colonial system. The attitude of India in particular was clearly defined by Nehru, who said that India would not recognize the government of Bao Dai, or for that matter any other government in Indo-China, until there was an administration with authority over the whole area. The future of Indo-China will in fact be decided, not by outside opinion, but by the success or failure of Emperor Bao Dai himself to assert his independent authority and in so doing to secure lasting popular backing; none the less these differences of approach to its problems within the Commonwealth at Colombo were highly significant for the Commonwealth itself. It can be argued that differences which preclude the emergence of any common Commonwealth front against Communism in Asia are a source of weakness. It may be so; but on the other hand it can be argued, with at least equal force, that, whatever the differences in emphasis at Colombo, all of the Commonwealth countries now enjoy the inestimable advantage of being able to formulate their individual policies in the light of internal Asian considerations of which they might otherwise have been insufficiently conscious. What is certain is that Colombo marked a phase in the evolution of a new Commonwealth. Its romance is now over; its history has begun. It is because the Commonwealth enjoys great opportunities for promoting understanding between East and West that the promotion of mutual understanding and the reconciliation of contrasting views confront it with duties and responsibilities not to be easily or lightly discharged.

In surveying the Commonwealth today, nothing is more misplaced than facile optimism except impatience. Time is needed for natural unforced growth of sympathy and understanding. 'I have survived', was the boast of the Abbé Sieyès at the end of the French Revolution. For the Commonwealth that is the first, though not the only, essential. Only by continuing to live creatively can it fulfil the mission now imposed upon it.

# 9

# The Triumph of Nationalism
in South Asia

In the spring of 1947 I was an observer at the Inter-Asian Conference in New Delhi. There by the deathbed of the British Empire in India the spokesmen of the new Asia planned how they would order most things new when once again the destiny of their continent passed back into their own hands.

## SENSE OF MISSION IN INDIA

Over the conference of 1947 hung the shadow of civil war in China and growing antagonism between Muslims and Hindus in India. None the less it was an exciting, even exhilarating, occasion, and it was with no little curiosity that on my return to Karachi and Delhi early this year I sought to discover to what extent the reality of independence had fulfilled the high hopes of four years ago. I found, as one might expect, opinion less sanguine about the future and far more aware now that the problems which confront both the Indian subcontinent and Asia as a whole (particularly the problem of food and mounting population) are susceptible of no easy solution. And with this went a growing realization that national rivalries were not confined to the West. But it would be quite wrong to suggest that I sensed an atmosphere of disillusion. Some hopes have not been fulfilled, but much has been achieved which gives solid and enduring satisfaction. Indians, for example, are gratified to feel that Delhi is now one of the great diplomatic capitals, not merely of Asia, but of the world; Pakistanis that their country, the largest of Muslim states, is playing a leading part in the counsels of the Islamic peoples.

A sense of mission undoubtedly influences the temper of Indian nationalism and its attitude to world affairs. It derives some at least of its strength from the contrast often drawn between the spiritualism of the East and the materialism of the West which suggests to eastern peoples that they may have remembered some things of great importance which the West in its preoccupation with material progress has forgotten. Because of this there is a certain confidence that Asia in the coming years is likely to influence the West, more than the West is likely to influence Asia; and that within the British Commonwealth of Nations the voices of its new Asian members, of India, Pakistan and Ceylon, are likely to weigh at least as much as those of its older European partners. The official statement issued after the Prime Ministers' Conference held in London in January 1951 suggests that in this they may not be altogether mistaken.

But, of course, to a nationally self-conscious people the triumph of nationalism is its own reward. In the West it is now axiomatic to write off nationalism, particularly other people's nationalism, as a bad thing. This makes it the more important to remember that in South Asia it has proved a powerful unifying force at a time when a process of political fragmentation seemed not unlikely to set in. With the disappearance of imperial rule, it seemed to many observers that South and South-East Asia would become a prey to disruptive forces, but in fact, in South Asia at least, these fears have proved largely unfounded. In the last years of imperial rule British statesmen were much preoccupied with the future of the innumerable quasi-autonomous princely states, which covered some two-fifths of the whole of the Indian subcontinent. But today princely India has disappeared. Some of its former rulers are now Governors of states in the Indian Union, many more are pensioned off, and all owe allegiance to the President of the Indian Republic.

### Pakistan, 'Creation of the Muslim Masses'

What is true of India is also true of Pakistan. The very existence of Pakistan derives from the strength of Muslim nationalism. 'There are not one but two nations in India', claimed Jinnah, the leader of the Muslim League; and when Lord Mountbatten arrived in New

Delhi in the spring of 1947, Jinnah warned him, as he had already warned his predecessors and the Congress, that unless the Muslim claim to a separate state of Pakistan were conceded, the subcontinent would be faced with the bloodiest civil war in the history of Asia. The warning could not be disregarded. Jinnah was in a very real sense the architect of Pakistan. But his warning carried the weight it did because of the strength of Muslim national feeling. Pakistan was the creation of the Muslim masses and it is sustained today by their enthusiasm. Still in Karachi are to be seen crowds of refugees whose little huts lie huddled together in a large area beneath the tomb of Jinnah and stretch right out into the desert of Sind. Yet, despite such desperate overcrowding, despite the difficulties of setting up a new government in a new capital, despite the sufferings and fantastic problems of the early years, the feeling of the masses in Pakistan has in no way changed. Indeed they are proud of what has been achieved and are resolved that Pakistan shall survive.

Undoubtedly much of the strength of Pakistani nationalism at the present time derives from fear, whether exaggerated or real is beside the point, of India. I was in Karachi during the Commonwealth Prime Ministers' Conference of last January which Liaquat Ali Khan, after protracted hesitation, decided to attend. Unmistakable there at that time was the feeling that any alternative was to be preferred to Hindu rule; there was also the feeling that the Kashmir question, whose satisfactory solution seems to most Pakistanis almost a condition of the continued separate existence of their country, was the criterion by which their attitude to the Commonwealth, to the United Nations and to world affairs was to be judged. But it would, in my opinion, be a mistake, for that reason, to think of Pakistani nationalism as something negative. I believe it to be at root a strong and positive force.

CONTINENTAL COMMUNITY

Despite a continuing antagonism between India and Pakistan, which obscures the extent of their common interests, nationalism in South and South-East Asia is closely allied to a sense of continental community. The peoples of that part of Asia feel that they have long been ruled, and in some cases exploited, from without, and that their common liberation forms a bond of unity greater than any which links together the countries of western Europe. This sense of continental community, which found intellectual expression in the Inter-Asian Conference, finds a more popular outlet in Asian games, in Asian lawn tennis championships, where you may hear the cry 'come on Asia', when, for example, a Filipino is playing an American. It comes most strongly to the surface when the independence of any Asian people appears to be challenged from without. Colonialism in Asia is dead. 'You may like it or dislike it', said Nehru, 'but like an earthquake it has happened just the same.' None the less, not all suspicions of the designs of the former colonial powers have been stilled. A couple of years ago the future of Indonesia was regarded throughout the continent as a test of the reality of the western withdrawal. Today Indo-China means a good deal to India and to Pakistan. Though informed opinion will admit that the situation is confused, it is far from convinced that opposition to French rule was not in the first place nationalist; and that it was not French intransigence that drove the nationalists into unwelcome alliance with militant communism.

In a broader field this continuing suspicion of the West is reflected in many ways. Early this year I found that misreported statements from Washington had revived such fears, and their continued existence is indicative of the psychological mistrust that remains the most formidable barrier between East and West. Because of it western economic and financial aid is often regarded as a dubious asset. No one in Asia received more assistance from the United States than Generalissimo Chiang Kai-shek. Yet, as leaders in South Asia have noted only too well, neither he nor China would appear to have benefited greatly from it. Deeper still there is the feeling that financial assistance from a power so wealthy as the United States would almost certainly involve some limitation upon national liberty of action. Even when faced with large-scale famine in Bihar the Indian government has not shown itself prepared to accept supplies of food from America on conditions which seemed to it inconsistent with full independence.

Nor is there lacking criticism of the ideological grounds for which western assistance is most freely given irrespective of the integrity or national standing of the recipients. I remember a Pakistani friend who had heard that dollar aid was being offered to Afghanistan to counter reported communist infiltration there, saying that while there was no Communist Party in Pakistan it was time that one was created so that Pakistanis would also be assured of an equally sympathetic gesture from the West. Characteristic, too, is the story circulating in Asia in various forms about the Prime Minister who was anxious to secure a dollar loan and who, thinking it to be the best approach, informed President Truman's envoy that there were no communists in his country. This, however, was far from producing the desired result, the envoy remarking that clearly there was greater need for American aid elsewhere. Realizing his mistake, the Prime Minister thereupon appealed to the Prime Minister of a neighbouring state for the loan of some of his communists. This was curtly refused with the observation 'they are far too valuable to us.' Yet no one familiar with living standards in that part of the world can fail to recognize the immense good which western, and especially American, technological aid could achieve. In a very real sense the raising of living standards there is more likely than defensive measures to limit the spread of militant communism. For this reason, if no other, it is supremely important that the causes of mistrust should be thoroughly investigated and, where possible, removed.

### Fear of Chinese Expansionism

If South and South-East Asia is united by such exaggerated fears of outside interference, it is not equally united in a more positive sense. This has been a great disappointment. The 1947 'blood bath' in the Punjab was a very unwelcome reminder that even in the day of liberation, communal and national passions burned as bitterly in Asia as ever they had done in Europe. Nor has it been overlooked that the smaller states of South-East Asia regard, not without misgiving, the growing populations and the expansionist outlook of their greater neighbours. One reason why Ceylon is so contented a member of the British Commonwealth is that she regards her membership as a reinsurance against undue population pressure from India. Far more widespread in South-East Asia is the fear of Chinese expansionism. This was apparent in 1947 even when control was slipping from the grasp of the dying nationalist regime, and it is much more pronounced today when Chinese communism seems likely to march hand in hand with Chinese nationalism.

This fear of China does not leave even a greater state, such as

India, unaffected. There was in 1947 a latent sense of antagonism between India and China, a feeling that between these two lay the prize of political leadership in South and Eastern Asia. With the coming into power of the Chinese communists there followed a honeymoon period in Indo-Chinese relations. It would perhaps be a mistake to say that it has ended, but certainly early enthusiasm is fading. The Indian Note to the Chinese government about Tibet produced a rejoinder whose asperity aroused no little resentment in New Delhi. And, while outwardly relations remain cordial, a good many Indians now feel that they cannot wholly discount the possibility of Chinese aggression against Burma or Malaya or even Indo-China, which would endanger the security of India itself.

Yet, despite some things that I have said, the most outstanding feature of nationalism in South Asia hitherto has been its essential moderation. It may be because it is the nationalism of the intellectuals and the politicians that has so far been in the ascendant and that, as power passes to the peasants and the workers, their nationalism will be more exclusivist and intolerant. It is hard to judge. All one can say is that hitherto India and Pakistan, however self-consciously nationalist in outlook, have not questioned the duty that a state owes to the wider community of nations nor have they lacked enthusiasm for the United Nations and the ideal of one world for which it still stands. Both, too, have retained the link with the British Commonwealth of Nations. With true statesmanship Nehru declared on the morrow of the 1949 Prime Ministers' Conference, which decided that India, as a Republic, should remain a full member of the British Commonwealth of Nations, that this was not a time when links between nations should be broken. And today in Delhi, in Karachi, and in Colombo membership of the British Commonwealth of Nations, although not unquestioned, is accepted by administrators and ministers as part of the working order of things.

This is a very remarkable fact made possible by the moderation of Asian nationalism and reflecting lasting credit on British statesmanship. Nor is it without immediate practical significance. The Colombo Plan, worked out in cooperation by the members of the Commonwealth, suggests how living standards in underdeveloped areas may be gradually improved through mutual self-help and planning. In the diplomatic field India, alone of Commonwealth countries, has been represented by an Ambassador in China and his reports on the situation there, according to Nehru, have been made available to other Commonwealth governments in the ordinary process of Commonwealth consultation. Whatever one may think of the merits of the advice which Panikkar, the Indian Ambassador, has presumably been giving, it is clearly a tremendous advantage to the members of the British Commonwealth that they should have the opinion of an Asian government upon the development of the crisis in Asia. And it affords, too, an encouraging example of how West and East can profitably work together on a footing of complete equality.

## RESPONSIBLE PARLIAMENTARY GOVERNMENT

As important as the continued membership of the British Commonwealth has been the adoption by the Asian dominions of the British system of responsible parliamentary government. This indeed may be regarded as one of the greatest triumphs of British political ideas. In New Delhi or Karachi or Colombo one can see today the procedure, the practices and the conventions of British parliamentary government being carried out much as they are at Westminster or Ottawa or Wellington. Within a few months India will hold her first general election. Some of the constituencies will have no fewer than 750,000 electors and though Aristotle in his wisdom declared that size made no difference to the application of political principles, even he, I think, would feel that an election on this scale presented some very particular problems. The fact that it is taking place is not the result of chance but reflects a deliberate decision endorsed by most of the peoples of South and South-East Asia in favour of the form of government with which we are familiar in preference to the alternative system of which the Soviet Union remains the principal protagonist.

The importance of that decision is often overlooked. The countries of South Asia, linked to the West by history, are also linked to it through common national interests. However much they may feel emotionally part of Asia, their history and their seafaring tradition give to them a window on to a wider world. Because of it they have something of that sense of tolerance and balance which for some reason maritime peoples have so often displayed. Certainly they like the link with the British Commonwealth because they believe that the Commonwealth possesses those qualities itself. 'The most liberal force in world politics today'— that is how an Indian described to me the British role in world affairs at this time; and so long as Britain and the older members of the Commonwealth remain true to that conception of the part they should play, then I think it likely that the countries of South Asia will wish to go with them. Certainly it is a link which at the present time gives a unique opportunity to Commonwealth leaders for constructive statesmanship. Fundamentally it exists because in South Asia the Commonwealth, which itself rests on the principle of the government of men by themselves, is not the enemy of Asian nationalism but its ally. And it is the nationalism of these countries that is the dominant factor in their outlook. One can say with some confidence that no western policy in Asia is likely to succeed that is opposed, not merely to militant communism, but to Asian nationalism. Indeed one can go further and say that the strongest barrier within Asia to the evidence of militant communism is the strength of national sentiment. In itself it is not a sufficient barrier, but without it no sufficient barrier can be created.

# 10

# The Impact of Asian Membership

When, in 1947, India, Pakistan, and Ceylon became fully self-governing and yet chose to remain in the Commonwealth, Britain and the older European members found it a welcome, a reassuring, but not in itself, a very surprising, event. They believed that Commonwealth membership was something of advantage to self-governing nations; that it meant independence with something added to it. It was in precisely these terms that Peter Fraser, Prime Minister of New Zealand, recommended membership to them. But as seen from Asia this continuing membership is surprising.

The year of decision, 1947, was also the year of the Asian Conference, which heralded the disappearance of European rule, the triumph of Asian nationalism, and the resurgence of Asia in world affairs. Was it likely that in this dawn of a new age, in which the sentiment of Asian solidarity flowed strongly, that Asian countries would continue in association even on a footing of equality, with the former European rulers?

Burma, in fact, was not prepared to do so and in India itself there was a widespread presumption that with independence all ties with Britain would be severed, for complete independence was the proclaimed goal of the Indian National Congress. Moreover, during and just after the war, while the prestige of the Commonwealth had become perhaps greater than ever before in the western world, its relative power had declined. In 1942 Gandhi spoke brutally of the Cripps offer of dominion status to India after the war, as a post-dated cheque upon a bankrupt Empire. Why, then, did India and Pakistan remain?

It was Gandhi himself who had said in the thirties that he did not wish to break the bond between England and India but to transform it. Equality between the two countries was his demand, but once equality was conceded then he desired friendship. English thought, especially English notions of liberty, were part of his being—not for nothing was he once described as the last of the Great Victorians—and this conviction of one who was revered in India as the Father of the Nation was very important. The timing and the manner of the transfer of power also made a deep and lasting impression in both India and Pakistan. It was, so it seemed to them, something worthy of the traditions of liberal England on which so many Indians in the past had been nurtured. The Asians' calculation of advantage played a proper, but I do not think a decisive, part. Asian membership dates, after all, from the period of Britain's postwar exhaustion and recurrent financial crises. Something of what this meant was brought home to me not long ago in Lahore. In discussing the fare, my tonga driver asked hopefully if I was an American. On learning that I was not, he did his best to conceal his disappointment, saying that Britain was an old country with a fine culture but—his regretful smile implied—no money.

Asian membership of the Commonwealth is not something that even yet is taken for granted in Asia. It is something that still arouses curiosity. Chou En-lai, on his return from the Geneva Conference, was reported to have enquired closely in Delhi about the nature of India's ties with the Commonwealth—and in answer to have been told illuminating anecdotes about life at All Souls by that very distinguished scholar, the Vice-President of the Republic of India. Not long ago in Karachi, when I gave a lecture on 'Commonwealth Relations', I was flattered to see almost the whole of the Russian and Chinese embassy staffs in my audience. One would certainly not arouse this degree of attention in this country, but here the Commonwealth is part of an accepted order of things. In Asia, including Commonwealth Asia, it is not, and we must not let the fact of Asian membership confuse us about the facts of Asian opinion.

There are deep differences between India and Pakistan, or between India and Ceylon, on particular questions, but when Nehru said that India remained a member of the Commonwealth because of a belief that 'membership was beneficial to us and to certain causes in the world we wish to advance', he was thinking of causes that appeal equally to all the Asian members. Chief among them are the ending of colonialism, of racial discrimination in any form, the raising of living standards in economically backward areas, and the restoration of Asia to what is believed to be its rightful place in world affairs.

Colonialism in Asia drew to its stormy close in the Second World War. But colonialism elsewhere has not ended. It continues, particularly in Africa. At the United Nations the Asian members of the Commonwealth, their faith in national self-determination unimpaired, have championed the cause of self-government for all colonial territories. This has brought them into conflict with the colonial powers, including the United Kingdom. The cleavage in opinion is real, but there has been misunderstanding as well. It is widely believed in this country that Asian pressure has been for the immediate ending of colonial rule. This is not so. That is agreed to be impracticable. What Indians and Pakistanis would like to see is the doctrine of international trusteeship extended to all colonial territories, and they would like ultimate responsibility for the timing of the transfer of power vested in an international authority. Imperial powers, they argue, are apt to postpone indefinitely the handing over of power. Britain herself, they say, has not resisted the temptation in the past. In the words of the present Prime Minister of Pakistan, self-government came to the subcontinent of India 'with painful slowness'.

But it came. It was, at least since 1917, the goal of British policy in India. Today it is the goal of British colonial policy. That is now more widely understood in Asia, and British colonial administration earns generous tributes. There is also understanding of the difficulties of applying notions of international accountability with existing tensions at the United Nations. Indeed, the complaint most often heard is that at the United Nations, Britain, which in Asia and elsewhere has given convincing proof that she knows better, should keep discreditable company—the discreditable company of imperial powers who do not accept self-government as the goal of their colonial policy. Perhaps particularly in Pakistan you will find, for this reason, some misgivings about the North Atlantic Treaty, and about Britain's closer association with Europe, lest they should serve to bind this country more closely to the imperial powers of western Europe.

In respect of racial discrimination, something closely associated with colonialism in the Asian mind, there has been open and bitter dispute between the Asian members of the Commonwealth and the Union of South Africa. Here the weight of Commonwealth opinion comes down on the Asian side in point of principle, though the other members of the Commonwealth are more disposed to regard South African policies as a matter primarily of domestic concern and exercise greater restraint in public than India or Pakistan either wish or see fit to do. There is no doubt that the cumulative effect of pressure from Delhi, from Karachi, and from Colombo has been to make the older members of the Common-wealth more sensitive to the tide of world opinion in respect of colonial and racial questions. That is something in itself welcome in Asia, and indeed a strong argument there for continuing Commonwealth membership.

The Asian members were not responsible for initiating the Colombo Plan, but it is for their vast and under-developed part of the world that it has been initiated. In India or Pakistan today you may see, on model farms, tractors marked as having been supplied by Australia or Canada or New Zealand, as the case may be, under the Colombo Plan. You never see 'supplied by Britain', but that is because Britain contributes in a characteristically unspectacular way by the release of sterling balances. Sharing in the Colombo Plan, modest though it is in relation to needs, may well have strengthened Commonwealth ties, as it has certainly enlarged Commonwealth experience.

Most of all, perhaps, the presence of Asian members has made us more conscious of Asia as a whole. It is the continent in which lives some three-fifths of the human race, yet in recent times its role in international affairs has been extraordinarily small. Even today recognition of it comes slowly. On many occasions Nehru, who in these matters speaks for non-communist Asia, has complained bitterly of western powers seeking to decide the future of Asia without due regard to the opinions of Asians. The under-representation of Asia on the Security Council provokes great indignation. At one phase of the Korean negotiations the whole continent was represented by the Lebanon, 'that excellent but small country', to quote Nehru, and by the government of Formosa which 'represents no body in Asia but Formosa'.

INFLUENCING WORLD AFFAIRS

It is clear that membership of the Commonwealth is seen by Asia, and rightly seen, as one way in which Asian influence can be exerted on world affairs. It has left to the Asian countries full freedom to pursue their own policies, but at the same time through its intricate network of communication and consultation it has enabled Asian opinion to be taken into account in London, in Ottawa, in Canberra, before policies are formulated. For some years, moreover, India was the only member with a fully accredited diplomatic representative to the People's Government in Peking, and Indian interpretations of Chinese policy were regularly communicated to other Commonwealth governments. I believe that this influenced the United Kingdom in its decision to recognize the Peking government as the *de facto* government of China. Again, at the recent Geneva Conference, the Foreign Secretary kept in close touch with the contemporary meeting of Asian prime ministers at Colombo. Reassuring to them, such contact added also to the influence of Britain. The British Foreign Secretary could guide his course knowing, and being known to know, the thoughts of great Asian countries on the resettlement of Asia. This is something new in Commonwealth history. It is something important. Through Commonwealth membership the influence not only of the Asian members but of Britain herself in world affairs is enhanced.

Some consequences of this are to be seen in the attitude of other members to the Commonwealth itself. In Canada today the importance of the Commonwealth looms larger because of Asian membership. This is still more true of Australia and New Zealand— of Europe but not in it, in Asia but not of it. They see, in the Commonwealth, a means of reconciling the divergent pulls of history and geography.

Decentralization was the dominant feature in Commonwealth history long before 1947. But with the addition of the Asian members the process gathered renewed momentum. With their self-conscious nationalism, the Asians were concerned lest the new Commonwealth should prove to be no more than the old Empire in a different guise. They required convincing proof that it was not. This accounts for their insistence on full freedom to secede should they so desire, on their right to pursue wholly independent foreign policies even to the point of neutrality in the event of a war in which other members of the Commonwealth were engaged. This was understandable in the light of their history, but in fact by 1947 independence in every aspect of external policy was implicit in dominion status.

Only in respect of allegiance to the Crown has Asian membership brought about a clear departure from established convention. Till 1949 allegiance was a condition of Commonwealth membership; since that date it is no longer so. The breach with tradition was made so as to enable India, which had adopted a republican constitution, to remain a full member of the Commonwealth. Today India owes no allegiance to the Crown but she acknowledges the Queen as the symbol of the Commonwealth association and, as such, the Head of the Commonwealth. The draft constitution of Pakistan contemplates a republican form of government and it seems likely that in due course Pakistan's relationship with the Commonwealth will be expressed in similar terms.

Some have regarded this loosening of the fabric of Commonwealth unity with dismay. Menzies in Adelaide in 1950 lamented: 'The old structural unity of the Empire has gone; it has been succeeded by structural variety.' If the process continued, he feared lest former unity should give way to a purely functional association based upon friendship and common interest but necessarily lacking the old high instincts and instantaneous cohesion, 'which sprang', he said, 'from the fact that we were all over the British world, as indeed we remain in the old Dominions, the King's subjects and the King's men.' This indeed is a classic statement of the misgivings felt by many traditionalists. But part of the answer, surely, was to be found in Menzies' own words 'as indeed we remain in the old Dominions'? There has been no change in *their* relationship to Crown and Commonwealth; there has been a proper recognition that peoples of different culture and traditions did not share such sentiments; and that it would be at the least unwise, as Irish experience so forcibly underlined, to seek to impose an uncongenial symbolism in the supposed interests of unity.

If history has in the past brought together the members of the Commonwealth, it has for each of them different facets. K.M. Panikkar's book, *Asia and Western Dominance*, presents an Asian intellectual's reaction to European imperialism. I looked up 'Indian Mutiny' in the index and found under that entry a cross-reference reading '*See* Great Rebellion'. How much is implied in those few words! At the Commonwealth Relations Conference at Lahore, nothing was more apparent than the difference in approach to world affairs between the Asian and older members of the Commonwealth; and that such differences are to be largely attributed to differences in experience. The older members, for some time accustomed to the pains as well as to the satisfactions of sovereignty, presumed that the world remained what in their experience it had always been, a place of danger, discord, and power pressures. In their preoccupation with security their representatives talked with a fluency, shocking to their Asian colleagues, of the indispensability of horrible weapons of war to preserve peace; they even advanced the seeming paradox that American supremacy in atomic weapons was the condition of an advance in Asian living standards. To the older members, in the light of twentieth-century experience, the choice in foreign policy seemed to be no more than one between the bad and the worse, the bad being equated with peace-time expenditure on defence heavier than ever before; the worse with inadequate preparation to meet possible communist aggression. But for the Asian members—if I may pursue this deliberately heightened but not, I think, unreal contrast—whose experience of sovereignty in the modern world had been briefer, postwar communist expansion in eastern and central Europe seemed remote. Their outlook was overshadowed by past conflict with imperial powers; for them the greater fear was the entrenching of colonialism, and not the advent of a new and aggressive expansion.

A FASCINATING EXPERIMENT

These differences in history and experience make Commonwealth unity today something far more difficult of achievement than in the past. But they also make it more worthwhile. It is because the multi-racial Commonwealth of today embraces not merely so many peoples of the world but so much of its experience that it seems to me so fascinating an experiment in cooperation between nations. We have already learned much from the newer members, and we have contributed the traditions of law and responsible parliamentary self-government which constitute the foundations on which the Commonwealth rests. The security of these foundations in Asia seems to me crucial to the survival of the Commonwealth in its present form.

We can now best play our part in the working out of the Commonwealth experiment in international and in racial cooperation by being true to the liberal, democratic, humanitarian tradition from which the ideal of Commonwealth derives. A hundred years ago the Emperor Louis Napoleon, in a speech at Guildhall, could say: 'The eyes of all who suffer turn instinctively to the West.' He was thinking of the oppressed nationalities of Europe; today we must think of a wider world, and of economic and social as well as of political ills. Asian membership of the Commonwealth is, or should be, a constant reminder to us that it will be a dark day indeed when the eyes of those who suffer look elsewhere because they have looked to the West and found indifference there.

# 11

# The Commonwealth: Problems of Multiracial Membership*

The dominions whose status was defined in the Balfour Report and whose names were listed in Section I of the Statute of Westminster were predominantly European in respect of their population and wholly European in respect of their government. There were minorities of non-European origin in Australia, in Canada, and in New Zealand: there was a large non-European majority in the Union of South Africa. But neither minorities nor majority were in a position to exert a decisive influence upon government. In Canada and even in South Africa it was the cultural tensions between peoples of European stock that exercised a direct, and often decisive, influence upon national policy and perhaps for that reason it was not unknown, though discountenanced by Canadian scholars, for the term 'race' to be applied to relations between English- and French-speaking Canadians while on the lips of South African politicians the terms 'race' and 'racial' customarily referred to relations between British and Afrikaners.[1] That they did not

*The present article follows, with some amendments, Nicholas Mansergh's paper which was discussed on 25 March 1955 at the 5th Annual Conference of the Political Studies Association of the United Kingdom.

1. And not only on the lips of South African politicians. In the debate in 1906 on self-government for the Transvaal, the Under-Secretary of State for the Colonies, Winston Churchill, the leader of the Opposition, A.J. Balfour, and a young Labour member, J. Ramsay Macdonald, used it in this sense. The 'native question' was the phrase applied to relations between

warrant such a description if the term race were to be precisely defined was in a sense beside the point; it was a description that in South Africa at least was felt to have both traditional justification and a certain appropriateness. The term 'cultural' somehow seemed, and still seems, inadequate to express the intensity of Anglo–Afrikaner antipathies at certain critical periods in the history of the Union. But the multiracial membership to which the title of this paper refers is the full self-governing membership of peoples of different racial origin in the Commonwealth. It is something that dates from 1947.

In March 1954, the Prime Minister of Pakistan spoke of 1947 as a date in Commonwealth history as important as 1926 or 1867. It was from the British North America Act that the conception of dominion self-government derived; from the definition of dominion status in the Balfour Report that the contemporary Commonwealth might be dated. But, in the opinion of Mohammed Ali, non-European peoples had graduated with 'painful slowness' to self-government and to Commonwealth membership alike and neither had been attained in full measure till 1947.

The association between self-government and Commonwealth membership, to which Mohammed Ali referred, is one of the foundations of the multiracial Commonwealth that came into existence in 1947. Radical imperialists like Joseph Chamberlain, great pro-consuls like Lord Curzon had alike emphasized excellence in the art of government as the outstanding contribution of the British overseas. That British settlers in Canada or Australia or New Zealand should believe that they, too, inherited the traditions, and were entitled to practise the art, of responsible self-government was an occasion neither for surprise nor for concern. When other Europeans, non-British in extraction, claimed corresponding rights there was more reserve. Neither Afrikaners nor Irish were considered to be equally well fitted to exercise them, the former largely because they were too paternalist in their notions of government and too hostile to the British connection, the latter because they were too volatile. It is not often recalled that Campbell Bannerman's magnanimous gesture of 1906, when, to quote General Smuts, the

---

the peoples of European and African races. See *Parl Deb.* 4 series 1906, vol. 162, cols. 776–804.

Liberal Government 'gave us back in everything but name—our country'[2] by conferring self-government on the Transvaal and the Orange Free State, was condemned by A.J. Balfour as being so premature in its timing (largely because 'Downing Street was no less desirous of getting rid of the Transvaal than the Transvaal was of getting rid of Downing Street') as to constitute 'the most reckless experiment ever tried in the development of a great colonial policy.'[3] Unionist mistrust of the instability of the Irish is by comparison well known and needs no commentary other than the complaints of innumerable English journalists at the unchanging dullness of Irish politics in the last quarter of a century. Representative institutions and responsible self-government for non-Europeans, however, involved experiments more reckless than that denounced by Balfour in 1906.

It is one of the curiosities of Commonwealth history that it was the Indian National Congress that from the day of its first session in Bombay in 1885 demanded the extension of representative institutions to India and that it was the British exponents of what Joseph Chamberlain described as 'the best form of government' who expressed continuing doubts about the wisdom of acceding to the Congress demand. The oblique introduction of the representative principle in 1892, its extension in 1909, were widely regarded in Britain, and not only by conservative opinion, as a 'sop to impossible ambitions'. 'The notion', said Lord Kimberley, a former Liberal Secretary of State for India, in 1892, 'of parliamentary representation of so vast a country, almost as large as Europe, containing so large a number of different races, is one of the wildest imaginations that ever entered the minds of men.'[4] Lord Morley in 1909 thought it neither desirable nor possible nor even conceivable that English political institutions should be extended to India.[5] The Simon Commission in 1929 exuded the depressing sort of wisdom that springs from doubt and misgivings. 'The British parliamentary

---

2. J.A. Spender, *Life of the Rt. Hon. Sir Henry Campbell-Bannerman* (London, 1943), vol. 2, pp. 237–8.

3. *Parl. Deb.*4 series 1906, vol. 162, col. 804.

4. *Hansard*, cccxlii (1890), 93, quoted by Sir R. Coupland, *India: A Restatement*, p. 103.

5. *Recollections* (London, 1917), vol. II, pp. 172–3.

system . . . has been fitted like a well-worn garment to the figure of the wearer, but it does not follow that it will suit everybody. . . . British parliamentarism in India is a translation, and in even the best translation the essential meaning is apt to be lost.'[6] But while the Simon Commission talked somewhat spaciously of forms of responsible government other than the British, it is doubtful whether the British rulers of India, or indeed Indians trained under the British system, would have been well qualified to apply them. What is certain is that the British system is what the Congress wanted despite the misgivings of some of its older leaders and Muslim fears of the consequences of its adoption for minorities. It was also the system which had been proclaimed in 1917 to be the goal of British policy in India.

Dominion status traditionally has been deemed to be the outgrowth of domestic self-government and to this day full membership of the Commonwealth would seem to derive from the practice of that form of government. That this should be accepted in South Asia is the most important element in the multiracial Commonwealth. Liaquat Ali Khan spoke of the common practice of responsible self-government as the strongest bond of Commonwealth unity—an observation that prompts sobering reflections in the light of the suspension of constitutional government in Pakistan—and on this point his conviction was emphatically reaffirmed at the Commonwealth Relations Conference held at Lahore, 1954.[7] The Commonwealth is an experiment in cooperation between states of varied race and culture, and one condition of its success would seem to be the common practice (with variations to suit local circumstances) of the parliamentary system of government. Or to put the point in a less positive form, it is doubtful whether states adopting other forms of government would continue to find membership congenial.

While in retrospect the misgivings of the Simon Report may seem somewhat exaggerated in respect of Asia, the question, very important for the future of a multiracial Commonwealth, remains:

6. *Report of the Indian Statutory Commission*, vol. II—*Recommendations,* Cmd. 3569, 1930, pp. 6–7.

7. A report of its proceedings by the author of this paper has been published by the Royal Institute of International Affairs under the title *The Multi-Racial Commonwealth.*

do the conditions necessary for a comparable experiment in responsible parliamentary government exist in East, Central, or West Africa? There is in India, Pakistan, and in Ceylon a long tradition of civilization and culture, and though the great mass of the people still remains illiterate the experiment in responsible parliamentary government is taking place in societies where learning is respected and where there exists an elite from which leadership may be drawn. But in most parts of Africa there is no such heritage of culture. It may be, as some suppose,[8] that as a result the conception of responsible self-government will be the more readily assimilated because where there is no comparable, there can be no conflicting, cultural tradition. I find this argument unconvincing, and I believe therefore that in respect of government the multi-racial Commonwealth has its more difficult, though possibly less important, tasks still before it.

The forms and practice of government are of importance to the future of the Commonwealth not least because the working of the Commonwealth system is more closely associated with them than is generally understood. The machinery of Commonwealth cooperation is in fact tied to the procedure and practice of responsible parliamentary government. Mackenzie King in his speech to both Houses of Parliament at Westminster in 1944[9] spoke of a continuing conference of Cabinets. He used this phrase in a very precise sense. To him the important thing was not that ministers or even prime ministers but that Cabinets should confer. His objection to centralized machinery in war as in peace was firmly based on his opposition to anything that would impair the collective responsibility of individual dominion Cabinets to individual dominion Parliaments. If in the thirties he over-emphasized the doctrine that 'Parliament will decide' the objections he advanced early in the Second World War to proposals for the creation of an Imperial Council or the revival of an Imperial War Cabinet were well grounded in the tradition of responsible government. He disliked the notion of a minister or prime minister in London as member of some imperial body taking decisions without the opportunity of personal consultation with his own Cabinet colleagues. 'If the

8. e.g. Martin Wight, *Colonial Constitutions 1947,* Introduction.

9. Reprinted N. Mansergh, *Documents and Speeches on British Commonwealth Affairs*, vol. I, pp. 587–9.

Prime Ministers of the dominions', observed Mackenzie King in the Canadian House of Commons in February 1941, 'were meeting in an Imperial War Cabinet in London they would either have to act on their own exclusive responsibility without regard to their colleagues, or alternatively to hold up proceedings while they communicated with their governments at home. On the other hand, the existing arrangements permit the Prime Minister to consult his colleagues at once . . . a decision can be reached at once with the secure knowledge that it represents authoritatively and finally the government as a whole.'[10] What Mackenzie King advocated therefore was the elaboration of a system of cooperation which made it possible for Cabinets, thanks to modern methods of communication, to be consulted on all major issues of policy and to reach their decisions 'in the atmosphere, not of London, but of the dominion itself.' Too much has perhaps been written of the anti–Downing Street complex from which Mackenzie King was supposed to suffer and certainly too little of his understanding of the principles and the working of Cabinet government. The system of Commonwealth cooperation which he did much to build up not only derives from the principles of Cabinet government but is conditional for its effective operation upon the practice of parliamentary government by the member-nations of the Commonwealth.

In the postwar years continuing reliance has been placed upon consultation between Cabinets supplemented by informal exchanges of view between prime ministers and ministers. If meetings of Commonwealth prime ministers have superseded the former Imperial Conference, that is largely because by their character and composition they make possible cooperation on a basis of discussion, whilst leaving, in practice as in theory, decisions to governments and to parliaments. Important in itself as showing how the notion of responsible parliamentary government has been the determining principle in the evolution of the idea of Commonwealth cooperation, this development is also, in my opinion, immensely important in making membership of the Commonwealth congenial to Asian members with their marked insistence on the fullness of their national sovereignty. Indeed it would be possible to argue that had

10. *Canada H. of C. Deb.*1941, vol. I, pp. 811–13, reprinted Mansergh, *Documents and Speeches on British Commonwealth Affairs*, vol. I, pp. 528–32.

some more centralized machinery of Commonwealth cooperation come into existence during the Second World War, Asian membership after the end of the war would not have been possible on any lasting basis. There is little doubt that in fact it was experience at the Prime Ministers' Meeting of October 1948, the first at which the Asian members were represented, that went far to consolidate the opinion of Asian governments in favour of continuing Commonwealth membership.

The Commonwealth as we know it today is the outcome, but not the inevitable outcome, of history. It is not surprising that newer members—in the past South Africa and the Irish Free State, at the present time, India, Pakistan, and Ceylon—should entertain some fears lest the new Commonwealth should in fact prove to be no more than the old Empire writ large. It was because the members of the Commonwealth had acquired the right to secede should they so wish, to remain neutral in a war in which Britain was engaged and to pursue their own foreign policies independently of the policy of Britain or the older members of the Commonwealth, that India and Pakistan remained members of the Commonwealth. The existence of these rights, said the Prime Minister of Pakistan in 1954, was a condition of their continuing membership, but equally, experience of membership had lessened the emphasis upon them as it came to be understood that their existence was something that could be assumed. One consequence is that the Asian membership has today a more settled appearance than at any time since 1947.

In the constitutional field the Asian members have found the old dominion symbolism uncongenial. This is partly because of doubts instilled during the inter-war years about the extent of the independence which dominion status conferred, and partly because the monarchical symbolism which was then an essential part of dominion status appeared first to India and later to Pakistan to be incompatible with their own indigenous traditions. Walter Bagehot remarked that it was as difficult to adopt a monarchy as to adopt a father and in essence it was this simple fact that precluded the survival of older dominion forms in the new Asian members. The London Declaration of April 1949 which allowed a republican India at her own request to remain a full member of a Commonwealth of which the King was to be acknowledged as the symbolic Head involved no allegiance on the part of India to the Crown, and in no way impaired republican status. But it did preserve the symbolic unity of the Commonwealth. In 1953 the Pakistan Constituent Assembly passed a resolution recommending a republican form of government for Pakistan; and in February 1955, Pakistan, at her own request and with the agreement of the Commonwealth prime ministers assembled in London, also retained, as a republic, full membership of the Commonwealth. It seems that the government party in Ceylon, the United National Party, is likely in due course to make some similar recommendation. In general Asian membership has introduced a greater variety in Commonwealth constitutional symbolism and this variety, which reflects political and psychological realities, is likely to be accentuated as the multi-racial character of the Commonwealth becomes more pronounced. In this way new constitutional questions relating to the form of Commonwealth membership are likely to arise, but they may not be of a formidable character in themselves.

The constitutional relation of India and Pakistan to the Commonwealth constitutes a new departure but would seem to have advantages that outweigh its disadvantages. It is self-evident that there was no sentimental attachment to the monarchy in India and Pakistan such as exists, for example, in Australia, New Zealand, and Canada, and therefore, even had it been politically possible, it would hardly have been politically advisable to adopt a monarchical form of constitution since that would have had the almost inevitable result of making Commonwealth membership and allegiance to the Crown matters of domestic controversy in these countries. Of the dangers of such an outcome the history of Ireland has unmistakable lessons to teach. In this context it is to be noted that in South Africa the constitutional issue deeply divides the European population, whereas both in India and Pakistan there would seem to have been virtually unanimous acceptance of their respective republican constitutions. For that reason, while a republic in South Africa would seem to be inevitable, especially in view of the increasing preponderance of Afrikaans over English-speaking South Africans in the younger age groups, domestic divisions may have repercussions without as well as within the Union.

The adoption of republican constitutions by the Asian members reflects their political aspirations, their insistence on incontestable national sovereignty, and also their reaction against imperialism.

That is very marked and poses one of the major problems of multiracial membership in the Commonwealth at the present time. The limitation of the area of common experience as between the Asian and the older members of the Commonwealth has accentuated it. In the last two decades the older European and the newer Asian members have been beset by different cares, preoccupied with different problems, oppressed by the thought of different dangers, and seeking different ends, and one result is that the lessons they have learned from recent history are not the same. For the older members, experiences which condition their outlook are of the dismal and well-nigh disastrous consequences of appeasement in the nineteen-thirties, of the struggle for a year, alone and ill prepared, against the might of Hitler's Germany, and of victory followed by the re-emergence in Eastern Europe of a new and seemingly equally formidable totalitarian threat to peace and security. The lesson most deeply graven on their minds is of the need to unite in time in resolute resistance to aggression, wherever it may occur. But in Asian minds what remains uppermost is the struggle to overthrow imperialism in the nineteen-thirties, its largely successful outcome in the nineteen-forties, and uncomfortable reminders from South-East Asia that it is not yet ended. Where the former remember how the Nazi tyrant picked off his victims one by one, the latter recall the years of subjection to imperial rule. All the opprobrious significance of the term 'appeasement' in the West is invested in the term 'colonialism' in the East. They are two words that epitomize respectively the experiences of the older and of the Asian members. Their meaning is very different.[11]

These differences in experience have had two consequences. In the first place there is the distinctive approach on the part of the Asian members to world affairs and in the second place there is their hostility to the concept of colonialism. In respect of the first, there is in Asia a deep mistrust of western imperialism and it is directed mainly against the United States, now the greatest of the western powers. A few years ago American economic imperialism was the phrase that expressed it: more recently there has been active fear of American military adventures on the mainland of

11. These reflections were prompted by the discussions on foreign policy and defence at the Lahore Conference, and this paragraph is largely reproduced from the concluding chapter of Mansergh's report.

Asia, a fear which is accentuated by the feeling that the western world in general and the United States of America in particular have a certain continuing indifference to the welfare of Asia. Threats, for so they are regarded, of massive retaliation, have not lessened it. Asian countries are believed to be regarded in the West as pawns in the struggle for power, their peoples not the equals of Europeans. More than once since 1947 have I heard it said that the atom bomb would never, no matter how long the European War had lasted, have been dropped on a European people, and Chester Bowles's admirable report[12] on his Embassy at New Delhi confirms that this was no exceptional experience. Important in itself, it reflects a fear that is deep-seated and will not easily be removed. It is the product of past memories of colonialism coupled with a sensitive contemporary nationalism and a continentalism which feels that Asia as a continent has been long submerged and that the western world is still unwilling to see it occupy its rightful place in world affairs. Because such feelings are entertained Commonwealth cooperation in international affairs is something that today can never be assumed. It has to be sought, to be worked for. That is a new experience and a new problem, at least in its intensity for this country. But with the problem has also come opportunity; the opportunity of working together with leading countries in a new resurgent Asia on the basis of full equality for peace and welfare in Asia and in Europe. How great that opportunity may be recent events have underlined.

In theory, the Asian attitude to colonialism and the racial discrimination psychologically so closely associated with it, is one of uncompromising hostility. In practice, Indian and Pakistani opinion tends to make some exception in favour of the United Kingdom. This exception in no way detracts from their condemnation of colonialism as a method of government even for backward peoples, but it does reflect a recognition both of the quality of Britain's colonial administration and self-government as the goal of her colonial policy. While the Asian members would like to see greater authority vested in the United Nations, perhaps through a more liberal or even a strained interpretation of Article 73 of the Charter, they are prepared to recognize that the declared goal of British

12. *Ambassador's Report.*

colonial policy is something of which they can unreservedly approve and their criticisms are therefore directed to two things. In the first place, they doubt whether any imperial power, even Britain, is likely to transfer power to a colonial people at the first possible moment that it is ready to assume responsibility for its own affairs; and secondly they fear lest Britain's association with 'reactionary' imperial powers in the North Atlantic Treaty and other agreements for the defence of western Europe should deflect her from her declared policy of self-government for colonial territories.

The emphasis on colonialism and on racial policies means that the multiracial Commonwealth of today is peculiarly sensitive and perhaps peculiarly vulnerable to racial tensions. It is for that reason that South African policy, long a matter of dispute with the government of India, has recently assumed wider importance within the Commonwealth and without. The Indians and the South Africans are agreed on one point of principle, namely, that the Commonwealth itself should not set up as a judge or arbitrator in intra-Commonwealth disputes or over the domestic policies of member-nations. For that reason, the Indian and the Pakistani complaint (though the Pakistanis do not share the Indo–South African distrust of a Commonwealth tribunal) has been pressed not within the Commonwealth circle but at the United Nations. The treatment of South African citizens of Indian descent in Natal was India's first concern; but her representatives widened the issue by proposing an inquiry into the causes of racial tensions in Africa. There is no doubt of the importance which Indian opinion attaches to this proposal, and the Indian Prime Minister has gone so far as to suggest that unless these tensions are eased they might provoke a world war on racial lines. Indian criticisms have been confronted by the South African repudiation of the authority of the United Nations to debate South Africa's racial policies on the ground that they are a matter of domestic concern within the meaning of Article 2(vii) of the United Nations Charter. Within the Commonwealth South Africa, committed as she is to the maintenance of 'European' or 'Christian' civilization, to quote the terms usually used, finds it increasingly difficult to keep in step with a community of states that is becoming more and more multiracial both in membership and in outlook. It is for this reason that the question either of the admission of future members to the Commonwealth or of the future of the High Commission's Territories might cause doubt about South Africa's continued membership of the Commonwealth. Both, it is to be noted, are matters of controversy not with Asian members but with the United Kingdom, which is perhaps more deeply committed to the experiment of a multiracial Commonwealth than many of her people realize.

The question of admission of new members is of course a matter of general Commonwealth interest. Malan expressed more than once his violent opposition to the admission of a West African negro state to full membership. His protests led people to assume that the South African government would attempt to veto any such proposal for admission and instilled misgivings in West Africa that the South African government might be able to use a supposed veto power effectively. But in fact this is extremely doubtful. It is an unwritten obligation of membership that the strongly expressed views of the majority of members of the Commonwealth should be accepted and there is no possibility of a veto since there is no voting at Commonwealth Conferences. Indeed, a more careful scrutiny of what Malan said suggests that he himself recognized as much but wished, in the first place, to ensure that South Africa was fully consulted, and, in the second place, to be in a position to register a protest even though that protest proved ineffective—this partly on grounds of conviction and partly for reasons of domestic politics. But even if the possible dispute is thus narrowed, the underlying cause of dissension remains and the United Kingdom government will in due course, not in all probability by one dramatic decision about the admission of one particular African colony to full membership, but by a series of smaller steps, have to take up its stand. The very nature of the surviving colonial Empire, coupled with the existing multiracial membership of the Commonwealth, quite certainly, in my view, means that the United Kingdom government will come down in favour of admission of African territories now far advanced on the road to self-government, and so accentuate the multiracial character of the Commonwealth. Over a period of years this is bound to present difficult questions to any government in the Union of South Africa.

Because of this emotional racial setting the conditions of membership need some definition. At the Lahore Conference there was general agreement that they were five: a desire for membership, recognition of the Queen as head of the Commonwealth, a firmly established parliamentary system, sufficient size and resources to support the responsibilities of a sovereign state (for 'bogus nations' were not wanted within the Commonwealth community), and, finally, the agreement of existing members to admission. The outward sign of membership was attendance of the Prime Minister not by courtesy but as of right at Commonwealth prime ministers' meetings. In turn this would mean, if precedent is to be observed, a transfer of departmental responsibility for any colonial territory that graduated to full membership from the Colonial to the Commonwealth Relations Office. Suggestions, it is true, have been made to the effect that the dividing line between the responsibilities of the Colonial Office and of the Commonwealth Relations Office should disappear, and that there should be one large department dealing with relations and affairs in all parts of the Commonwealth. It seems doubtful, however, whether any such proposal is likely to achieve the ends its sponsors have in mind. In the first place, nationalists in what are now colonial territories will not welcome the disappearance of the distinction between departmental responsibility in the United Kingdom for relations with self-governing states and the discharge of administrative duties in respect of non-self-governing territories because, apart from anything else, it will make it the more difficult for them to decide when they have reached self-governing status and when they have been recognized by the United Kingdom government and other members of the Commonwealth to have done so. In the second place, the proposal seems to me ill-advised because relations between the self-governing members of the Commonwealth are so intimate, and, in my opinion, so fruitful, largely because there is a department in London specially concerned with them and with them alone. To merge that department in a larger department where the distinction between relations and executive responsibility might become blurred would seem inadvisable. Much more is likely to be lost than gained. On functional grounds, indeed, the case seems far stronger for the amalgamation of the Commonwealth Relations Office with the Foreign Office than for the amalgamation of the former with the Colonial Office. But neither is, I think, desirable.

There is, however, in view of the growing preoccupation with problems of subsistence, of development, of food, and of health among self-governing and non-self-governing members of the

Commonwealth alike, a case for the re-examination of methods of cooperation in economic, financial, and social policies, not so much with a view to creating any new machinery but so as to ensure the best use of the machinery that already exists. In the Statute of Westminster Commonwealth, the inhabitants of the dominions belonged for the most part to the western, high-standard-of-living section of the world; but in the newer multiracial Commonwealth economically privileged and economically underprivileged communities alike are members. The Colombo Plan, what it implies rather than what it is, portends a new field of cooperation for Commonwealth members and already it can be seen that the Plan is not only having some impact on living standards in South Asia but is also enlarging the experience of the Commonwealth as a whole. For the future that may be equally important.

The multiracial Commonwealth would seem to offer fruitful fields of study to many academic disciplines. The anthropologist and the sociologist as well as the economist, the historian, and the political scientist have much to contribute to an understanding of it. If, however, I am right in thinking that the Commonwealth, in conception and in practice, derives from the working of a particular form of government, then the study of that form of government and of its possible extension to territories where it has not hitherto been practised and where formidable and hitherto little-considered problems may confront it would seem deserving of our closest attention. Already we know that in the multiracial communities of Africa the Durham formula is likely to prove no magic solvent of them, while even in the more homogeneous territories of West Africa the grafting on of British political institutions to what is vital and vigorous in indigenous life and custom is something that requires an intimate knowledge of the local society and institutions. But the importance of the task and of the knowledge for its fulfilment can hardly be in question. The British colonial empire is one of many colonial empires of the present and of earlier times, but history would seem to furnish no parallel to the conception of a community of free and equal states associated in one Commonwealth. It is curious that this unique offshoot of British expansion overseas and of British political thought should be regarded in the land of its origin with an outward respect that barely conceals inward indifference.

# 12

# The Commonwealth and the Future

When historians are asked to write about the future, they are apt first to think of the past; it is there that they find assurance, and sometimes illusion, of knowledge; and it is there that they seek first for signposts along the road to the future. But even in so doing they are likely to reflect with Coleridge that history is like a lantern on the stern of a ship, casting its light only on the waves behind it and, more disturbingly, to recall Samuel Johnson's aphorism about indulgence in prophecy being the most gratuitous of all forms of human folly. Though there remain among historians an eminent and fortunate few who profess to see in the history of mankind a system, or grand design, within reach of human comprehension and who, in the face of passionate protestation from their professional colleagues, feel enabled as a result to infer what the pattern of the future may be, even they speak of it only in broad conceptual terms. But as for the great majority of us, mere 'antiquarians and chroniclers' as we were described once, we feel occupationally disqualified, as it were, from an assignment so foreign to our trade.

In the case of the Commonwealth, or the Commonwealth of Nations, as I would prefer to call it, were this not an age when brevity is all, there are more particular difficulties in essaying to forecast the future. This, I think, arises less from the pace of contemporary change than from the nature of the association itself. It has never been easy to foresee the future of the Commonwealth and those who have attempted to do so have usually been pretty wide of the mark. Some fifty years ago the Prime Minister of Canada, Robert Borden, noted in the Imperial War Conference in 1917 that the 'greatest intellects of the Empire in the past have miscalculated the conditions that would develop in the dominions, and have failed to foresee the relations of the Empire under the policy of developing full powers of self-government, which was supposed to have the effect of weakening, if not severing, the ties which unite the dominions to the mother country.' But that policy 'which was supposed to weaken the Empire . . . had really strengthened it' and further progress along the line of past development and towards 'an increasingly equal status' would help, so he continued, venturing himself into the realm of prognostication, to realize 'the idea of an Imperial Commonwealth of United Nations'.[1] Borden's comments provoke two contradictory reflections. Firstly, if the prophets were wrong in the past, how can they expect to be right in the present? And secondly, if Borden himself could foreshadow in 1917 with reasonable accuracy the pattern of development in succeeding decades, why can it not be done now?

When the Canadian Prime Minister spoke, there were four dominions, to which a fifth, the Irish Free State, was shortly to be added, all racially homogeneous in respect of government, even if there were in Canada and South Africa cultural divisions, and in the case of South Africa alone a racial problem of the greatest complexity. But for the five governments, that is to say the United Kingdom and the four Dominions, represented in the Imperial War Conference in 1917, there were substituted at the Commonwealth meeting held in London in September 1966, twenty-two free, equal, and independent states—the United Kingdom, Canada, the Commonwealth of Australia, New Zealand, India, Pakistan, Ceylon, Ghana, Malaysia, the Federal Republic of Nigeria, the Republic of Cyprus, Sierra Leone, Jamaica, Trinidad and Tobago, Uganda, Kenya, Malawi, Malta, Zambia, Gambia, Singapore, and Guyana, to which list is to be added the United Republic of Tanzania (which decided not to be represented), and Botswana, Lesotho, and Barbados, which have since become members. These member states were not aspiring to equality in status; they were

1. See A.B. Keith, ed., *Speeches and Documents on British Colonial Policy 1763–1917* (London, 1918), vol. 2, pp. 376–7.

equal. They were not seeking to assert their autonomy; they were independent. They were not united in explicit or implicit support of a mother country; they were each one, including the United Kingdom, self-evidently occupied in the furtherance of their own interests or opinions. It is, therefore, not only the number but also the variety of interests and viewpoints which makes any forecast of the future of the Commonwealth so problematical by comparison with 1917. To all of its member states the Commonwealth is a superstructure, the usefulness of which at any given time is to be determined by individual concepts of state interest. It may be thought inherently improbable that such a superstructure can continue indefinitely to advance the purposes of all the member states. It would be unrealistic, accordingly, to contemplate a future in which membership was constant. There will be additions, and present indications suggest there will be possibly more significant subtractions. If this seems too obvious to merit statement, it is well to remember that in 1917, or indeed down to 1939, while the first was contemplated, the notion of the second, in the form of secession, remained something to be discussed theoretically rather than something to be given practical effect. More important for the future will be shifts in national interests and attitudes, though it is to be noted that impersonal factors—historical, geographical, economic—generally allow of less freedom of national manoeuvre than commentators are apt to suppose. In some few instances, however—for example at this present time in respect of British membership of the European Economic Community (EEC)—there is by the nature of the cases a specific handicap for the forecaster in the lack of strictly contemporary or near-contemporary evidence of state policies, on matters with a direct bearing on the development of the Commonwealth. Here all is apt to be altogether speculative.

The Statute of Westminster Commonwealth, with its emphasis upon common allegiance, free association, and equality of status, which was foreshadowed by Borden in 1917, endured till 1947. It was then, with Asian membership, that the modern Commonwealth may be said to have come into existence. It did not, however, come into existence so to speak of its own momentum. The critical decision was that of India. It was taken after debate and much discussion. Essentially, it was a decision reached by party and government, or perhaps one should say governments, in view of the participation of other Commonwealth governments, if not in its making, then in its final formulation in 1949. Reasons of state, considerations of prudence, and idealist concepts of international relations went to the making of that decision. They have been sufficiently analysed elsewhere. In the context of the present, when the Commonwealth connection is under critical scrutiny in India, sharper than at any other time since independence, rather than review them once again, it may be profitable to reflect upon the objections to India's membership of the Commonwealth as they were expressed to me when I was in Delhi as an observer to the Asian Relations Conference in the spring of 1947. If their formulation was specifically Indian, their significance was general.

The four principal objections to India's membership of the Commonwealth advanced at that time may be grouped as follows. (1) It might mean something less than full independence and be accordingly inconsistent with past Congress pledges. (2) It would mean association in common membership with South Africa, and because of South Africa's racial policy, even under the Smuts regime, be at once undesirable and uncongenial. (3) It would mean association in a community of states in which the only great power and the traditional leader and guide, Great Britain, was also the greatest of the colonial powers at a time when the ending of colonialism was to be the chief aim of Indian foreign policy. (4) It would mean more generally association, through consultation and perhaps by consequent implied, if not explicit, commitment, with western-dominated foreign policies.

How do these objections look today?

The first, on the fullness of independence, no longer remains a preoccupation. In every respect, members of the Commonwealth are, and have been for some time, altogether independent. Neither in South Asia nor in the East African states have I heard any suggestion to the contrary—allegations of neo-colonial influences being unrelated, so far as I could judge, to Commonwealth member-ship. There is one novel question sometimes posed in Britain itself, namely where there is undue limitation upon Britain's independence and freedom of action in its African policies as a result of its exposure through Commonwealth membership to pressure from African states. The implications of the question are potentially anti-Commonwealth. For the rest, in so far as there is debate, it has moved from the issue of whether a Commonwealth member is independent to that of whether Commonwealth membership continues to be an asset to member states in the furtherance of their several and separate policies, or whether, at least for some of them, it is inhibiting or even something of a liability. In the shorthand of twenty years ago, the question might be put—does Commonwealth membership mean independence plus or independence minus?

The South African problem, the second on my list, remains, but it is no longer a problem of Commonwealth membership. Asian and, later, African membership, modifying traditional concepts of Commonwealth, intensified the foreseeable and foreseen sense of incompatibility between South African and Asian and African membership, and the issue was duly resolved with South Africa's enforced secession in 1961. It was correct, therefore, to foresee and forecast conflict between Indian and South African membership of the same Commonwealth, but it was not sensed that it would be India, chief among the new members, that was to prevail. This indeed was generally recognized to be a triumph for the new concept of Commonwealth, and on South Africa's departure, Commonwealth prime ministers, for the greater part, vied one with another in their acclaim for the consequent strengthening of Commonwealth ties and the new positive sense of purpose and direction the Commonwealth had thereby acquired. That was a mere five years ago. The occasion had also a theoretic importance. In 1961, the Commonwealth prime ministers collectively decided that there was one issue, racial discrimination, on which the traditional Commonwealth doctrine of non-interference in domestic affairs should not, and would not, in effect apply. It remains to be seen, now that the breach has been made, whether their successors widen it or not. Historically, one would expect this at least to be attempted. In a recently published work on Britain and the old dominions, Miller has commented upon indications of Australian sensitivity to signs of a possible weakening of the domestic non-intervention tradition with the progressive enlargement of Commonwealth memberships though he has also noted, by contrast, that the Canadians, seemingly untroubled by any such considerations, remain convinced that such expansion in membership provides means of access to Asia and Africa that might not otherwise exist.[2]

In 1947, the third problem, that of colonialism, and particularly of the British colonial empire, loomed larger than South Africa. It was felt then that, given the changes in world power and the climate of opinion especially in the Labour Party in Britain, colonialism in its Commonwealth setting was a question chiefly of time. And even those who ventured to advance such an opinion, hardly supposed that the winding up of the British colonial empire would proceed at the pace at which it has done. Under the British parliamentary system, no government, should it so decide, is so well placed to effect rapid, even revolutionary changes as a conservative one. Parnell understood this in 1885, when he sought to secure a Conservative alliance to carry Irish Home Rule, and Gladstone understood it equally well when he gave the Conservative leader, Lord Salisbury, direct encouragement to concede it. Indeed, he pointed out to Salisbury that two momentous reforms earlier in the century, Catholic Emancipation and the repeal of the Corn Laws, had been carried by Conservative governments, though understandably he refrained from reminding him that the price in both instances had been the splitting of the Conservative Party. But Harold Macmillan, disregarding all discouraging precedents, carried through imperial policies potentially as, or almost as, controversial without semblance of serious division within Conservative ranks and with the assured support of the Labour and Liberal Opposition. Early in 1960 he went to Africa. On 9 January, at a State banquet in Accra, he spoke of the wind of change 'blowing right through Africa'. No great significance was attached to his words. But on 3 February, before an unreceptive audience in the Houses of Parliament in Cape Town, he talked once more of the winds of change which he had felt on his African travels.[3] This time the phrase had a telling, dramatic impact. He remained, however, understandably silent about the change of wind in Whitehall and in Westminster. That silence was a source of misconception. For

2. J.D.B. Miller, *Britain and the Old Dominions* (London, 1966), p. 211. It is to be noted that Miller does not himself think Australian reservations well grounded.

3. Reprinted in Nicholas Mansergh, ed., *Documents and Speeches on Commonwealth Affairs 1952-1962* (London, 1963), pp. 347–51.

long, British settlers in Africa, and especially in Kenya and Rhodesia, had contemplated uneasily the return of a Labour government, which they thought not unlikely to apply the South Asian precedents of the forties, with a fixed timetable for transfer of power, to Britain's African possessions. That a Conservative government should deliberately adopt such a course was something that seemingly occurred to none of the settler leaders, as their writings, notably the autobiographical records of Michael Blundell in Kenya, published under the appropriate title *So Rough a Wind*, and of Roy Welensky in the Rhodesian Federation,[4] make abundantly clear. For this a price was paid in the deep-seated mistrust of British settlers in Africa and, above all, in Rhodesia for the British government, whatever its political complexion.

Britain's resolve to liquidate its African empire—a resolve probably correctly dated to 1959—as quickly, or as some Left-wing critics even allege, for example, in the case of the three former High Commission territories in South Africa, more quickly than circumstances and conditions reasonably allowed, was little understood in the United States or even in other Commonwealth countries. Indeed, long after Britain had decided to liquidate its empire, it was widely presumed that it was anxious to retain what remained of it. It was not. It was anxious to wind it up. This was a matter of deliberate policy. At one of the rapidly succeeding constitutional conferences which paved the way for independence, the Conservative Secretary of State for the Colonies said: 'We do not want to hustle you into independence.' When a politician finds it necessary to say that he does not want to hustle his audience, it can reasonably be assumed that that is precisely what he has in mind. 'As the 1960s progressed and the pace of constitutional development increased', noted the former African correspondent of *The Times* of London,

the British Government seemed to lose control over the situation, to be following a trend rather than initiating and pursuing a definite properly conceived policy of disengagement. There were several signs of this. For

4. Sir Michael Blundell, *So Rough a Wind: The Kenya Memoirs of Sir Michael Blundell* (London, 1964), and Sir Roy Welensky, *Welensky's 4000 Days: The Life and Death of the Federation of Rhodesia and Nyasaland* (London, 1964).

one thing, there was the fundamental change in the accepted criteria for independence. For another, there was an increasing readiness to see the preparations for independence as a proper exercise of Lancaster House Conferences, as a challenge to chairmanship rather than a duty to find a constitutional framework genuinely acceptable to the people of the country concerned and relevant to their needs and conditions.[5]

This was just, but was it realistic? Could a process of decolonization on this scale be phased? In any event, in 1966, the Colonial Office, long dwindling away, finally ended its separate existence. With it there was removed the 'colonial barrier to Commonwealth cooperation'. It had proved, after all, to be only a matter of time. If it be urged that there was still colonialism in Rhodesia, the first thing to be said, whatever view may be taken of British policies after the Unilateral Declaration of Independence (UDI) in November 1965, is that this was not British colonialism but settler rule. If it be alleged that the outlook of the British government was still colonialist, because it did not take more drastic action against the illegal regime in Salisbury, that is no doubt a serious allegation but it is also a questionable inference and an issue which has little or nothing to do with colonialism as a factor in Commonwealth relations and as it was debated in India in 1947. Nor is it to be overlooked that in respect of Rhodesia, however deep the divisions within the Commonwealth, the British government, while retaining ultimate responsibility, consulted with their Commonwealth partners in a way that would have been thought inconceivable in 1947. This is not a claim for virtue but a statement of fact. There has been throughout the Rhodesian crisis a Commonwealth committee in London reviewing the effectiveness of sanctions.

So far, so the argument may be thought to run, the future of the Commonwealth might look more rather than less assured in 1967 than in 1947. Have not all doubts about national independence been removed? Has not South Africa been compelled to leave the Commonwealth because of the incompatibility of its racial policies with a multiracial society of states? Has not Britain, the greatest of the colonial powers in 1947, wound up its colonial empire? Does not the removal of these barriers open up, as was so eloquently stated in so many quarters at the time of South Africa's secession,

5. W.P. Kirkman, *Unscrambling an Empire: A Critique of British Colonial Policy 1956–1966* (London, 1966), p. 13.

new possibilities for friendly and fruitful cooperation? The answer in theory is no doubt in the affirmative; in practice almost certainly in the negative. The reason, in my view, has little or nothing to do with Rhodesia, which, viewed against the background of the Commonwealth as a whole, remains certainly a critical but still a comparatively small and presumably ephemeral issue. It is against a world background that the future of the Commonwealth is rightly to be assessed.

The future cohesion of the Commonwealth is most closely dependent upon attitudes and the formulation of policies in that large area of international affairs, and here I come to the fourth and last of the difficulties foreseen in 1947, where the deeper, long-term differences between member states have their source. The point may be illustrated from the history of Indo–British relations. At the moment they are probably best described as cool but correct. The coolness derives immediately from supposed British attitudes interpreted in the light of British statements made during the Indo–Pakistani conflict of the autumn of 1965. Both India and Pakistan are at once neighbours and members of the Commonwealth. In some quarters disappointment has been expressed that over the years the Commonwealth, and particularly Britain, should have contributed little to the resolution of differences between them. In others, there has been the feeling that the Commonwealth, and again Britain in particular, has shown partiality. There has been resentment and on both sides, perhaps particularly the Indian, disillusionment with the Commonwealth. Yet, it may be asked whether the Commonwealth, as a society of independent states loosely associated in a concert of convenience—the phrase is J.D.B. Miller's[6]—could ever hope to unravel and resolve differences, so deep and yet so intimate as those between neighbouring states that were at one time or other part of a single polity? The precedents, so far as they go, suggest a negative answer. In the case both of Anglo–Irish and Indo–Pakistani relations, the Commonwealth, in itself no more than a superstructure, had little to offer, and it was probably the wiser course for statesmen in other Commonwealth countries to reconcile themselves in such cases to a prudent sense of the

6. J.D.B. Miller, *The Commonwealth in the World* (London, 1958), pp. 275-7.

limitations of their own knowledge and potential contribution. This would certainly seem to have been the conclusion of Arnold Smith, the Commonwealth Secretary-General, when approached with urgent suggestions for a Commonwealth peace mission to help bring to an end Indo-Pakistani hostilities in September 1965. He felt that the United Nations, with its overriding responsibilities in peace-keeping and peace-restoring, was the appropriate body and that even the appearance of rivalry between the United Nations and the Commonwealth 'would be a profound disservice to both'.[7]

The recurrent strains in India's relations with the Commonwealth, and again particularly with Britain reaching near breaking-point at Suez in 1956, would seem, however, to have a broader basis. Both Britain and India are great powers with world-wide interests. At almost every point in international affairs—the Cold War, alliances and defence pacts in every region of the world, Vietnam, Sino–Soviet relations, nuclear weapons—they have a common but not necessarily a like concern. Nor have they, as a matter of history, thought alike on many of these issues. How, indeed, could it be otherwise, given differences of experience, economic circumstance, and geographical situation? Since, therefore, there are bound to be divergences, the contribution of the Commonwealth is limited to encouraging the formulation of authentic differences in terms of common understanding. If the Commonwealth is not successful in making that contribution, its future in respect of Indian, and presumably other, membership is doubtful. Is it? It is argued in India that the Commonwealth, by fostering certain presumptions, even illusions of grandeur, on the British side, far from helping, is a hindrance. The same argument, also, has been advanced in Britain, though there it is usually presented in terms of the existence of the Commonwealth, the nature of which is insufficiently understood, creating a sense of unreality and thereby leading Britain to an exaggerated idea on the part of the public of what Britain could or should do.[8] Against the old myth

7. Arnold Smith, 'The Need for the Commonwealth', *Round Table* (London), vol. 56 (1965-6), p. 225.

8. *The Future of the Commonwealth: A British View* (London, 1963), p. 3. (Report of a conference held at Ditchley Park, Oxfordshire, 25-7 April 1963—Ed.)

of Commonwealth is put the new reality of the Common Market. In so far as these arguments have substance, inevitably they diminish the future prospects of the Commonwealth. It will, however, be noted that both rest upon a supposed state of mind, and even if it be conceded that the supposition in both cases is well grounded in fact, states of mind are inconstant factors in politics.

There are, of course, many factors in the contemporary Commonwealth relationship, which were not foreseen or even considered in 1947. No one, it may be thought, contemplated a Commonwealth of twenty to twenty-five member states within two decades. No one perhaps then, or even now, is in a position to assess on the basis of experience what such enlargement in membership may mean. In Delhi, as in London, it is very easy to overlook the measure of reliance upon, and consequently the value of the Commonwealth connection to, some of the smallest of the new recruits. Indeed, in order to appreciate it, it is necessary to look at the Commonwealth, let us say, from Maseru, the capital of Lesotho (formerly Basutoland), with its still largely pastoral society, with its dependence in trade and for employment for surplus population upon the South African Republic, and its meagre resources in materials and in men—the population is under a million—and see from such a standpoint what the Commonwealth relations may mean in quite practical terms. Nor is Lesotho an isolated example. There are many small states now in the Commonwealth, the smallest being Gambia, with a population of some 300,000, indifferently equipped to support the responsibilities and trials of international status. The consequences of an abrupt disappearance of Commonwealth support for these states might have disruptive, even disastrous consequences. In part, this accounts for African pressure for the constitution of a Commonwealth Secretariat. The African states, having no doubts about status, have no reason to entertain inhibitions about a central administrative organization. They have for the most part need of aid efficiently channelled to them. They believe the Secretariat can help to ensure this. In so far as it succeeds, the Secretariat may foreshadow, in conjunction with the new Commonwealth Foundation, the Commonwealth Education Unit, and other parallel organizations, a new era in economic and social cooperation. Does the Secretariat also imply the coming into existence of a wider area of effective action for Commonwealth conferences, now that they are vested with limited administrative means for giving effect, subject always to the agreement of individual governments, to their collective conclusions? On the basis of limited and largely Rhodesian precedents, the answer may well be—despite continuing theoretic objections and watchful scrutiny on the part of some governments—in the affirmative.

It is important, moreover, to think of Commonwealth foundations not merely in terms of politics or economics. There is a considerable and growing field of technical and professional cooperation. In the academic world, the tide is flowing all one way—in the direction of greater Commonwealth interchange, interest, and cooperation. This is manifested in the academic world, in Commonwealth scholarships, in the creation of study centres such as the recently established Centres of South Asian and African Studies at Cambridge. It is well always to ask ourselves whether these developments in the academic, like comparable developments in technological or professional, field or in respect of aid and trade, would have taken place in the same way and on the same scale if there had not been a present-day Commonwealth inducement? I think not. And to my personal view is to be added the weighty opinion of the Secretary-General of the Commonwealth Secretariat. 'The richer Commonwealth members', he has written, 'have given hundreds of millions of dollars in economic aid and technical assistance to their less rich partners. This aid, this interest in one another's problems, should no doubt have been forthcoming with or without Commonwealth contacts. But I am by no means sure that it would have been.'[9]

What is required in attempting to assess the future of the Commonwealth is no less than an essay in political accountancy. On the debit side there appear some large items:

(1) Political tensions, notably between Britain and India, and Britain and a number of African states, some of whom broke off relations with Britain over Rhodesia and several of whose governments have from time to time threatened to secede from the Commonwealth as a means of applying pressure on London, are more general and more marked than at any time before in the history of the Commonwealth.

9. A. Smith, 'The Need for the Commonwealth', p. 223.

(2) The increased questioning on every side whether a Commonwealth can continue to subsist under such strain. That questioning is widespread not only in African states, and in India, but also in Britain itself, where, and it is well to be candid on this point, some African attempts to force the hand of the British government by threatened secession have recoiled unfavourably upon the concept of Commonwealth.

(3) The possibility or prospect of ultimate British membership of the Common Market, while by no means necessarily incompatible with the Commonwealth connection, will subject it inevitably to a period of political and economic readjustment and may tend further to diminish Britain's interest.

(4) There is the psychological heritage of Empire—something neither to be over- nor under-estimated—which is apt to stir emotions and revive memories of imperial rule in times of tension or crisis.

(5) The progressive disappearance of a uniform pattern of government may, it is sometimes argued, impair the effectiveness of Commonwealth cooperation. Mackenzie King used to speak of a continuing conference of Cabinets; it may be doubted now how continuing or comprehensive is the conference and certainly it is no longer one only of Cabinets.

What is there that might be placed on the credit side?

(1) First and foremost is the fact that the Commonwealth is an association of many states, alone of its kind and assured on that ground of considerable continuing backing. Few of us, certainly of the older generation, would face untroubled the thought that this experiment begun in 1947 had finally failed.

(2) The Commonwealth on the non-political level is showing signs of vitality and development and with the establishment of the Secretariat and other standing bodies, equipping itself with the means of promoting greater cooperation in professional fields.

(3) It is significant that the African states, in their repudiation of imperialism and their suspicion of neo-colonialism, remain none the less the strongest advocates for giving more positive content to the Commonwealth connection.

(4) No more Rhodesias! There can be none and with the close of that episode will come, therefore, the final ending of the colonial–racial question in Commonwealth relations.

How does the balance sheet add up? Each man remains his own

political accountant and it is a greatly cherished privilege. Temperament in this case has something to do with the final balance sheet; actual experience, contact with the Commonwealth at work, even more. For all the frustrations, and intentions of past and present years, there is no doubt in my mind at least that it was right to have attempted the experiment of a multiracial Commonwealth and that despite frustrations and setbacks on balance it has contributed much over the past two decades to the resolving of colonial and racial issues and to wider international understanding. Institutions, like men, must hope to serve their own generations. More than that it is presumptuous and unstatesmanlike to ask. By that test of service the Commonwealth must stand or fall. It is not a political absolute. In the professional and social fields of which I have some knowledge, it passes that test, to my mind, without question and beyond doubt. In the realm of higher politics it is not possible to feel any such measure of assurance. There, statesmen need to think what are the purposes required of such an association at this time and by this generation and whether and in what ways the Commonwealth may be used to serve them.*

* Originally published in *International Studies*, vol. 9, no. 1 (1966). Copyright © Jawaharlal Nehru University, New Delhi, 1996. All rights reserved. Reproduced with the permission of the copyright-holder and the publishers, Sage Publications India Pvt Ltd, New Delhi, India.

# Part III. Reappraisals

# 13

## Jawaharlal Nehru: The Spokesman of Liberal–Internationalism

I Ie could hardly at this time be described as a politician at all. He was a revolutionary. Whenever there appeared some tenuous hope of settlement, he was always at hand to urge extreme courses, and his efforts were reinforced by a beautiful appearance and a glowing eloquence. . . . He was at this time an agitator who thrived on tumultuous meetings where motions subversive of British rule were passed amid wild excitement. He was one of the foremost agents of the new 'propaganda war' which, indifferent to truth, organized hatred with ice-cold logic.[1]

The period was the later 1920s; the man Jawaharlal Nehru, most gifted son of a distinguished father; the writer, Lord Birkenhead in his biography of Lord Halifax, who as Lord Irwin had served as viceroy, looking forward with well-intentioned, liberal–imperial gaze to a dominion status for India which would concede autonomy within the British Empire, but not the complete independence which the younger Nehru demanded. Other, and firsthand, judgements from the Raj were more temperate but not dissimilar. In the tense aftermath of the Cripps Mission, Lord Linlithgow remarked that 'Nehru may be a considerable orator and in many ways he has the qualities of a leader. But he is torn at all times by an internal conflict of ideals and he is too lacking in consistency ever to be the sort of basis on which one could build with confidence', while Wavell who worked closely with Nehru, especially in the Interim Government, said he 'could not help liking him. He is

1. The Earl of Birkenhead, *Halifax: The Life of Lord Halifax*, London, 1965, pp. 220 and 243.

sincere, intelligent and personally courageous. .... But he is unbalanced. ....' Or again a year later, 'cultured, intelligent, highly strung, usually likeable but quite unstable. ....'[2] The last Viceroy with whom Nehru formed a friendship which was of historic moment, while altogether more appreciative of his gifts, also had occasion to observe his moods and emotions over and above physical tensions which drove him to near exhaustion. But even with the passage of time, *Swaraj*, Indian membership of the Commonwealth and Nehru's standing in the world, Englishmen of conservative temper found it hard to efface earlier impressions of the handsome young Indian with his English schooling and his imperial friends,[3] who left his affluent home in Allahabad to challenge the British Raj with weapons forged in the armoury of English liberal thought and sharpened with an edge of Marxist dialectic. To Smuts, who had fought against the British, all might be forgiven and more than forgiven, but against Nehru, who had suffered long years of imprisonment, even when an elder statesman of the Commonwealth, much was remembered. Both were intellectuals, both graduates of Cambridge, the one in Law, the other in Natural Sciences, both were at once nationalist and internationalist, both were leaders, as Mackenzie King so emphatically was not, of charismatic appeal. But where Smuts—and herein perhaps from the point of view of continuing British sensitivities lay the crucial difference—was a traditionalist in social as in racial policies, Nehru was at once a national and a social revolutionary, deeply influenced by Marxism though certainly in later life highly critical of its rigid conceptual framework and hostile to its dialectical certitudes. Moreover, he came to power with little experience of administration and possibly no great aptitude for it—hence his reliance to a degree not yet clear upon Mountbatten in his first turbulent post-partition months of office—and this was reflected in things he did and how he did them. Where Smuts devoted his gifts to immediate and definable purposes—the winning of war, the refashioning of the Commonwealth, the drafting of a constitution

2. Mansergh and Lumby (eds.), *India, The Transfer of Power 1942–47*, vols. I–IV, London, 1970–, vol. I, no. 148; Mansergh and Moon (eds.), *India, The Transfer of Power 1942–47*, vols V–VII, Appendix, vol. VIII, no. 493.

3. The Rt. Hon. Lord Butler, *Jawaharlal Nehru: The Struggle for Independence*, Cambridge, 1966, pp. 8–11.

for a new world order—Nehru, in pursuit of aims that might appear equally commendable, advocated means and employed arguments which were in many cases not only revolutionary in much of the thought that lay behind them but abstract in their conception or presentation. Non-alignment, the Panch Shila or Five Principles, areas of 'non-war', coupled with pained rebuke and admonition to those who sought security in alliances and built up strength against possible aggression—all these were attitudes or policies or, and perhaps most of all, language which many in Britain found it hard to stomach. In the past it had been the British who had lectured others on the folly of their ways—they found it in consequence doubly difficult to bear with equanimity the admonitions of another couched in intellectual–moral terms. They noted inconsistencies, or detected them where none existed. They were apt to associate and to confuse Nehru's with Gandhi's views on non-violence, and having done so, to point an accusing finger at Nehru's policy in Kashmir or Indian absorption of Goa by the use or threat of force. Nehru's immediate and unqualified condemnation of the Suez adventure, coupled with delayed and qualified denunciation of Russia's rigorous suppression of the contemporary Hungarian revolt—in itself an error of judgement, indicating a political imbalance deriving from over-sensitivity to the type of imperialism against which he had struggled and insufficient sensitivity to mani-festations of one with which he was unfamiliar—rankled, in many minds besides that of Sir Anthony Eden. On many occasions Nehru gave hostages to political fortune by his practice of relating international affairs to first principles and expressing his opinion on how they ought to be conducted. To conservative pragmatists the first was an irrelevance and the second, when actions of theirs had fallen short of the prescribed standard, hard to forgive.

Many of the things that made Jawaharlal Nehru suspect to the right served to enhance his standing with liberal–internationalists of the left. Over Smuts there hung the shadow of native policy (or lack of one), and while liberals and nationalists alike welcomed Smuts's insistence upon a Commonwealth decentralized to the limit, he remained for them an enigmatic figure, enlightened in his concepts of a world order, but the protagonist of a white sub-imperialism in Africa: too preoccupied with preserving intact the domestic jurisdiction of national states to be the authentic herald of a new international society concerned to uphold and to advance human rights: over-much occupied with power politics to give sufficient attention to the claims of the weak or the downtrodden. In Nehru they found their ideal. Eloquent and sensitive, he possessed at once personal magnetism and the gift of effortless leadership. His credentials as an opponent not only of imperialism— he had spent almost nine years in jail*—but in the thirties of Nazism, Fascism and Japanese militarism, were impeccable. On his European travels he had scorned the advances of Mussolini, sensed the deeper significance of the civil war in Spain, looked down with critical regard from the Gallery of the House of Commons upon Neville Chamberlain speaking in the dramatic debate which preceded his flight to Munich and felt that there was a man in whose countenance there seemed to be 'no nobility', who looked 'too much like a businessman', who was very evidently 'not a man of destiny but a man of the earth, earthy.'[4] He had warned his contemporaries, in the language of a Churchillian internationalist, of the awful consequences of the rise of militarism in Europe and Asia, and he recalled, when on trial for sedition at Gorakhpur in 1940, that there were few Englishmen who had denounced Fascism or Nazism with the same consistency and outspokenness as he had done. Having seen 'with pain and anguish how country after country was betrayed in the name of this appeasement and how the lamps of liberty were being put out', had he not the more reason for resentment that 'the hundreds of millions of India' should be thrust in 1939 'without any reference to them or their representatives into a mighty war' fought 'in the name of freedom and self-determination'?[5] When eight years later the hour came for him, as Prime Minister of an independent India, to tread the stage of history he showed his

---

* The exact period, as recorded in the display at the Nehru Memorial Museum, was 3,262 days, i.e. nine years less twenty-three days. Nehru's first period of imprisonment was in the Lucknow District Jail from 6 December 1921 to 3 March 1922: his last and longest (following upon the 'Quit India' resolution) from 9 August 1942 to 15 June 1945 at Ahmadnagar Fort. There were three periods, with short interludes between them, each of two years in the early thirties.

4. Jawaharlal Nehru, *The Unity of India*, London, 1941, pp. 290–3, and Mansergh, *Survey of British Commonwealth Affairs* 1931–1939, pp. 359–60.

5. Jawaharlal Nehru, *The Unity of India*, p. 397.

ability, as was noted at the time, to rise to great responsibilities. 'He has developed', wrote Rajagopalachari to Sapru in April 1948, 'in a most remarkable way. . . . You must have seen this about Jawaharlalji with natural pleasure and gratification.'[6] In that same year Mackenzie King in London discussed with him India's future relations with the Commonwealth, King indicating his belief that emphasis should be placed upon the 'Community of Free Nations' and what was common to the community 'rather than having emphasis upon the Crown'. He was greatly impressed and found that Nehru 'reminded him a little of Sir Wilfrid Laurier in his fine sensitive way of speaking . . .',[7] a high tribute indeed from such a source. While Nehru always lacked capacity for sustained and purposeful administration, few could match his sense of style or occasion. From the midnight hour on 14–15 August 1947, when the Congress kept 'its tryst with destiny', to that memorably moving broadcast six months later on 30 January 1948 which told India and the world of Gandhi's assassination—'the light is gone out of our lives, and there is darkness everywhere' for 'our beloved leader, Bapu, as we called him, the Father of the Nation, is no more'; from crowded demonstrations in the capitals of Asia, from Prime Ministers' Meetings in London, at which his attendance was unfailing, to the dramatic symbolism of Delhi's Republic Day celebrations on 26 January each year, to the receptions of potentates and presidents, prime ministers and revolutionary leaders from all over the world, at dusk in the Red Fort where, presiding over the ceremony, immaculate in Gandhi cap and white achkan, with a red carnation in his buttonhole, he rarely failed to leave upon his hearers the impress of his personality and his pervasive sense of the movement of history.

Jawaharlal Nehru was a prolific writer, with autobiographical reflections, deepened in the seclusion of his prison years, in almost every work. The breadth of his appeal lay in his ability to reflect the aspirations of his time, as much as of his own people and to speak in their own terms, both to the villagers of India in their millions

6. Sapru Papers, letter dated 22 April 1948.

7. J.W. Pickersgill and D.F. Forster, *The Mackenzie King Record*, 4 vols., Toronto, 1960–70, vol. IV, p. 404.

and to the new political elites of the cities. He was enabled to do so because he spoke quietly and directly, a microphone always with him, in a personal way—as though he were among close friends, obviously happy to communicate his thoughts to them—and also because, as has been truly said, both as a man and in his style of speaking he 'transcended sophistication with a certain natural simplicity.'[8] Secularist and humanist, Nehru was the spokesman of a liberal reformist approach at once to the divisions of community and caste at home, and to questions of peace and war abroad. He never wavered in his faith in the parliamentary process in India and, deploring the long-range abusive, propagandist dialectic of the great powers in the Cold War, urged quiet discussion in conference even of the most intractable issues. There was a transcendent quality in his appeal to the intellectuals, to the sometimes self-consciously enlightened, to younger generations finding neither psychological satisfaction nor congenial refuge in the alliances of the Cold War years and who, weighed down by the menace of nuclear annihilation, responded wholeheartedly to Nehru's concern to harness the twentieth-century technological revolution to the service of the over-populated and under-nourished areas of the former colonial world. The new, more sanguine, more meaningful, more idealistic and, be it added, simpler approach to the complexities of international relations which they looked for, they found, as nowhere else, in the utterances of India's Prime Minister. The aristocratic, westernized high-caste Kashmiri Brahmin thus became the mouthpiece of the new, classless societies of the mid-twentieth century. He hated war, and denounced the armaments and alliances which threatened to bring it nearer to Asia. He was the proven enemy of imperialism; he was the angry champion of the underprivileged, and he was outraged by the pretensions of racialists whether in Asia or in Africa. When the Mau Mau rebellion erupted in Kenya in 1953 he regretted the violence but he came round to the opinion that the African had no alternative to violence.[9] 'I am not', he said,

8. Nehru told the author in 1947 that he never went on any speaking tour without a second microphone by way of reinsurance. The quotations are from Marie Seton, *Panditji. A Portrait of Jawaharlal Nehru*, London, 1967, p. 174.

9. S. Gopal, *Jawaharlal Nehru. A Biography*, London, 1979, vol. II, pp. 167-8.

interested at present in petty reforms for the Africans, that is a matter for them to decide. I am interested in standing by people who are in great trouble and who have to face tremendous oppression. . . . I should condemn of course every species of violence and give no quarter to it. But I shall stand by the African nevertheless. That is the only way I can serve them and bring them round to what I consider the right path.

If Jawaharlal Nehru loomed so large in the world and the Commonwealth of the fifties that was because, while moving on a world stage, he continued to express with insight and foresight so many of the feelings and aspirations of this time.*

While Nehru's appeal was world-wide, his heart came to beat with the continent and the people to whom he belonged. There was, it is true, an earlier time when with his westernized education he felt that he had 'become a queer mixture of the east and west, out of place everywhere, at home nowhere. . . . I am a stranger and alien in the west. I cannot be of it. But in my own country also, sometimes, I have an exile's feeling.'[10] But in maturity, and under Gandhi's influence, his roots struck deep in his native land.

---

* On a number of occasions, Nicholas Mansergh had interviews with Nehru. In his article 'Letters that we ought to burn' Mansergh mentions conversations in 1951 and 1958. (The article is reprinted in N. Mansergh, *Nationalism and Independence: Selected Irish Papers*, Cork University Press, 1997, pp. 241–9.) Amongst Mansergh's personal papers there is a record of an interview with Nehru in April 1954. From this it is clear their talk covered three subjects: the sequence of events leading to independence and the reasons why India remained in the Commonwealth; the strength of parliamentary government in India; and the date when the partition of India became unavoidable.

As regards the first subject, Nehru evidently said that two things had been all-important, namely the way power had been transferred and the role of Mahatma Gandhi. India found the Commonwealth a useful bond, shared information was valuable and the meetings were helpful. India was able to work especially with the United Kingdom, Canada and the United Nations. On the second subject, Nehru pointed out that India's experience of parliamentary government was on the whole encouraging and there was no suggestion of any alternative. Democratic procedures were spreading downwards to the village council level. On the third subject, Nehru said that until August 1946 he had believed in the unity of India. The conversation then moved on to the difficulties of bringing the Muslim League into the Interim Government in 1946 and to the League's actions once in the government.

10. Jawaharlal Nehru, *An Autobiography*, London, 1936, pp. 597–8.

Constantly, as Prime Minister of India, he returned to the theme of the awakening of Asia and of India after a long sleep; of the attention after long neglect the West must pay to Asian interests and Asian opinions; of the 'torment in the spirit of Asia', 'the tremendous ferment of change' in a continent whose growth had been arrested for some two centuries.[11] While there was much that dismayed or distressed him in this stormy resurrection of a continent, he did not doubt that with national freedom and the ending of the 'dire poverty' of so many of her people, Asia would become 'a powerful factor for stability and peace'. 'The philosophy of Asia', he said, 'has been and is the philosophy of peace.''India', he said at another time,

may be new to world politics and her military strength insignificant in comparison with that of the giants of our epoch. But India is old in thought and experience and has travelled through trackless centuries in the adventure of life. Throughout her long history she had stood for peace and every prayer that an Indian raises, ends with an invocation to peace.[12]

The sceptics remained unconvinced, but for a time at least a Gandhian image was partially superimposed not merely upon a nation, but a continent. It was tarnished by Indian intransigence in Kashmir and Indian action in Goa, and destroyed by the Chinese attacks upon the Indian frontier. In each case Nehru's reputation was damaged, and these events must now be commented on.

The Maharaja of Kashmir acceded to India. The circumstances were debatable, but the Indian title rested upon the legality and the finality of that accession. Nehru, the liberal, offered a plebiscite. There was no obligation upon him to do so. Nehru, the Kashmiri and nationalist, found a succession of reasons, some convincing, others unconvincing, for ensuring that, in circumstances that had admittedly changed, the offer was not given effect. For his own reputation it would have been better had he rested his case throughout upon the signature by the Maharaja of an Instrument of Accession in the form approved by the India Independence Act, 1947. But Nehru desired, over and above the sanction of law, the

11. *Jawaharlal Nehru's Speeches*, 1949–53 (2nd imp.), Ministry of Information and Broadcasting, Delhi, 1957, pp. 159, 189 and generally 158–60, 179–93.
12. Ibid., pp. 127 and 124.

approval of the people of Kashmir. This, in a sense satisfying to world opinion, he did not secure. Likewise Nehru desired to gain possession of Goa by persuasion; in the end, confronted with Portuguese intransigence and under political pressure at home, he was persuaded to sanction force. To the nationalist in him the acquisition of Goa represented the fulfilment of the national movement for independence and, in this instance again despite many hesitations, Nehru's nationalism proved stronger than his sense of an internationalism that conceived of change only by peaceful means. On his own nationalist argument, little weighed by critics in the West, his error may well have been in delaying so long. In the late forties the take-over by a newly independent India of the small Portuguese enclaves in the subcontinent might well have been accepted by the world at large as a further and inevitable step in the liquidation of western colonialism in Asia. But once decision was deferred to a point in time when the national movement had lost its initial momentum, and an air of stability had been recreated, the liquidation even of so minor an outpost of European colonialism by forcible means was received in the West not with resigned acquiescence but with a storm of protest. There remained the liberal image of a pacific Asia, to be brutally shattered by the Chinese invasions across the Indian border in October–November 1962. Many had forewarned Nehru, not least Acharya Kripalani in the Lok Sabha,[13] but cherishing illusions of Sino–Indian friendship he had not taken their words to heart. He had, *per contra* allowed himself to be beguiled by Chou En-lai at the Bandung Conference in 1954 and twice persuaded by K.M. Panikkar, speaking with the authority of Indian Ambassador in Peking, to let generalities about imperialistically determined frontiers go by, when his own instinct was to question and, if need be, to challenge them, while opportunity was favourable. Disaster came, writes S. Gopal, 'not because of Nehru's unrealistic assessment of China's strength or his failure to attach importance to the frontier issue but because he allowed his own views and those of his senior advisers, to be set aside by an ambassador who rationalized a shirking of unpleasantness'—

13. India, *Lok Sabha Debates*, 2nd ser., 1959, pt. 2, vol. XXXIV, coll. 8006–12, and Mansergh, *Documents and Speeches on Commonwealth Affairs 1952–62*, pp. 590–4.

something which helps to explain but not to exonerate Nehru's inaction. The bitter disillusionment that in 1962 drew from him the confession 'we were getting out of touch with reality in the modern world'[14] must have been heightened by the recollection of lost opportunity. Therein was reflected the tragedy of more than a man, or even a country. It was a hope of the new independent Asia that had been undermined.

Nehru reinterpreted the idea of Commonwealth to fit his own philosophy of international relations. The Commonwealth was an association of governments and peoples brought together by history which—and this to him was of first importance—gave to India, as to other Asian members of it, equal standing with members of European origin and afforded to Asian governments opportunities, not otherwise open to them in quite the same way, of influencing world politics, particularly in respect of Asia. The Commonwealth was a means, more generally, of associating in fruitful partnership the technological achievements of the West and the age-old wisdom of the East. It was a bridge between peoples and continents. It must be made, at the deepest level, multiracial. It was, also, something of an example to the world of Gandhian principles applied to relations between states in circumstances that might ordinarily be expected to lead to estrangement or lasting hostility. Mahatma Gandhi, remarked Nehru, 'taught us a technique of action that was peaceful: yet it was effective and yielded results that led us not only to freedom but to friendship with those with whom we were, till yesterday, in conflict.'[15] And later, addressing the Canadian Parliament, Nehru returned to the same theme.

I am convinced [he said] that this development [India's republican membership] in the history of the Commonwealth, without parallel elsewhere or at any other time, is a significant step towards peace and cooperation in the world.

Of even greater significance is the manner of its achievement. Only a few years ago, Indian nationalism was in conflict with British imperialism and that conflict brought in its train ill-will, suspicion and bitterness, although because of the teaching of our great leader Mahatma Gandhi, there was far less ill-will than in any other nationalist struggle against foreign domination.

14. *Annual Register*, 1962, p. 66 and Gopal, *Jawaharlal Nehru. A Biography*, vol. II, p. 181 and generally pp. 176–81 and 243.

15. *Jawaharlal Nehru's Speeches*, p. 124.

Who would have thought then that suspicion and bitterness would largely fade away so rapidly, giving place to friendly cooperation between free and equal nations? That is an achievement for which all those who are concerned with it can take legitimate credit. It is an outstanding example of the peaceful solution of difficult problems and a solution that is a real one because it does not create other problems. The rest of the world might well pay heed to this example.[16]

Nehru was apt to dwell more positively on the nature of the initial achievement of Indian membership in freedom and equality than on subsequent practice. This was partly because he wished to define beyond doubt or dispute the limits of Commonwealth action or cooperation. 'Presumably', he said in 1950, 'some people imagine that our association with the Commonwealth imposes some kind of restricting or limiting factor upon our activities. . . . That impression is completely unfounded. . . . We may carry out any policy we like regardless of whether we are in the Commonwealth or not.'[17] He underlined, against Pakistan, the principle of non-intervention in domestic affairs, and India's objection to any Commonwealth tribunal or any Commonwealth mediatory responsibilities in intra-Commonwealth disputes. And against the aligned members of the older Commonwealth (and Pakistan after 1954) he emphasized India's non-participation in common war or defence policies. 'We have never discussed', he stated categorically to the Lok Sabha in June 1952, 'defence policies in the Commonwealth, either jointly or separately.' He was equally explicit about India's political and constitutional independence. 'The Republic of India', he said, 'has nothing to do with England constitutionally or legally.' Indeed the attraction of the Commonwealth was its freedom from the notions of obligation or commitment. 'Our association with the Commonwealth is remarkable in that it does not bind us down in any way whatsoever . . . .'[18]

Was Indian membership then to be thought of only in terms of negation? The answer to that in part is that it was often expressed in terms of negation not to concede advantage to its critics. But on essentials Nehru did not retreat from his initial constructive approach. He, more than any other man, had brought India into

16. Ibid., p. 126.
17. Ibid., p. 272.
18. Ibid., pp. 223–5.

the Commonwealth and he stood by his action. He believed he had good reasons for so doing. They were not, however, reasons that by their very nature allowed of public exposition. 'We do hardly anything', he said in December 1950, 'without consulting the countries of the Commonwealth.' He believed such consultations to be useful in themselves and valuable for the opportunities they presented. To those who wanted India to leave because of South African racial policies Nehru replied in 1952 that in principle this was one of the reasons why he thought India should remain. And why? Because by remaining 'We have better chances of being able to influence the larger policies of the Commonwealth than we otherwise would. Being in the Commonwealth means a meeting once or twice a year and occasional consultations and conferences. Surely, that is not too great a price to pay for the advantages we get.' He never doubted in those early years that those advantages were substantial, not least among them being that as India was open to other influences so also there was 'the possibility that we may also greatly influence others in the right direction.'[19] That right direction was greater world understanding of Indian and Asian problems, of the strength of anti-colonialist, anti-racialist sentiment and the concern of mankind for peace. And the measure to which the Commonwealth was moved along it is recorded in many of its collective conclusions and sometimes in phrases or sentiments in official communiqués which bear unmistakably the impress of Nehru's thoughts and use of language. If the sense of developing partnership never recaptured its earlier part-emotional appeal after the Suez crisis of 1956, when Nehru, however, firmly resisted demands for secession even from the conservative Rajagopalachari on the ground first that India had been in no way inhibited in word or action by membership, and second that any severance of the relationship should be the outcome of cool consideration not angry reaction to a particular crisis,[20] it had not wholly departed. 'I wish I could paint to the House', said Harold Macmillan on his return from a Commonwealth tour in 1958,

a picture of the thousands of people gathered in Shah Jehan's great courtyard in the Red Fort. Here there was something more than the traditional

19. Ibid., pp. 225 and 272–3.
20. S. Gopal, *Jawaharlal Nehru. A Biography*, vol. II, p. 288.

courtesy of the Indian people. I felt both then and in the meetings I had
with the Indian Prime Minister . . . and his colleagues, a real sense of
partnership in the truest sense of the word.[21]

If, on the Indian side, it was Gandhi who had laid the foundations
of partnership, it was Jawaharlal Nehru who had built upon them.
Even if it should prove that his service was chiefly to his own generation it remains an honourable one, reflecting largeness of mind.

Nehru will be remembered for failures of judgement no less
than for his insights into the minds of men—in pre-partition days
his share of responsibility for the rejection of proffered Muslim
League cooperation in Indian Provincial governments in 1937, for
the opportunities given to the Muslim League to strengthen its
position during the war, for the Congress failure to sense the reality
of the Muslim threat to partition India until it was imminent,
remains to be precisely assessed but was certainly considerable.
After 1947 as Prime Minister of an independent state Nehru is
open to the charge of mistaking the enunciation of high-sounding
principles for foreign policy, of disregarding the likely price of
non-alignment in terms of isolation, of blindness to the threat of
Chinese aggression in the fifties, of alternating resolution and irresolution in Kashmir. The indictment is formidable, yet in essence it
is so because Nehru was a natural leader with ideas, themselves
inconstant, at times irreconcilable, often pursued with insufficient
regard for the realities of India's power or his own position, but
for all that often stimulating, original, and uplifting in their purposes
and beneficial in their consequences. One of those ideas was India's
membership of a multinational, multiracial Commonwealth. It
was in his lifetime amazingly fruitful. But for him, India almost
certainly would not have become the first republican member state
of the Commonwealth, and but for Indian membership almost
certainly elsewhere in Asia and, still more, in Africa would not in
their turn have opted also for membership. In the consequent
addition of anti-imperialist Asian and African states to a
Commonwealth which had grown out of an Empire, by procedures
that became so conventional as to cease to cause remark, an idea
achieved its most spectacular triumph. Not Smuts, not Mackenzie

21. Mansergh, *Documents and Speeches, 1952–62*, pp. 762–4.

King but Nehru was the principal architect of that achievement. Nor was he only chief among the creators of the new multiracial Commonwealth; he was in 1956, as his biographer writes, 'also in its first major crisis, its saviour.'[22] In the short term nothing can detract from the greatness of his contribution; in the longer run its endurance will depend upon the reality of those virtues—the touch of healing, the equal association of races, the readiness and the capacity of the richer Commonwealth states to assist the poorer— which in his more sanguine moments Nehru believed the new Commonwealth might come to possess.

22. S. Gopal, *Jawaharlal Nehru. A Biography*, vol. II, p. 288.

# 14

# Indira Gandhi: Heiress of the Indian Revolution

Indira Gandhi was the third in a great Indian political dynasty. The Nehrus were of high-caste Kashmiri Brahmin descent. Indira's grandfather Motilal Nehru sacrificed his westernized clothes and the furnishings of his Allahabad home in one dramatic gesture—he made a bonfire of them on the lawn—in order to join the Congress, later becoming the President and serving Indian independence dressed in homespun khadi.

Her father, Jawaharlal Nehru, 'The Light of Asia' as he was called surprisingly enough by Churchill, was with Mahatma Gandhi, architect of that independence. 'I am more than Prime Minister', he once remarked, 'We'—pointing to his ministerial colleagues—'are the heirs of the Indian revolution and the mantle of its greatness hangs about our shoulders.'

He was in fact both artificer and heir. Indira in a very particular sense was its heiress. With her assassination the political glamour of the independence years has finally departed.

I met Indira Gandhi with her father first in 1947 when Jawaharlal Nehru took me to lunch after a morning session of the Asian Relations Conference which he had invited to meet in New Delhi to mark the approaching end of colonialism in Asia. She was then thirty years of age.

With other Congress members she had served a period of imprisonment and I thought then it had left scars more marked than long years of it had on her father. Attractive and lively, her interests as I recall were cultural rather than political in any pronounced way.

During the first ten years of Nehru's premiership she did indeed eschew politics and it was not until the later fifties that she entered the arena. When she did, she became immensely active notably in travelling around the vast expanse and crowded cities of that great democracy in support of the Congress programme and candidates.

Thereafter, her advance was rapid through the Presidency of the Congress in 1964, a junior but key Ministry for one who knew how to use it, in information and broadcasting to the Premiership in 1966.

As Prime Minister, Mrs Gandhi had from the outset grassroots backing in abundance. She was her father's daughter. But she had to face a great deal of criticism in the Lok Sabha (House of the People). Listening to exchanges from the gallery at that time I wondered if she would long survive. She looked frail and uncertain; her critics formidable.

But she soon changed all that. Indeed, the remarkable thing is that she established her authority not only once but twice, with the unhappy years of the 'Emergency' when she stretched her exercise of emergency powers up to or questionably beyond the limits of the constitution by her actions, helping to split the Congress. It was at this point that she reached the ebb tide of her fortunes.

Experience of government under a well-intentioned but indecisive Opposition was a contributory factor in her restoration to power in 1980 but even so it was an astonishing essay in political recovery.

I asked my taxi driver from the airport shortly after the election to account for the result. He replied that he had just voted for Mrs Gandhi so as to bring an end to profiteering, exploitation and overcharging. He then asked me for double the authorized fare.

By the 1980s Mrs Gandhi was of world stature. While problems at home, not least in the government of the state, and particularly the Punjab, mounted, she had throughout a sure touch and at the end had acquired immense prestige in respect of foreign policy.

When Bangladesh broke away from Pakistan, Mrs Gandhi sent in Indian troops at the request of the Bangladesh regime but with a rare sense of timing judged exactly when to withdraw.

There was reluctant admiration in the description of her at that time as 'Empress of India'. Outside the subcontinent she remained true to the principles of foreign policy set out in the Panch Shila (the Five Principles) by her father, chief among them being that of non-alignment, that is to say no commitment to great-power alliances but freedom to determine peace or war in the light of India's own interests at the time.

When, with the Soviet invasion of Afghanistan, the threat of war came close to the subcontinent, Mrs Gandhi became one of the key figures in international affairs. Night after night in the winter of 1979-80 Mrs Gandhi would appear on television welcoming visitors from all over the world, from small border states as Nepal and Sikkim, from France and Hungary, from the Soviet Union and from Yugoslavia, where her co-leader of the non-aligned movement, Tito, was dying.

The counsel Mrs Gandhi apparently gave was that while the Soviet Union should withdraw, such withdrawal was more likely to be effective by diplomatic representations over a period of time than by public denunciation, her emphasis in the language of the crisis being on 'defusing', on stabilizing and de-escalating the crisis as against striking attitudes, such as moving aircraft carriers or banning Olympic Games.

Not all her visitors agreed. There were, as it was diplomatically phrased, differences in interim perceptions but generally she earned great respect for her sureness of touch and her vision. Last year, Mrs Gandhi presided over the largest gathering yet of non-aligned nations and over the largest Commonwealth conference hitherto.

She did so as to the manner born—as indeed she was—and in her position and person, fittingly symbolized the magnitude of the mid-twentieth century anti-colonial revolution.

The judgement of later generations on Mrs Gandhi's domestic problems will be, I suspect, heavily marked with light and shadow; her foreign policies with respect for sureness of judgment and breadth of view. Her assassination has deprived the world of a leader of commanding stature.

# Part IV. Retrospect

# 15

## The Partition of India in Retrospect

On the subcontinent at least the partition of India has not passed into history. It touches too painfully on sensitive nerves for that. The area of friction, it is true, has been progressively reduced in the intervening years—the armed forces and civil service have been divided, government property and resources distributed so far as they ever will be, even the Indus Waters dispute resolved by treaty in 1960 with the assistance of the International Bank. But reduction in the area of dispute has led to no corresponding diminution in its intensity. Kashmir remains and not only Kashmir. Behind Kashmir lie different interpretations of what happened in 1947 and of the deeper meaning of partition.

In the view of Britain and Pakistan there were two successor states to the British Raj: in the predominant Indian view there was rather a successor state and a seceding state. The distinction is more than one of semantics. If there were two successor states then each was equally entitled to division of resources and authority within the prescribed terms of reference. If, however, there was one successor state from which territories were carved to form a seceding state, then the presumption was that resources and authority descended to the successor in so far as they were specifically allocated to the seceding state. In British statute law the issue may be readily disposed of. Under the provisions of the India Independence Act, 1947, described in its preamble as 'An Act to make provision for the setting up in India of two independent Dominions . . .' there were two successor states. Article 1(1) read:

'As from the 15th day of August, nineteen hundred and forty-seven, two independent Dominions shall be set up in India, to be known respectively as India and Pakistan'.[1] But could the issue be settled by reference to British statute law alone? The Indian National Congress thought not. It claimed that the Dominion of India should continue as the international personality of pre-partition India, and the Indian Reforms Commissioner, V.P. Menon, advised the Viceroy, after consulting the Legislative Department, that post-partition would remain identifiable with pre-partition India. 'It was our definite view', he wrote, 'that neither variation in the extent of a State's territory, nor change in its constitution, could affect the identity of the State.'[2] In respect of international status this opinion was accepted (or in the case of Pakistan acquiesced in after protest and with reservation), with the result that India after independence remained a member of the United Nations and all international organizations whereas Pakistan, as a new state, sought such membership *ab initio*.

Psychologically the question of succession or secession was not, and is not, as simple as it appeared either in British statutory enactment or in international practice. The respective designations of the two states were in themselves significant. They were called India and Pakistan, not Hindustan and Pakistan, as Jinnah and the Muslim League deemed logical and desired. The reason was clear. Behind the name India lay the claim consistently advanced and never discarded, not even at the moment of partition, by the Indian National Congress that it was representative, not of a class nor of a community, but of a nation and that that nation was India. When the All-India Congress Committee met in Delhi on 14 June 1947 to approve the 3 June plan for partition, the resolution accepting partition contained these words: 'Geography and the mountains and the seas fashioned India as she is . . .'[3] Acharya Kripalani, the President of the Congress, issued a statement on the eve of Independence, 14 August 1947, saying it was a day of sorrow and destruction for India.[4] Kripalani was a man of Sind. But he was

---

1. India Independence Act, 1947 (10 and 11 Geo 6, ch. 30).
2. V.P. Menon, *The Transfer of Power in India* (Bombay, 1957), p. 404. See generally, pp. 404–7.
3. Quoted in ibid., p. 384. See ch. 1, pp. 7–8.
4. Maulana A.K. Azad, *India Wins Freedom* (Bombay, 1959), p. 207.

also the President of the Congress. His emotional reaction to partition was widely shared. It precluded neither acquiescence in the existence of Pakistan nor peaceful coexistence with her. But it rested upon considerations and derived from assumptions about partition and its meaning which neither were, nor in the nature of things could be, shared on the other side of the border.

At the time differences in the interpretation of what was taking place were accentuated by psychological unpreparedness for it. Contrary to what is often suggested, the advantages and disadvantages of partition as a solution of India's majority problem had not been carefully weighed or long considered before it took effect. It is easy to be misled by words. But dialectical exchanges about controversial proposals are not in themselves sufficient evidence that those proposals are being advanced, criticized or rejected in terms of political actualities. Certainly it was the case that after the Lahore resolution[5] of the All-India Muslim League in March 1940—the so-called 'Pakistan Resolution' though the term Pakistan did not in fact appear in it—partition had its passionate protagonists, its outraged opponents and those who, with Mahatma Gandhi, acquiesced with resignation in a prospect less distasteful to them than the thought of enforced minority inclusion in a unitary state. But the debate was not practical and purposeful but rather long-range and emotive. The language used on the one side was that of Muslim homelands and a Holy War to defend them; on the other, to employ the phrase Gandhi made his own, that of the vivisection of Mother India. There is no evidence of consideration before 1947 on the part either of advocates or opponents as to what partition would mean in terms of administration and, still less, apart from generalities, in terms of economics or of social disruption. So much indeed was understandable. The Muslim League was fighting to establish 'an impossible' aim; the Congress to defeat a stratagem which its leaders believed down to the 'Great Calcutta Killing' of August 1946 (and in some cases into 1947) to have been adopted in order to secure a strong negotiating position for the entrenchment of Muslim minority rights within an independent India. When the records of the Congress are made public and more especially when

5. Reprinted in Cmd. 6196, *India and the War*, and in Sir Maurice Gwyer and A. Appadorai, *Speeches and Documents on the Indian Constitution 1921–47* (Bombay, 1957), vol. II, pp. 443–4.

the files of the India Office in London are made available for study, it will be of interest to learn in each case of the date of the first serious analysis of the likely overall consequences of a partition of India.

It was not so much the complexity as the nature of relations in India on the eve of partition that made foresight difficult and discouraged realistic appraisal of future possibilities. The more important of those relations were without exception triangular. There were the three principal communities, the Hindus, the Muslims and the Sikhs, in descending order of magnitude; there were the three political groups, the princes, the Muslim League and the Indian National Congress in ascending order of importance; and there were the three arbiters of national destiny, the British, the Congress and the League. In each triangle there was the pre-disposition—it is almost a law of politics—of the lesser to combine against the greatest. The League thus looked more kindly than the Congress on the pretensions of princes; almost to the last, until indeed Jinnah became convinced in 1946 that Lord Wavell was to be regarded as the 'latest exponent of geographical unity', the League was apt to be more understanding, or at the least less unreceptive, of British proposals than the Congress. At one time indeed, before Gandhi took up their cause, the League seemed prepared to champion the outcastes, and until early 1947 there were intermittent and still undisclosed negotiations with the Sikhs, thought to have been on the basis of Sikh autonomy within an undivided Punjab. The British, for their part, showed a preoccupation with the outcastes, and with minorities generally, which the Congress thought was hardly altogether altruistic. There was also a continuing Congress suspicion, only dispelled in the period immediately before partition, of British predisposition towards Muslims. Behind allegations or assertions, difficult as they are for the most part to substantiate, lay the inconsistencies, the dissembling, and the tactical devices inseparable from triangular political situations. Purpose and reality were difficult to disentangle from stratagem and manoeuvre, even at times by those engaged in employing them. In the maze of tactics the sense of direction was apt to become clouded. The existence of so many variants seemingly discouraged cool appraisal of realities—not least in one notable instance on the part of the Government of India and the India Office in London.

Successive British governments and Viceroys, it now seems evident beyond dispute, gravely overestimated the power and authority of the Indian princes. Even the Labour government was in part the victim of such miscalculation, and, as for the Viceroys, only the last, perhaps because he was himself of royal blood, proved in this respect to be without illusions. Over the years this British over-estimate was a complicating factor of importance on the Indian scene. Within a few months of the transfer of power the princes were shown to be, as Gandhi had earlier claimed, at any rate not much more than 'British officers in Indian dress'. And if *some* among a number of estimable and public-spirited rulers were not shown to have been 'sinks of iniquity' as Nehru had once alleged, that was partly because the Political Adviser to the princes, Sir Conrad Corfield, in May 1947, to the subsequent annoyance of Mountbatten and the anger of Nehru, ordered his subordinates in the Political Department to extract from the files confidential reports reflecting unfavourably on the public or private behaviour of the princes—'eccentricities' was the favoured term in respect of the latter—and burn what has been calculated to have been four tons of them.[6] But earlier in the same year, 1947, there were those who conceived, or cherished, the hope that in an independent India, the greater, at least, of the states might have an autonomous existence. There were enquiries from princely officials about the nature of external association, and in Bombay businessmen discussed prospects of development in Hyderabad and Travancore on the assumption that as autonomous units they might be the most stable and solvent parts of a new India. Eighteenth-century analogies were fashionable and, if they were too artificial to carry much conviction, at least they were illustrative of a trend in British thinking—and one incidentally wholly in conflict with British interests in the creation of one, or if need be, two strong, stable successor states after independence. Nor was the predisposition of the British both at the official and the unofficial level to exaggerate the importance

6. Leonard Mosley, *The Last Days of the British Raj* (London, 1961), pp. 162–5, tells the story and on p. 163 assesses the weight of the material destroyed. In the Preface he states that he put questions to Sir Conrad Corfield amongst others without their being responsible for what he subsequently wrote. The incident is also recorded in Michael Edwardes, *The Last Years of British India* (London, 1963), pp. 186–9.

of princes without its lasting importance. It was the princes, not, as the Congress had urged,[7] the peoples of the States who, by virtue of being empowered to sign, or not to sign, Instruments of Accession to either of the successor powers on the lapse of British paramountcy, were placed in a position to determine the destiny of the States. That authority is alleged to have been given to them by the Labour government partly to appease the Conservative opposition at Westminster. Whether this was so or not—and *prima facie* it would seem questionable—the fact of princely decision made prediction about States' accession difficult in some cases and virtually incalculable in Hyderabad, and, even apparently to princely advisers, in Kashmir.[8] Assuredly there were obligations of honour and nostalgic notions of a 'gorgeous East' but in essence continuing British reliance upon the princes sprang from long indulged preoccupation with the tactics of a triangular political situation.

In the struggle for power on the highest plane, that is to say between the British, the Congress and the League, it was the British who were familiarly cast in the role of the third party. In the Congress view the British in India had followed for some forty years before partition a policy of divide and rule. 'It has been the traditional policy of Britain', complained Gandhi, after the Congress rejection of the August offer of 1940, 'to prevent parties from uniting. "Divide and rule" has been Britain's proud motto. It is the British statesmen who are responsible for the divisions in India's ranks and the divisions will continue so long as the British sword holds India under bondage.'[9] This was the language of politics, not history. Thoughts of 'divide and rule', however, were not absent from the minds of twentieth-century British officials and statesmen. So much is clear from files dealing with the Liberal administration of the pre–First World War years and not necessarily only in relation to India. Nor was it absent in the thirties and forties. Lord

---

7. e.g. The Resolution of the Congress at the Ramgarh session, 20 March 1940: 'The Congress cannot admit the right of the rulers of Indian States . . . to come in the way of Indian freedom. Sovereignty in India must rest with the people whether in the States or the provinces . . .' Cmd. 6196.

8. Cf. Wilfred Russell, *Indian Summer* (London, 1951), pp. 102–5.

9. D.G. Tendulkar, *Mahatma: Life of Mohandas Karamchand Gandhi* (Bombay, 1951–4), vol. VI, p. 11.

Zetland, who was Secretary of State for India at the outbreak of the Second World War, noted, without sharing, the satisfaction which evidence of communal division gave among 'diehards', Churchill by no means least among them,[10] while the Viceroy, Lord Linlithgow, largely because of it, thought of dominion status for India as a still distant goal. 'No-one', wrote the Viceroy in 1939,

can, of course, say what, in some remote period of time, or in the event of international convulsions of a particular character, may be the ultimate relations of India and Great Britain: but that there should be any general impression that public opinion at home, or His Majesty's Government, seriously contemplate evacuation in any measurable period of time, seems to me astonishing.[11]

No doubt the Congress leaders sensed that such was the Viceroy's mind. In general the more the British government showed itself preoccupied with the position of minorities and with communal divisions, the more suspect it became to the Congress. If, as Gandhi argued, the communal problem was insoluble so long as the third party remained, and if, as the British argued, they could not go until it was resolved, might that not mean they would stay forever? Or to pose the dilemma in a broader, impersonal context, how was the British view that the resolution of the communal problem was a necessary precondition of their departure to be reconciled with the Congress conviction that their departure was a necessary precondition of its resolution?

There was, however, an alternative analysis. It was suggested to the Round Table Conference in 1931 by a distinguished Muslim. For the 'divide and rule' of Congress, he substituted 'we divide and you rule'. Pushed to its logical conclusion, this meant, presumably that the divisions at root were domestic. At the Round Table Conference, logic was not pressed to such extremes. Princes and Muslims were at one in proclaiming that they had no wish to create 'Ulsters in India'. But was this really so? In respect of some of the princes (and their friends) it seems questionable; in respect of the Muslims it posed the fundamental question: were they a

10. Marquess of Zetland, *Essayez; the Memoirs of Lawrence, Second Marquess of Zetland* (London, 1956), p. 292.
11. Ibid., p. 265.

community, the second largest within India, or were they a separate nation? If they were the former, then the pattern of a self-protective policy might have been expected to be, as indeed it was at least down to 1940, limited cooperation with the British and the Congress in the working out of a federal structure, in which the position of the Muslims, at least in Muslim-majority provinces, was entrenched against a centre certain to be dominated, under any form of representative government, by representatives of the great Hindu majority in the country. But if the Muslims were not the second largest community in India, but a separate nation, then any such policy of limited cooperation was precautionary and preliminary to a demand for a separate national recognition. In these matters words are not conclusive. But they are important particularly when invested with the force which Jinnah gave them at the Lahore meeting of the League in March 1940. He castigated the British for their conception of government by parties functioning on a political plane as the best form of government for every country. He assailed *The Times* for having earlier concluded, after recognition of the differences, not only of religion, but also of law and culture, between Hindus and Muslims, that in the course of time 'the superstitions will die out and India will be moulded into a single nation'. For Jinnah it was not a question of superstitions or, therefore, of time, but of fundamental beliefs and social conceptions—'The Muslims are not a minority as the word is commonly understood. . . . Muslims are a nation according to any definition of the term, and they must have their homelands, their territory and their state.'[12]

If there is indeed substance in Jinnah's contention then, it follows that the British must be acquitted of any final responsibility for the partition of India; or in the language of contemporary dialectics, it did not much matter in this respect whether the third party stayed or went. Had the British, indeed, succeeded in imposing unity, then the consequence, again accepting the fundamentals of Jinnah's analysis, might well have been, as he threatened in 1947, the bloodiest civil war in the history of Asia. For the essence of his

12. See ch. 1, pp. 18–20. Reprinted in Gwyer and Appadorai, *Speeches and Documents on the Indian Constitution*, vol. II, pp. 440–2 and in Nicholas Mansergh, *Documents and Speeches on British Commonwealth Affairs 1931–52* (London, 1953), vol. II, pp. 609–12.

argument was that it was the unity of India that was artificial and imposed; the division natural. And by way of epilogue it is worth noting that one of the Congress High Command, the formidable Vallabhbhai Patel, infuriated by League intransigence and possibly also under the influence of Mountbatten's persuasive powers, argued with Maulana Azad in May 1947 in favour of partition by saying 'whether we liked it or not, there were two nations in India.'[13] If, on the other hand, Jinnah's analysis is to be questioned in its essentials, then the arguments for a more probing analysis of the aims and purposes of British as well as Congress and League policies are conclusive. More immediately it is to be noted that while Jinnah staked his claim for Pakistan in March 1940, there was no certainty whether its dramatic presentation was a stratagem or a literal statement of his objective. Reports of some contemporary conversations he had in Lahore suggest that, for all the vehemence of his language, he may have remained himself undecided.[14]

Whatever the Lahore resolutions portended for the future, they indicated for the present a shift in Muslim priorities. While the Congress continued to fight on one front against the British to secure independence, the Muslim League was engaged on two fronts against the British and against the Congress; and after 1940 the second assumed ever greater importance. Here was an open challenge to the claims of the Congress to represent Indian Nationalist opinion. When the Congress governments in the provinces resigned after two and a half years of office in December 1939 on the issue of non-cooperation in the war, Jinnah proclaimed Friday, 22 December 1939, a Day of Deliverance from 'the tyranny, oppression and injustice' from which Muslim India had suffered under Congress rule. The source and origin of Muslim grievances is not in dispute. It lay in the fact that the Congress, after its massive victory in the 1937 provincial elections had formed one-party governments in provinces, in which the Muslim League had expected coalition governments, in which they would be partners. This repudiation and rejection of the League derived fundamentally from the Congress conviction that it represented all-India. There was no need accordingly for political concessions to a minority

13. Azad, *India Wins Freedom*, p. 185.
14. Personal information.

grouping or, more particularly, for recognition of a ministerial role for the League which anyway had fared poorly in the elections. Muslims there would certainly be in the government—but they would be Congress Muslims or League Muslims who had renounced the League and joined the Congress as a condition of office. This general presumption was reinforced, so both Jawaharlal Nehru and Rajendra Prasad have told us in their recorded reflections,[15] by a conviction that the conventions of British cabinet government should prevail. If there were League members of the provincial government in, for example, the United Provinces and Orissa, what then became of notions of collective responsibility? 'Congressmen', so Rajendra Prasad recalled, 'thought it contrary to the spirit of Parliamentary democracy to appoint any outsider in their Ministry.'[16] If Muslims were to serve, then first claim, as party stalwarts were quick to emphasize, lay with those Muslims who were loyal members of the Congress and not with supporters of the League. Yet in retrospect, as written records suggest and personal conversations underline, most of the prominent Congress leaders remained preoccupied and even questioning as to the correctness of their 1937 conclusions. And at the time one of the Congress leaders, not surprisingly the perceptive and courageous Congress Muslim, Maulana A.K. Azad—who was to serve as President of the Congress throughout the war years—challenged and fought in vain to prevent or reverse these exclusivist decisions dictated largely by party loyalists in the provinces. What was at issue was a question of political judgement, neither more nor less. On any reckoning the decision would seem in retrospect ill-advised. Whether it was more than that is a matter of opinion. But it may reasonably be asked, did the partition of India then derive from so trifling a cause? Were there not fundamental forces at work? An error, or a series of errors in tactical judgement is one thing, the source of a political event so momentous as partition ordinarily another.[17] Or to put the issue in another way—was partition implicit in the

---

15. Jawaharlal Nehru, *The Discovery of India* (Calcutta, 1946), pp. 320–2; and Rajendra Prasad, *Autobiography* (Bombay, 1957), pp. 444–8; and personal conversations.

16. Prasad, *Autobiography*, p. 446.

17. See ch. 1, pp. 11–12. See also Azad, *India Wins Freedoom*, pp. 160–2, and Penderel Moon, *Divide and Quit* (London, 1961), p. 14.

Indian scene or not? If it were, tactics were of secondary importance and only if not, of first significance.

Before the concept of Pakistan could pass from the realm of stratagem to that of near reality, certain conditions had to be fulfilled. The first was that the Imperial power should become increasingly sensitive to the claims advanced by the Muslim League. This in fact happened. It is attributed by V.P. Menon, and others who have followed him,[18] to Congress policies of non-cooperation and non-participation in provincial government during the war. It is an opinion to be accepted with reserve. Non-cooperation during the war was almost certainly a condition of Congress cooperation after the war. Immoderate policies ensured the ultimate triumph of moderation. By reason of their adoption there were no significant surviving enemies on the left after the war; whereas wartime cooperation would almost certainly have divided and therefore weakened the Congress in the face of the League, more rather than less. But, if explanation must remain speculative, the step-by-step advance on the British side to Muslim League claims is hardly disputable. The British statement that accompanied the August offer of 1940 remarked: 'It goes without saying that they [the United Kingdom government] could not contemplate transfer of their present responsibilities for the peace and welfare of India to any system of government whose authority is directly denied by large and powerful elements in India's national life.'[19] Not surprisingly in a changed, and from the point of view of the British government, a weaker position, the Cripps Mission went further in this respect than the August offer. The contemplated dominion constitution was subject to 'the right of any Province of British India that is not prepared to accept the new Constitution to retain its present constitutional position', or should such non-acceding provinces 'so desire, His Majesty's Government will be prepared to agree upon a new Constitution, giving them the same full status as the Indian Union.'[20] The introduction of 'this novel principle of

18. Menon, *The Transfer of Power*, p. 97; cf. also T.G.P. Spear, *India* (Michigan, 1961), p. 405, on the Congress rejection of the Cripps offer, 1942.

19. Statement of 8 August 1940. Reprinted in Mansergh, *Documents and Speeches*, vol. II, pp. 612–14.

20. Cmd. 6350. Reprinted in ibid., vol. II, pp. 616–17.

non-accession' was followed, after two conferences at Simla, with the purposely vague recommendations of the Cabinet mission in 1946, outlining a three-tier constitutional structure with a Union government at the apex and in an intermediate position three groups of provinces, the one comprised of predominantly Hindu, the remaining two of predominantly Muslim provinces, dealing with all such subjects as the provinces comprising each group might desire to have dealt with in association, and, at the base, the provinces themselves dealing with all other subjects and possessing all the residuary sovereign rights.[21] Certainly this was not tantamount to Pakistan, for the Cabinet Mission had considered and deliberately rejected partition. But the Council of the Muslim League was not mistaken in considering that in these proposals there lay 'the basis and the foundation of Pakistan'.

The second condition preliminary to the achievement of Pakistan was the consolidation of Muslim opinion behind the League. Despite the difficulties inherent in the geographical distribution of the Muslim population and in the reluctance of more Muslims than may now be supposed to contemplate partition, this condition also was substantially fulfilled. To appreciate the extent to which this was so, it is necessary only to place side by side the results, in so far as the Muslim League was concerned, of the elections of 1937 and of 1946. Where at the earlier date, even in Muslim-majority provinces, the League had made an indifferent showing, by the later date it was polling in most, if not all, cases close to its maximum natural strength. This was a remarkable achievement in terms both of leadership and organization. One element in it was the dramatiz-ation of issues. This was a rewarding technique—but one which exacted a sometimes terrible price. The League proclaimed its day of deliverance, its days of protest, and finally on 16 August 1946, Direct Action Day, on which the black flags of the Muslim League fluttered over Muslim homes—and in Calcutta provided the occasion for what has gone down to history as the great Calcutta killing, nowhere described with more sickening realism than in the restrained pages of General Sir Francis Tuker's *While Memory Serves*.[22] Well may one ask, was Pakistan unattainable without

21. Cmd. 6821. Reprinted in ibid., vol. II, pp. 644–52.
22. Sir Francis Tuker, *While Memory Serves* (London, 1950), ch. XII, 'The Great Calcutta Killing'.

communal violence on a scale unparalleled in all the years since the Mutiny? There was a further condition of partition. The League had to be equated with the Congress or, as Jinnah would have phrased it, Pakistan with Hindustan. In numerical terms this meant the equation of minority with majority. It had happened elsewhere. It had happened in Ireland when the six counties of Northern Ireland and the twenty-six counties of Southern Ireland were given equal representation in the Council of Ireland, that 'fleshless and bloodless skeleton', as Asquith termed it, proposed in the Government of Ireland Act, 1920.[23] In arithmetical terms such parity could not be defended in either case. But, so Jinnah argued, the debate was not about numbers nor even about communities but about nations. Nations were equal irrespective of their size. He secured his aim at the Simla Conference, 1946. League and Congress representation was then equated, with a sharp protest by the League at the nomination by the Congress of a Muslim, Maulana Azad, as one of their representatives. It was 'a symbolic affront'. Jinnah was indeed the most formidable proponent of a two-nation theory yet to appear within the confines of the British Empire. Positively his demand was for unequivocal recognition of the separate nationality of Muslim India which, in Bengal at least, was far from self-evident; negatively it was for the reduction of the Congress claim to speak for all India to a Congress right to speak for Hindustan. Nehru was written off as a Hindu imperialist; Gandhi as a man with whom it was possible to negotiate, because by vast self-deception he had convinced himself he was a spokesman of something more than Hinduism; Maulana Azad, that prototype of Congress Muslims, denounced as a renegade or even a quisling; the idea of a secular state ridiculed as part of a design of characteristic Hindu subtlety to fasten Hindu rule upon the whole of India. Again, however, there was implicit in Jinnah's demands a price even for their formulation. The League could challenge claims of Congress to speak for all India most effectively, only by becoming ever more firmly imprisoned within the rigid concept of a communal state.

Finally, there was one last condition of partition. To the Congress demand that the British should quit India, Muslims

23. United Kingdom, *House of Commons Debates 1920*, vol. 127, col. 1112.

responded with the demand that they should divide and quit—and in that order. Here again the League were largely successful. It is true that the division for which they asked was not the division they received. The full demand was for an independent state of Pakistan comprising two areas, one in the northwest consisting of the Punjab, Sind, North-West Frontier, and British Baluchistan, the other the northeast consisting of Bengal and Assam. Accession to that demand would no doubt have created a viable state. But the demand rested upon community and as the Cabinet Mission concluded 'every argument that could be used in favour of Pakistan can equally, in our view, be used in favour of the exclusion of the non-Muslim areas from Pakistan.'[24] There followed the partitioning of the Punjab and Bengal, and Jinnah was left with what he had once contemptuously dismissed as 'a mutilated, a moth-eaten and truncated Pakistan'.

The last phase was ushered in with the appointment of the Interim Government. Lord Wavell presided over its deliberations with a splendid, if unhelpful, soldierly reserve. It was only after it had been in existence some time that the Muslim League decided to join. The Congress had then to decide on a reconstitution of the government, and in particular on the more important posts to offer to the League. Under strong pressure from Sardar Vallabhbhai Patel, anxious understandably to retain control of the Home Department and with it of relations with the princes, and against the warnings of Maulana Azad, the principal portfolio they offered was that of Minister for Finance. When Chaudhary Mohammed Ali heard the news in the Department, it is said he told Jinnah it marked a great victory for the League. So in some respects it proved. The post was filled by Liaquat Ali Khan, and when Liaquat became the Finance Minister, records Maulana Azad, he obtained the possession of the key to government. Every proposal of every department was subject to his scrutiny. 'Not a Chaprasi could be appointed in any Department without the sanction of his Department.'[25] What is more, Liaquat drafted a budget the onus of which fell, as it was intended to fall, heavily upon the wealthy supporters of the Congress. And while to descend to trifling matters, it may be questioned whether tact mattered much at this late stage, it is still

24. Cmd. 6821.
25. Azad, *India Wins Freedom*, p. 167.

worth noting that the Congress ministers were not diplomatic in their handling of their new League colleagues. It was the practice of Congress ministers to foregather for tea before the sessions of the Interim Government. The invitation to the new League Muslims to attend these gatherings came from Nehru's secretary. They were offended. They never attended. But then, of course, they might not have anyway.[26]

With the statement of 20 February 1947 the British government regained the initiative. The statement[27] put an eighteen-month time-limit, till June 1948, on British rule in India. For weeks it was subjected to the most careful and suspicious scrutiny in Delhi, but it was found to be without trace of equivocation. The time-limit enhanced the prospect of Pakistan, but it diminished the chances of its orderly creation and establishment. Some five or six weeks later I had a conversation with Liaquat Ali Khan. The coming into existence of Pakistan was presumed, but Liaquat underlined that the time-limit was too short. A capital had yet to be chosen, government and administration to be organized, the inheritance of British India to be divided. Within a matter of weeks the time-limit was foreshortened by nearly a year. 15 August 1947 was fixed as the date of the transfer of power. The effect was to heighten the double impact made by the statement of 20 February. Pakistan was brought that much nearer; its early administration made that much more difficult.

The initiative regained by the British government was exploited by the last Viceroy. No one who was in Delhi at that time is likely to underestimate his contribution in giving a sense of purpose and direction on the British side at a time when, with relaxing control, communal tensions might have merged into civil war and led to partial disintegration. History was being made, and he brought drama to the making of it. Perhaps there was some element of illusion in the new understanding he established with the Congress leaders. Nehru, so Michael Edwardes has suggested, thought of Mountbatten as a straightforward English socialist, 'a sort of Philippe Égalité in naval uniform.'[28] What was important, however,

---

26. Ibid.
27. Cmd. 7047, reprinted in Mansergh, *Documents and Speeches*, vol. II, pp. 659–61.
28. Michael Edwardes, *The Last Years of British India*, p. 95.

was the understanding that was established. Moreover, in smaller as in greater things Mountbatten sensed the time for change. He was always 'taking tea with treason', if one may borrow from the terminology of denunciation employed against Lord Irwin's reception of Gandhi in the early thirties, and in his Vice-Chancellor's office at Delhi University, Sir Maurice Gwyer derived some wry amusement from studying the lists of those who now at long last were being entertained in the Viceroy's house.

The first Mountbatten plan, sometimes irreverently known as the 'Dickie Bird Plan' and involving the transfer of power to individual provinces, was considered by the Cabinet in London, but angrily rejected by Nehru as likely to lead to disintegration. Its only merit—if merit it were—was that it would have allowed opinion to be tested on the possible emergence of an independent and united Bengal. The second plan, dominion status for two successor states, was devised on his own account of it by V.P. Menon,[29] the Reforms Commissioner, and in substance it won acceptance. Never in all its history, it may be thought, has the Commonwealth idea made so momentous a contribution to the settlement of so great a problem.

Two last questions remain. The first is why the Congress leaders at the last agreed to partition. The answer, I think, is threefold. They had ambitions for India and those ambitions could not be fulfilled without strong central government. So long as the majority of Muslims were within a united India, that meant that strong, central government was out of the question. The second, strongly held by Vallabhbhai Patel, but by no means universally shared by his colleagues, was the belief that Pakistan would not endure long. He was convinced, records Maulana Azad, who was not a friendly witness, that Pakistan was 'not viable' and would 'collapse in a short time'.[30] Nehru also, though less categoric, did not think it could last.[31] The third dominant consideration was time. The Congress leaders had struggled long for independence, they were now ageing men and they were not prepared to delay independence

29. Menon, *The Transfer of Power*, pp. 358–65. See also Alan Campbell-Johnson, *Mission with Mountbatten* (London, 1951).

30. Azad, *India Wins Freedom*, p. 207.

31. Michael Brecher, *Nehru, A Political Biography* (London, 1959), pp. 376–7. Nehru, Brecher notes, did not believe Pakistan was a viable state and that 'sooner or later the area which had seceded would be compelled by force of circumstances to return to the fold'.

further. Here indeed was a root difference between Congress and the League and a source of strength to Jinnah. He was prepared to let independence wait upon division, while his opponents for the most part were not prepared to let it wait upon unity.

Not all of them, however, were agreed on this count. To the last, Maulana Azad remained convinced that time was on the side of unity.[32] One or two years' delay, and the Cabinet Mission Plan with its weak centre and its provincial groupings would prove acceptable. Patel was against him, so was Nehru, and at the last Gandhi himself appeared resigned to partition. Azad as a Congress Muslim had his own reasons for insistence upon the unity and his own grounds for misgivings about the consequences of partition. But if in this he was percipient, it may well be questioned whether he was realistic in his own recommendations. He advocated delay, the deferment of independence for one year or more as might be necessary. But was the Indian Civil Service and the British Army in India equal to the responsibilities such delay would undoubtedly involve? Were the British public at home prepared to sustain the effort that might be needed? If not, who was to govern India in the mean time? The Muslim League, Gandhi suggested, was a desperate but not an original device—Rajagopalachari had proposed it in 1940 also to avert partition. The Congress would not hear of it. Most of all, was the Maulana right in his presupposition that with time passions would cool? Was it not more likely that with procrastination they would be further inflamed? Was it not more likely that, far from diminishing the ambitions of princes, subtracting from the violent negatives of the League, adding to the readiness of the Congress to compromise, all would disappear? And what of the Sikhs, who accepted partition in June 1947? Their leader, Master Tara Singh—that prophetic-looking figure, whose words so belied the benignity of his flowing beard—in late February 1947, brandishing an unsheathed sword at a mass rally in the Punjab cried 'Oh! Hindus and Sikhs, be ready for self-destruction. . . . I have sounded the bugle. Finish the Muslim League.'[33] It was a few

32. *India Wins Freedom*, pp. 207–27.

33. Quoted Brecher, *Nehru*, p. 339; Moon, *Divide and Quit*, p. 77. See also Ian Stephens, *Pakistan* (London, 1963), pp. 131–6 and p. 182 *et seq.*, where there is an understanding account of the Sikh predicament and the Sikh reaction to it.

years later that he enunciated his creed, 'I believe in chaos.' All the evidence of one's own eyes in early 1947 suggested that if the momentum of events were slowed down, the risks of chaos in central and northern India were at the least unlikely to diminish. If there was mistiming about the settlement, it may well be that it was some ten years too late, rather than one or two years too soon. Tragedy, however, there was and no doubt within the same time-table some part of it might have been avoided. But what some critics, at least, are apt to overlook is that once partition was to be the solution, then the possibilities were not simply tragedy or no tragedy in the Punjab, but also tragedy and even greater tragedy than in fact occurred.

To conclude, a first reflection is that the triangular situation, from which partition emerged, in itself limited the freedom of manoeuvre, even the most purposeful or enlightened of leaders enjoyed. Their utterances and their actions, it may in these circumstances be supposed, had generally speaking less significance than it is now customary to attribute to them. They were in a measure, not always fully realized, the prisoners of a pattern of politics, which always pressed in upon their liberty of action.*

---

*As late as April 1947 Mountbatten was still hoping to convince Jinnah of the 'full stupidity of Pakistan', a colloquial word which had no meaning according to Nehru. How then did Pakistan become accepted? The documents of N. Mansergh and P. Moon (eds), in *India. The Transfer of Power 1942–47*, vol. X, HMSO, 1981, suggest four reasons. The first is the supreme skill of Jinnah as a negotiator. However frustrating and difficult others found him, he never made a concession which compromised his main goal. Nehru had to admit Jinnah was 'one of the most extraordinary men in history' whose 'success in life arose from never agreeing to anything.' The second reason was that Mountbatten's recommendation to bring forward the date of the transfer of power without League acceptance of a united India left the British government with no alternative other than to hand over 'to more than one authority'. The early date had the great advantage of ridding Britain of responsibility for an unruly country, putting more pressure on the Indian politicians, and implying a successful conclusion to the extensive negotiations. An additional factor is indicated by the Cabinet papers, which show how important it was in the minds of Ministers, and especially the Prime Minister, to keep the subcontinent in the new Commonwealth. To his advantage, Jinnah made an early announcement that Pakistan would remain in the Commonwealth. Finally,

A second reflection is more academic in kind. A few months before partition I discussed the problems of India with a prominent business supporter of the Congress. We talked, as nearly always at that time, about the triangular relationship and the third party. But after a while I sensed, however, that the conversation was not going along in the accustomed groove. There was denunciation of the third party. Somehow it did not seem to fit the third party. It was only after a while that I realized that it was not the British who were being denounced; it was the Muslims. They, it appears, were to be regarded—and it was consistent with Congress claims to speak for all-India—as the third party in India. Could they be wished off the scene, eighty millions of them, then all would be well in the new-found friendship of Britain and Congress India. It has since occurred to me that this Congress spokesman was perhaps too well grounded in British interpretations of the history of the subcontinent. He assumed, as we are apt to assume, that the most important event in its modern history has been the impact of expanding Europe. But the partition of India suggests that this was not really so. In the last resort it was not the British, it was the Mohammedan invaders of India, who possessed the more enduring political influence.

And finally there remains the question, also academic in its ordinary presentation, but fundamental to partition in India and elsewhere. What is a nation? How is it to be identified? Is there some criterion by which it may be judged whether or not there were two nations in the subcontinent? Or is it the case that political science does not deal in such absolutes and that only history by way of trial, error and much suffering can supply the answer?

---

concern about the divided communities in the North-West Frontier Province, the Punjab, and Bengal, drew Mountbatten, the Congress and the League into extensive discussions about provincial problems. Jinnah was in the favourable position of having the negotiations frequently concentrated on the provinces of his future country. This excluded a realistic discussion about the powers of central government, so necessary for the unity of India (*History*, vol. 67, June 1982, pp. 285–6, review by W. Golant, Department of History, University of Exeter).

# 16

# India and Pakistan:
# Whither Have They Turned?

There was a time when historians of Europe wrote and lectured confidently on periods in the Dark or Middle Ages, the Renaissance, the Age of Enlightenment and so on—but under critical probing of what happened beneath the surface, that assurance has been dented. It is the degree of continuity that survives even in revolutionary situations which is now apt to be emphasized to the point, or beyond it, when credibility is strained. Much in each case depends on the eye of the beholder and his perspective in time. If his interest is in social systems, for example, he may well find, as he would in contemporary India and Pakistan, continuity more pronounced than if it were in high politics, international relations, and war. In the international dimension (with which this article is concerned)—and especially where, as in the Indian subcontinent in 1947, there was manifestly a new departure—assessments made even a generation ago are likely to be subject to significant revision. In the 'glad, confident morning' of independence, there were concepts of potential Indian and Pakistani roles in international politics; thirty-six years later, there is a more prosaic crystallization of interests, accompanied, it may be, by some hardening of the diplomatic arteries. To what extent or in what respects did this imply a retreat from, or belie, earlier aspirations?

The editors, in their invitation to me to contribute to this last issue under their distinguished auspices, prompted these reflections by reminding me of the concluding sentences to the chapter on

Asian membership of the Commonwealth in the second volume of my *Survey of British Commonwealth Affairs*,[1] and asking me how I would seek to answer the question therein posed in a literary allusion more wide-ranging than historians, myself included, would only rarely be so incautious as to employ. The sentences read: 'Independence to which they [India and Pakistan] had aspired so long was theirs at last. The world awaited with interest the use that they would make of it.

> To Mecca hast thou turned in prayer
> With aching heart and eyes that burn:
> Oh, Hajji, whither wilt thou turn
> When thou art there, when thou are there?

The passage overall does, I think, faithfully reflect the questioning of its own time not only in the subcontinent but also in the Commonwealth and in the world at large. It was after all as important then to assess correctly whither new states of such magnitude would turn, as it is interesting now to consider the extent to which assessments made at that time have measured up to events.

At the first (and last[*]) inter-Asian conference which Nehru, in an inspired initiative, called to meet in New Delhi on the eve of independence, the view was widely entertained by Asian leaders, about to assume but still unburdened by office, that the impending end of colonialism in South Asia would prove a landmark in world history as momentous as the French or Russian revolutions. The parallel, at first seemingly extravagant, was advanced on the argument that the withdrawal of the greatest of European empires from South Asia would necessarily lead to the ending of colonialism, first in South-East Asia, then in Africa, and elsewhere throughout the world, and in so doing would transform the pattern of world politics. The assumption at least by and large did prove correct. Colonialism, if not dead, was doomed; the process which began with the transfer of power in India gathered momentum, as increasingly those who sought to sustain colonial rule appeared to be

1. *Survey of British Commonwealth Affairs; Problems of Wartime Co-operation and Post-War Change 1939–1952* (Oxford University Press, 1958), p. 261.

[*] A commemorative conference, forty years later, was called to meet in New Delhi in 1987 and was attended by the author.

fighting on the wrong side of history. In creating this climate of opinion it was the first step, the transfer of power in India, that remains by far the most important in historical perspective and which in one respect provided the prototype for much that followed, by showing how such transfer might be peacefully achieved as between withdrawing European imperial powers and successor national rulers.

At the heart of peaceful transfer lay the Commonwealth connection, whose contribution and evolution had its own surprises. The Muslim League had long made known its desire for Commonwealth membership for the emerging Pakistan, but the Congress was committed to Purna Swaraj or complete independence for India. Yet in the summer of 1947, India turned towards dominion status, in the first place as an interim device to facilitate an immediate transfer of power, and then in 1949, as the last Viceroy, Lord Mountbatten, had envisaged as a possible consequence, to Commonwealth membership on a more lasting basis. Despite Kashmir, Suez, racial issues, war with Pakistan, Rhodesia, India has remained a member and indeed acted as host for the most recent Commonwealth Conference in November 1983. There were few, very few, in Whitehall or elsewhere, Mountbatten apart, who anticipated a link that might endure at least for a generation. None, so far as I recall, envisaged a Commonwealth of which India remained a member, but from which Pakistan had seceded, even though that secession was not based on the merits of membership, but was in protest at recognition by Commonwealth states of the independence of Bangladesh in 1972. Overall, however, India's accession and Pakistan's secession represented a twofold departure from general expectation.

In listing the occasions of tension which over the years seemed likely to place continued Asian membership in jeopardy, there is an omission which would have seemed astonishing to most delegates to the Asian Conference in 1947. Why, they would have asked, have you omitted the deepest of all sources of division—colonialism? And the question would have been much to the point. India and Pakistan (in respect particularly of the Muslim states along the North African littoral) were at that time not only intent on independence—in the case of Pakistan from Hindustan as well as Britain—for themselves: they were also the champions of freedom movements wherever they emerged in the territories of the western colonial empires. Of those empires the British remained the greatest. How could India and Pakistan reconcile their anti-colonialist crusade with membership of a Commonwealth in which Britain was the dominant partner? In Whitehall, as the records show, there were gloomy departmental prognostications of likely consequences, leading in some instances to the conclusion that Asian membership by reason of colonial and related racial issues would be a divisive influence and therefore something to be discouraged.

The reasoning was logical, yet the sequel did not endorse it. For this four reasons may be adduced. Firstly, while Britain was still the dominant partner in the Commonwealth, Australia and New Zealand among other members were with the anti-colonialist lobby in the United Nations, stridently in the case of Australia with Herbert Evatt as its spokesman. Secondly, while the concepts of trusteeship held by the British and the majority of the United Nations members differed fundamentally in their notions of responsibility as between the administering power and the Trusteeship Council for the timing of the advance of dependent territories to independence, both subscribed to the concept. Thirdly, the manner in which Britain had transferred power in South and South-East Asia was widely viewed in a favourable light that was enhanced by the resistance to change of the so-called reactionary colonial powers in the area, France and Holland; fourthly, and flowing from that, there was the influence of anti-colonial Asian states at play from their vantage point within the Commonwealth. The strains were there, though much less pronounced on the straight issue of independence and its timing than generally foreseen. It is indeed the case that colonial racial issues, as in Rhodesia, and a question with strong colonial–racial overtones, namely Suez, brought the Commonwealth relationship seemingly close to breaking point. Yet, even in respect of these issues, it did not break. That nowadays is apt to pass unremarked. But in historical retrospect, it seems of much moment and to be deserving of exploration. Was it in part to be attributed to the fact that colonial and related issues were viewed not exclusively in an Anglo–Indian but also in a Commonwealth setting, in which other member states, most notably Canada at the time of Suez, were thereby enabled to play a mediatory role? If so, then here too the Commonwealth as a whole played a role more significant than expected.

In retrospect, membership of the Commonwealth would seem

to have best served Indian interests as such in the earlier years. It hastened and eased the passage to independence, it served to counter exclusive Pakistani influence from within (which was itself an important factor in India's opting for membership), it enabled India to shape a foreign policy westward-inclined but without any unequal bilateral relationship with the United States. Above all, by carrying no Cold War commitment, it left open the way to non-alignment, the *Panch Shila* being formulated in the preamble to the Sino–Indian agreement on Tibet in April 1954, and most important, to the feeling out of a working relationship with the USSR such as exists today. Commonwealth membership was at its most effective in the role it enabled India to play in securing a cease-fire in Korea. In terms of international politics, the importance of membership to outward appearance has perceptibly declined in more recent times, though the Commonwealth dimension remains to be deployed as and when it is in India's interest to do so.

At the time of independence, while British attention was given to Indian and Pakistani Commonwealth membership and its implications, Indian thoughts were turning to India's world role. Its first concern was regional and common to most states in the area: to preserve South and South-East Asia as an area of 'no war'. There was, however, a more positive side to it. In the phrases of the time, Asia and India—Nehru did not always distinguish between the two—awakening after a long sleep, were about to bring a new, a more rational, and, above all, a more temperate and understanding voice to international affairs. The great powers, with their global rivalries, their brash assertions of interest, their division of the world into blocs with insensitive rebuke to those who adopted an independent stance, and their deployment of force, were so far as possible to be restrained by the resolve of uncommitted states to urge peaceful means of settling differences, the merits of which would be decided as they arose and not determined by engagements previously entered into. To be non-aligned, as the stance came to be known, was not to be neutral. Neutrality was a role appropriate to small powers, like Ireland, or states geographically exposed, like Sweden, but not to a major Asian state. Freedom from obligations to great power alliances was one thing, prior commitment to stand aside another. That would be unworthy retreat from world responsibilities. Non-alignment, by contrast, allowed freedom of action when crises arose based upon India's own unfettered judgement, at the price, be it added, of a good deal of great power resentment and potential misunderstanding. In these respects, India's aspirations, despite phases of disillusion, have remained constant. Its was a new voice in world affairs and its leaders believed that a part of their mission was that India should be heard.

When Mahatama Gandhi came to address the Asian Relations Conference,[2] he was hailed by the leader of the Chinese delegation as 'the beloved teacher, the saviour of India, the father of a continent!' Yet the Chinese did not desire fatherly or other leadership of the continent, in other than a figurative sense—unless, indeed, it were Chinese. The rivalry between India and China was implicit in the later proceedings, and while a decision was taken to hold biennial conferences with the next to take place in China, it was never implemented. The Indians preferred no further conference to one held in China; the Chinese to another held in India.

Yet despite incipient rivalry within Asia, the image of a non-violent India guiding the destinies of post-colonial Asia was an important factor in the first decade of independence and, though somewhat tarnished since, it is not without strong appeal among the non-aligned nations to this day. It was associated with a twofold assumption: the first that India itself was in a general unspecified way committed to Gandhian doctrines of non-violence internationally as well as at home; and the second that Asian states were peace-loving and free from traditional *inter se* rivalries in a way that European states were not.

Discussing revolutionary violence, in his 1971 Rede lecture[3] in Cambridge, Herbert Butterfield remarked that contemporaries tend to judge a revolution by its atrocities, while a later generation not only is apt to overlook them, but is sometimes even too impatient to glance at them, preferring rather to judge a revolution by its ideals. Apart from the two partitioned provinces, Bengal and, above all, the Punjab, which paid in mass migration and terrible slaughter the greater part of the immediate price of partition, this view has proved true, so far as I can judge, of the post-independence generations in India though not, I think, of those in Pakistan. Externally

---

2. *Asian Relations: being a Report of the Proceedings and Documentation of the First Asian Relations Conference, New Delhi, March–April, 1947* (New Delhi: Asian Relations Organization, 1948).

3. *The Discontinuities between the Generations in History* (Cambridge University Press, 1972).

also what happened in the Punjab has been regarded as a predictable, and by Gandhi predicted, calamity with historical interest now focused on what was and what was not done by the British in advance, and by the Indian and Pakistani governments subsequently, to reduce in scale something which, given partition, could not have been altogether averted. Critics of India's actions in respect of Hyderabad and Junagadh at the time and of Kashmir down the years have, however, consistently drawn particular attention to a lack of conformity in each case with India's own peaceful professions. Was non-violence susceptible only of selective application? Did it apply where scrupulous regard for it would delay or preclude the fuller realization of the national ideal, independence with unity? These were matters put to the test most severely in the subcontinent in an improbable (as it still seems to me) but demanding context.

When power was transferred on 15 August 1947, small pockets of foreign rule remained. It did not occur to me at the time that the lesser imperialisms of France and Portugal should, or could, survive the greater in the subcontinent. More important, this had not occurred either to the French chargé d'affaires, who remarked to a member of the British High Commission on 13 August 1947, that he himself 'saw the impossibility of the situation of the French establishments in the new India' and that he had been making representations to the French government indicating the utmost importance of surrendering them to the Indian Union quickly and with good grace. 'Unfortunately', he continued, a French government preoccupied with prestige looked upon withdrawal 'as trailing the tricolour in the mud.'[4] Nine years accordingly elapsed before the Chamber of Deputies approved the transfer and then, as K.M. Panikkar, ambassador in Paris at the time, told me, it was successfully commended to a critical chamber only by a prime ministerial announcement that it had been agreed that the governor's residence in Pondicherry would be preserved for all time as a centre of French culture and civilization in the East!

The Portuguese, however, displayed no such adaptability; on the contrary they enunciated the doctrine that Goa (with their other possessions) was part of the metropolitan territory and thus could

4. Nicholas Mansergh and Penderel Moon (eds), *The Transfer of Power 1942–47: Constitutional Relations between Britain and India* (12 vols., London: HMSO, 1970–83), XII, no. 450.

never be alienated. For that reason, there was no point in exchanging views: there was nothing to exchange them about. The sequel was mounting national feeling throughout India, calls for popular action in the form of satyagraha by volunteers, casualties and violence in Goa on Independence Day, 15 August 1956, followed, after much searching of conscience, by a pronouncement by Nehru that one government should not use satyagraha against another, and finally, five years later, in December 1961, by his further pronouncement that India's patience was exhausted and that armed intervention sufficient to bring about Portuguese capitulation would be deployed. The West was loud in its denunciation of this departure from non-violence by the state which was at once its enunciator and professed adherent. The criticisms were warranted. Nehru, amid more important preoccupations, had shown lack of foresight. He should have pressed urgently for the settlement of the comparatively trifling question of foreign possessions in India on 15 August 1947. Even a display of force would then have seemed the not unnatural outcome of a still unfolding national revolution, whereas fifteen years later it attracted odium as a departure from self-professed principle. Politics, among other things, is a matter of timing—something a chargé d'affaires understood rather better than prime ministers.

The second assumption, that of Asia as a continent of peace-loving states, carried with it its own peculiar hazards, chief among them that Indians might believe it. At an Institute of Pacific Relations Conference in 1958, a good deal was heard about India's tradition of peaceful relations with China—a common allusion being to the thousand miles of common frontier and the thousand years of peace between them. In 1959, in reply to warnings in the Lok Sabha from Acharya Kripalani, Nehru discounted the prospect of armed Chinese intervention—the real danger was not, he said, of 'armies pouring in', but of words being said in Beijing about the frontier which 'we cannot possibly accept, admit or agree to . . . it would be a tragedy if we, who stood up against the cold war, . . . should surrender to its voice and technique' in the face of Chinese provocation and discourtesies. He added, very characteristically: 'Cold war is an admission of defeat. . . . It is not, if I may say so with all respect to the participants of the cold war, a mature way of considering a question . . . cold war is the negation of non-violence.'[5] When the Chinese border incursion came in 1962, the impact was greatly heightened by the unexpectedness of armed assault. Nehru, his own most severe critic, confessed 'we were getting out of touch with reality in the modern world'; though on the evidence, as set out by his biographer,[6] Nehru was by no means unaware of the risks, but ill-advisedly subordinated his own views and those of his advisers to those of India's ambassador in Beijing, K.M. Panikkar. None the less for most Indian leaders[7] the shock was psychologically traumatic. It was a hope not only of India but of newly independent Asia which had been undermined.

For Pakistan at the moment of independence there was by contrast greater and necessary concentration on the domestic front. The state started from scratch—a capital to be chosen, an administration to be established. The second required not only the often very able Muslims who migrated from the new India but also essential equipment. The latter was not readily obtained. In early August 1947, Lord Mountbatten reported from Calcutta that 'as usual' in seeking to effect a fair division of resources between the two successor states, division of certain mechanical office equipment was causing a 'complete deadlock', with the formidable Indian Home Minister, Sardar Patel, 'flaring up' at the suggestion of a printing press going to Karachi where there was only one. 'No one', Patel declared, 'asked Pakistan to secede', and he had no intention of allowing them another press from India.[8] Yet such office equipment and paper—I have a clear recollection of the still continuing desperate shortage of the latter in government departments in Karachi in 1951 when I called on I.H. Qureshi,[9] who had ministerial responsibility *inter alia* for the great mass of refugees who sought refuge near the capital and whose identities had to be recorded—are things without which modern government

5. Lok Sabhà, *Debates*, 2nd series, 1959, pt. 2, vol. 39, cols. 8118–22; reprinted in N. Mansergh (ed.), *Documents and Speeches on Commonwealth Affairs 1952–1962* (London: Oxford University Press, 1963), pp. 595–9.

6. S. Gopal, *Jawaharlal Nehru: A Biography* (3 vols., Cambridge, MA: Harvard University Press, 1979), II: *1947–1956*, p. 181.

7. The Vice-President of India, Dr Sarvepalli Radhakrishnan, would not have been among them, judging by a conversation with the author in 1958 on the likely course of Chinese frontier policy.

8. Mansergh and Moon (eds.), *Transfer of Power*, XI, no. 39, and XII, nos. 287 and 302.

9. Later Vice-Chancellor of the University of Karachi.

cannot effectively function. Of this Liaquat Ali Khan, Jinnah's deputy—in so far as he had one—in the Muslim League and first Prime Minister of Pakistan, was well aware. In the spring of 1947 he felt that for administrative reasons transfer, even by June 1948, was too early, though later for political reasons he felt transfer could hardly be too soon. But the handicap of shortages in vital resources remained, and I suspect conditioned the early history of Pakistan in a way that is not retrospectively sufficiently allowed for.

In March 1947 I asked Liaquat how he viewed the prospect and policies of the then emerging state. The relevant part of my record reads as follows:

Question: How will Pakistan work? Are you reasonably confident that the particular political problems it presents—including the territorial separation of its component parts—can be overcome?

Answer: It will work quite satisfactorily though in the early stages there will be considerable difficulties. I have in mind a close federation between East and West Pakistan with a capital in each but a unified system of government, of social services and of taxation. It might be that one capital would be administrative and the other parliamentary (I had made this suggestion). Throughout the whole area the League is satisfactorily holding its position and it will be able to maintain law and order. There has never been one India. That was a creation of the British and if one India were forced upon us the danger of outside intervention would be far greater in that other powers anxious to fish in troubled waters would be able to engage the sympathy of a persecuted minority. If the Muslims remained in a united India their treatment by the Hindus would be unendurable.

Question: Do you think there is a serious risk of civil war?

Answer: That all depends on how power is handed over. If it is handed over to two separate authorities equally, it may be avoided. The choice lies with the British. But there must be two constituent assemblies, one to draft a constitution for Hindustan, one for Pakistan.

Question: Do you think that it would be possible to reach any arrangement about unified defence and unified conduct of external affairs?

Answer: Of course within the two Pakistan areas there will in fact be complete unification. They will be part of one state. So far as the relations between Pakistan and Hindustan are concerned, an arrangement could be made which would enable a close agreement to be reached about defence and external affairs.

Question: Do you think that Pakistan will wish to continue any relationship with the British Commonwealth?

Answer: There are only three great powers. The Soviet Union is an uncertain factor and her materialism is repugnant to Muslims. We have seen a certain amount of the United States in recent years. Their soldiers came to India and they went away again. We did not dislike them, we just feel that there is nothing in common. Therefore we are likely to think first of Britain as an associate since we know her. Once Pakistan is established, arrangements can be made to cover all security questions on a wide basis.

These fundamental aims were realized. There was a separate constituent assembly responsible for drafting the constitution for the separate and independent state of Pakistan duly established on 15 August 1947. The problems of the territorial separation of its two parts were not overcome in the longer term however—something that may be partly attributed to the assassination of Liaquat in 1954 and with it, the untimely removal of a guiding hand at once strong and tolerant, though *per contra* it might be contended that it was inherent in the division and recalled that Mountbatten in May 1947 had foreseen a day when a separate Bengali state might apply for membership of the Commonwealth.[10]

The implications of the answers to my third and fourth questions in so far as they related to defence remained much in mind. In fact no arrangement was concluded with India on defence before 15 August—a fact which was viewed with concern by the British chiefs of staff, while to enquiries from the British chiefs of staff as to what steps, if any, were to be taken for external defence after 15 August, the answer was 'none'.[11] Britain and India, however, as well as Pakistan were resolute in their intent to uphold imperial frontiers, and Afghan claims on the North-West Frontier were

10. Mansergh and Moon (eds.), *Transfer of Power*, X, no. 553.

firmly repudiated. There was awareness of the Baluchis across the border as well as in Baluchistan. In the background was the greater fear of Russian infiltration into Afghanistan. A neighbour to Pakistan, Afghanistan is not for India a far away country of which little is known. On the contrary, it is a country whose past is interwoven with that of the subcontinent from the eleventh-century invasions of Mahmud of Ghazni through the Lodi kings, an Afghan dynasty that ruled in Delhi for a century down to 1526, to the years of British rule when Afghanistan was the centrepiece in the Great Game played, but never to a finish, between the British and the Russian empires, which had no common frontier because of the long tongue of Afghan territory stretching eastward to China. The purpose of the Game was essentially negative, that of ensuring that Afghanistan remained a buffer and did not become a base. But now all that is changed. Afghanistan has become a base with uncertain foundation and unpredictable consequence. Kipling and rumours on the frontier of a 'grey-coat coming' have a fresh appropriateness:

> . . . Of the Russians who can say?
> When the night is gathering all is grey.

In the reported words of President Karmal, the Russians are in Afghanistan to stay until 'plots and conspiracies of regional reaction, imperialists and expansionists are ended forever.' Well, however interpreted, that certainly suggests they will be there for some time!

The crisis in Afghanistan was not only close geographically and in historical setting: it exposed for the first time to the eye of a wider public the consequences of the lack of a 1947 tripartite or post-1947 bilateral understanding between India and Pakistan on defence. A recipient since 1954 of American aid, Pakistan, after apparent contemplation of a more hazardous course on the strength of that assistance, has seemingly decided upon prudent restraint in the face of the Russian occupation. At the outset the diplomatic reaction in Delhi was muted. The Indian view early in 1980, as conveyed to a stream of high-level visitors from West and East and from neighbouring states small and large, was that the Russians

11. Ibid., XI, no. 487. See also ibid., IX, nos. 544 and 55.

should withdraw from Afghanistan, but that expression of this view should be tempered by understanding of Russia's fears, and that such withdrawal was more likely to be effected by diplomatic representations over a period of time than by public denunciations or military or naval manoeuvres with more than a hint of menace attached to them. Indian emphasis accordingly, and in the language of the crisis, was on stabilizing, on defusing, and on de-escalating with concomitant condemnation of the United States, China, and Pakistan for taking steps, striking attitudes, hegemonizing—a shaft directed at Beijing—or using language likely to destabilize the situation or to escalate tensions. Not all of the distinguished visitors to Delhi concurred in Indian views—there were what were discreetly termed differences in interim perception—with the Muslim states, the King of Nepal, and the Yugoslav Foreign Minister (mindful no doubt of the implications for his own country) in greater or lesser degree insisting that Russia should first withdraw and then be given all reasonable assurances and understanding, as against the Indian view that the reverse order alone offered a realistic prospect of success.

Despite conversations, the Afghan crisis underscored yet again the gulf that separated Pakistan, aligned as it was with the United States, Britain, and other western powers by treaty and other commitments, from a non-aligned India. 'India', Mrs Gandhi was reported as saying on 2 October 1983, 'feels more threatened by American upgraded forces in Pakistan than the presence of 100,000 troops in Afghanistan. . . . I don't see we are threatened by Russian troops though we would like them not to be there.'[12]

At the last, looking back over the years since independence, the most striking change is psychological. Asia has re-emerged in world affairs. Delhi has become one of the great diplomatic capitals. In 1983, India acted as host to the seventh summit of non-aligned nations, the largest that has yet assembled, and to the second Commonwealth heads-of-government meeting to be held in Asia, with the Indian Prime Minister presiding at both. In this respect, Jawaharlal Nehru's hopes, as conveyed to the Asian Relations Conference, have been amply, even dramatically, fulfilled. In its own way that symbolizes the magnitude of the anti-colonial revolution in world history.

12. As quoted in the *Daily Telegraph*, 3 October 1983.

# Epilogue—India in the 1950s

# 17

# A Visit to India and Pakistan

In the white marble palace of the Mughal Emperors in Delhi's Red Fort, I had some difficulty in determining the exact site of the famous Peacock Throne. This was not altogether surprising, for it had been carried away in 1739 by the Persians and melted down in Teheran to replenish the coffers of Nadir Shah. In the hall of Special Audience where once it stood no trace of it remains. But it must have been of surpassing splendour. Two peacocks in solid gold so inlaid with precious stones of varied colours as to resemble living birds gave the throne its name. The seat and the canopy were of gold ornamented with diamonds, rubies and emeralds. So at least my guidebook told me. But it was not the account of this fantastic oriental splendour nor its exact site that interested me so much as the tacit acceptance by the writer of the act of Persian spoliation. The melting down of the Peacock Throne seemed to him a matter for regret but not for indignation. That was reserved for an Englishman, a Captain Johan, afterwards Sir Johan—the improbable name and the impossible title seem only to make the deed the more deplorable—who after the Mutiny removed inlaid panels of exquisite design from the Durbar Hall to serve as marble tabletops in some English suburban home. The writer of the guidebook may not be too certain on points of detail but I respected his judgement. To melt down the spoils of conquest was the traditional perquisite of Asiatic conquerors, but to make imperial mural decorations serve as tabletops savoured intolerably of alien bourgeois philistinism. Who but a Victorian Englishman could think of anything so sensible—and so outrageous? The story had, however, a tolerable ending. Lord Curzon was outraged and brought about the appropriate act of restoration. Of that I am glad. Great crimes are so often but tastelessness so rarely forgiven. Indeed I have often looked back in gratitude to the minor achievements of Lord Curzon. His is not a name to conjure with in present-day India. The figure of the most imperial of pro-consuls conceals that of the restorer and protector of historic monuments. Yet in that role his name lives on. I remember commenting to a venerable custodian on the beautifully kept lawns surrounding some imperial tomb. 'Ah', he said in trembling piety, 'that was the work of the great Lord Curzon.' Was Curzon not really more character-istically English in his sense of the past than Captain Johan, and was he not most English in the care he lavished on lawns and gardens?

How many times on returning from India have I not been greeted with the half-anxious enquiry 'Well, how are things now?' It is distressingly difficult to give a satisfying answer; especially when, as is so often the case, my questioner has spent more years in the old pre-1947 India than I have months in the new. Politics, corruption, the working of the parliamentary system, communism, Nehru, the bearing of the armed forces—all these are possible topics. But each requires more than a few impressionistic phrases and none is all-sufficing. So usually I talk about gardens, or to be more exact, about the state of gardens. I believe that that is what most Englishmen who knew India at least want to hear about. If they lived within the charmed, if not always charming, official circle at New Delhi it is of the upkeep of the Mughal Gardens at what was once the Viceroy's Palace, and is now the President's official residence, that they will first wish to learn; if their memories are of the market-place then an account of the contemporary and once more orderly appearance of the flower beds in Connaught Circus will ensure attention. By one's report on the public gardens in the great cities most Englishmen in their hearts will judge the state of India.

I know nothing of the history of gardening in India; it was always, I suspect, the luxury of a leisured few. But it was perhaps some small consolation to a subjugated people that their conquerors were lovers of gardens. This was as true, perhaps more true, of the Muslims than of the British. The naming of the garden at the Viceroy's House, the Mughal Garden, was an implied tribute to precursors in gardening as in conquest. I often think that the affinity between Englishmen and Muslims is symbolized by their common love of gardens. And of the two the Mughal rulers had perhaps the better sense of landscape. English gardens in India sometimes look a little self-consciously English with the colour effects violently accentuated. Or so it seemed to me this spring, a newcomer from England, my eyes till then familiar with shy flowers along the Cambridge Backs, the snowdrops, the crocuses

> pale purple as if they had their birth
> In sunless Hades fields . . .

Of course there was colour too in the Mughal Gardens—one need go no further than the flower beds in the 'Life Bestowing Gardens' at Delhi's Red Fort to realize that. But it was the lawns with trees that gave shade as welcome as that of a great rock in a desert land, the marble channels with flowing water that intersected them, and the cool splashing fountains that made, and still make, the Mughal Gardens such delightful havens. None that survive is more enchanting than the Shalimar Gardens outside the city walls of Lahore. There a month or so ago I attended a garden party in honour of the young King Feisal of Iraq, and as the wail of Panjabi pipes mingled with the sound of gently falling water from some three hundred fountains, the guests (if they were not too hot) could think back nostalgically to the golden days of the Emperor Shah Jehan when the gardens were laid out. It is a tempting thing to do, especially in Lahore, a frontier city now a little too conscious perhaps of a greater past and of the lost opportunity of the present. Tradition and its cultural heritage marked out Lahore as the capital of Pakistan; it was geography and strategic considerations that gave the honour to the dusty, parvenu airport city of Karachi.

Englishmen are peculiarly prone to romanticize about empires dead and gone, whether another's or their own. We are, indeed, I suspect, embarking upon a period of romantic reappraisal of British rule in India. No topic lends itself more happily to such treatment. The wonder that for so long a small European island people should have controlled the destiny of the great subcontinent of South Asia is something that will and should never die. As Macaulay sensed in its early phase, it is one of the great dramatic episodes of history. But it is over, and it is right that we should be very conscious, despite a proper pride in the record, that it has ended.

In India and Pakistan today British people are popular. They are popular because British rule has ended and still more because of the manner of its ending. Who in the thirties and particularly in the summer of 1942, the summer of the Quit India resolution, would have dared to prophesy that the British would leave India not in some violent cataclysm but amid the plaudits of a people whose high hope was that the last Viceroy might be persuaded to remain as the first Governor-General of a new dominion? Despite the disaster and tragedy that accompanied partition that was one of the political miracles of our time. Lord Mountbatten had much to do with it—a conqueror greater than Clive because he won the hearts of the people, an Indian friend remarked—Attlee's sense of timing perhaps even more and Mahatma Gandhi most of all. There could, a Congress Minister suggested to me, have been another ending, an ending in which Nehru was forced into the role of Ho Chi Minh in Indo–China and Britain became involved in a long, thankless war in which she would have lost the goodwill of all Asia. Or, as I was tempted to reply, was British faith in the principle of self-government so deep-rooted that so disastrous a climax would in the end always have been averted?

In the gallery of the House of the People one finds some reason for such a reassuring answer in the sense of continuity. Until April this year I had not attended a parliamentary debate in Delhi since 1947 when I had happened to be present at the last session of the Legislative Assembly under British rule. There were changes. The official members were gone; the European representatives were gone and the Muslim League had gone though individual Muslims remained. But there seemed little change in procedure. The Indian Republic was the heir to British parliamentary institutions in India—an heir long anxious to enter into his heritage and on the whole satisfied with his experience of it. To the older Congress leaders no other form of government now seems conceivable while among the younger, even among the Communists, one hears of no openly suggested alternative. Experience of one general and many state and local elections is regarded as reassuring. Younger men may criticize, not without apparent justice, the arrogance of some ministers, and the indifferent use made of certain parliamentary procedures notably of the parliamentary question, but, no doubt about it at all, there is an undeniable impressiveness in the free debates in the House of the People. There are gathered together representatives of the most populous democracy on earth to discuss, as in my hearing, pressing domestic problems of food production and irrigation or to listen with unanimous approval to Prime Minister Nehru dismissing in those quiet persuasive tones the notion, fantastic and intolerable, that small enclaves of foreign-dominated territory should survive on Indian soil.

Parliamentary self-government in India and in Pakistan is, of course, an experiment. An observer, however encouraging he may think the start, is well advised to be cautious in his prognostications of the future. We do not know enough. 'You can as little judge of the feelings and inspiration of the people of India', said G.N. Curzon in the House of Commons sixty two years ago with his Viceroyalty still before him, 'from the plans and proposals of the Congress Party as you can of the physical configuration of a country which is wrapped in the mists of early morning, but a few of whose topmost peaks have been touched by the rising sun.' That is still largely true. 'Long years ago we made our tryst with destiny', said Nehru as the clock moved towards the midnight hour in the Constituent Assembly on 14 August 1947, when the pledge was to be redeemed. But with its redemption the Congress Party had fulfilled its manifest destiny. Till then the champion of a people's freedom it remains a political party without a party's programme. Across the border it has seen in recent months the election landslide of East Bengal when the Muslim League, the party which had brought Pakistan to birth, was swept aside by a combination of dissatisfied elderly politicians and impatient, impetuous young men. Is that for the Congress, too, the writing on the wall? Or will their deeper roots and more established leadership save them from so ignominious an overthrow? Such questions are easily asked, not easily answered. What one can say is that despite corruption and scandals there is still in India a spirit of hope and aspiration. It may be that it is only the topmost peaks one sees, but their configuration suggests that what lies still shrouded in mist is a land rich at least in human experience and in intimate knowledge of the life of man.

It is a land rich perhaps in little else. Sometimes I could wish that western people who prescribe what India ought to do could spend a few hours, not in a new community centre where visitors are now customarily taken, but in an ordinary Indian village to see how life is lived. No sensitive person will lightly banish from his mind the sight of such wretched poverty borne sometimes with humour, more often seemingly with fatalistic dignity. Nor will he fail henceforward to understand what Gandhi meant when he said it was equivalent to robbery to eat delicacies in India when the millions did not get a full meal. It may be that you or I might reach the same conclusion about the course of action India should take in world affairs, but at least we should have reached it the hard way. Such sights, too, are a useful reminder for those who are disposed to take a romantic view of British rule. Unity, honest administration, impartial justice, the seeds of representative government—these were the blessings it brought and of these the first, unity, proved transient. They were great and important things. But for good or ill the planned raising of the standard of living was not the first concern of the British rulers of India. Perhaps it was something no alien government could do; perhaps more simply it was that the age of the welfare state was not yet. But as a matter of history the British rulers of India were driven if you will, into the closest association with the princes, the great landowners, the rising business class. These were their natural allies. The poor had justice—no mean thing—but they remained destitute. I remember one morning in April standing in the white marble pavilion that projects out over the eastern wall of the Red Fort at Delhi where in Mughal times the Emperor came daily at dawn to salute the rising sun and to receive the salutations of his subjects. It was a ceremony revived by King George V after the Coronation Durbar of 1911. Below the pavilion is the jungle that comes right up to the red walls of the fort where the jackals call at night, beyond is the river and a tarmac road where slow, white oxen drag their heavy loads. Except for the motor transport the scene is as it was when Mughal Emperors and an English King looked out on now far distant dawns. Below me under the shade of a thorn tree I saw an outcast lying on the sand, clothed in some rough sacking, a woman beside him with a heavy veil of sacking over her sleeping face. They and their like had been lying there in the days of British and of Mohammedan rulers. The Empires have gone; they remain to confront the Hindus, now lords again in Hindustan, with their most testing challenge.

# 18

## Are Elephants Democratic?

The sixty-third session of the Indian National Congress was held in the frontier province of Assam in January 1958. The party's President, U.N. Dhebar, was accorded a memorable welcome, with a procession of sixty-three richly caparisoned elephants leading a mile-long procession which travelled with slow and ponderous dignity the nine miles from the river front at Gauhati to Pragjyotishpur where the Congress sessions were held. But while Congressmen enjoyed the spectacle, some among them were troubled in mind and conscience. Was such ostentation fitting for a party devoted to social reform and economic development? How was it to be reconciled with the teaching of Mahatma Gandhi, the father of the people, whose continuing influence was plain for all to see in the simple, homespun dhotis and white cloth Gandhi caps of the Congress delegates? Were elephants, the pride of princes and of emperors in bygone days, democratic? The Congress, and even the ordinary citizen, if the correspondence columns of the newspapers may be taken as a guide, felt that there was here a question with some disturbing implications for the ruling party of the new India.

The answer to the question would not have been far to seek if it could have been given in purely economic terms. In the northern provinces of India a yoke of oxen may be bought for some Rs 700–800; a single camel, a sufficient substitute for them for Rs 550, but who would think it worth while there to quote the current market price of elephants? A peasant in Rajasthan is as likely to be able to buy and to feed an elephant as a factory worker in Birmingham to buy and run a Rolls Royce. '*Le sol tremble sur le passage des cortèges des Maharajahs*'* reads the brochure on India of one of the great European airlines and this association of elephants with men of great position and of greater wealth is well founded in economics as in history. 'It is reported recently from Karachi that Civil Servants who have lived ostentatiously, as for example by keeping an elephant as a pet, are to be the special object of the enquiry into corruption among Pakistani Civil Servants initiated by General Ayub's new military regime there!' Decidedly the ownership and associations of elephants have not been democratic! But here economics like history can do no more than provide the setting for a question which derived its meaning only from the psychological context in which it was posed.

The Indian state that came into existence on 15 August 1947 was conceived by its principal founders as a democratic and a secular state devoted above all to improving the lot of the poor, the outcast and the oppressed irrespective of community or creed. 'The service of India' said Jawaharlal Nehru on 14 August as the midnight hour and India's independence neared 'means the service of millions who suffer.' This was no conventional phrase but something that came from the hearts perhaps above all, of those who knew the West and therefore by comparison with it, the lack of any semblance of tolerable conditions of living especially in the countless thousand villages where, as Gandhi never tired of reminding his urbanized colleagues, the great mass of the Indian people lived and, all too often, died before they reached maturity. In the face of their daily want and suffering was not all ostentation or luxury to be shunned? Yet what if those who suffered most, delighted most in spectacle and high ceremonial? What, still more, if reasons of state demanded that conscious and spectacular efforts be made to weld into one people all the varied castes, communities, religious and linguistic groups loosely brought together under alien rule and now comprising the sovereign, independent republic of India, a state responsible for the welfare of more people than live in all Europe west of Russia? India has variety and colour astonishing to western eyes; a conscious pride in it may well be a condition of

* 'The earth shakes with the passing of the Maharajas' procession'—Ed.

India's survival as a single political unit. A uniformly austere democracy might seem to many the proper goal of their endeavours, but was it practical politics to pursue it too fervently if that meant disregarding the possibly counter-balancing claims of unity?

The Congress at its Gauhati meeting considered that 'a distressing aspect of the present educational system in India' lay in the fact that it did not 'promote any basic loyalties among students' and the Congress urged accordingly that 'young boys and girls should be made to realize the dangers of narrow and separatist tendencies like casteism, communalism, linguistic fanaticism, and religious intolerance' and that 'efforts must be made to develop a sense of basic loyalty to the unity and welfare of the Nation, tolerance and high standards of behaviour.' This is something that applies with equal force in many fields.

The Republic Day parades in the Indian capital on 26 January each year, combining informality with highly efficient organization, are well designed to stimulate pride in India: pride especially in so much diversity within a political unity. They offer a living panorama as the processional floats go by, of the multifarious occupations, characteristics and levels of civilization of the inhabitants of the states comprising the Indian Union; irrigation engineers from the Punjab succeeded by dancing tribesmen from the Naga Hills, coir weavers from communist Kerala followed by factory workers from Bombay and, most striking contrast of all, camel corps from the desert of Jaisalmer going by with jet aircraft of the Indian Air Force breaking the sound barrier overhead. India is a state, old in its consciousness of nationality but young in its experience of nationhood and not readily to be fitted into the simpler categories in which the countries of Western Europe may be classified. It is a nation because a congeries of peoples living within the subcontinent desire that it should be a nation. But it is a nation that is founded not in uniformity but in variety, and in dialogue with the West the complexity and richness of that variety seems the most important fact of all to remember. Often westerners speak of 'the subtlety' of the Indian, or more usually, of the Hindu mind without considering whether this may not be the reflex of a highly complex national and cultural heritage.

Few who know India would care to deny that there is something identifiable, even if undefinable, in what is termed the 'spirit of

India'. But it is compounded of so many things that even the impact upon it of the great economic, political and social changes of the last generation is difficult to measure. Apart altogether from the self-evident unevenness of such impact—it is remarkable with what passive, dignified resignation Indians accept the fact of development even in a neighbouring village without seemingly expecting that they too will, or should also, immediately and likewise benefit—India as a whole has an absorptive capacity which at the least blurs the outward manifestations of change. At root it derives from a tolerance that is founded on the conviction that what is essential to Hindu life and thought will not, indeed cannot, be touched or still less destroyed. Such tolerance is widely extended to western ideas but its very source makes it hard to judge how far they may be said to have interpenetrated traditional ways of thought.

Even before the British abdication of power it was apparent at the inter-Asian conference which assembled in Delhi in the spring of 1947 in an atmosphere of aspiring and soon to be triumphant nationalism, that there was an unmistakable Indian desire to maintain such friendly links with Britain as did not impair in any way the full measure of restored Asian independence, whether in the political, the economic or the cultural field. This desire, so rare in the relations of empires with subject peoples, coupled with the manner of the British withdrawal, made possible the Indian decision two years later to remain, as a republic, a member of the Commonwealth of Nations and for Indian leaders subsequently to take a certain proprietary pride in a relationship which seemed to Nehru at least to be an example of magnanimity from which other nations might well draw useful lessons. 'Did the Romans, I wonder, ever return to Britain?' enquired Harold Macmillan of his hosts in Delhi in January 1958 and the posing of the question as well as the tumultuously enthusiastic reception the British Prime Minister was accorded showed that for once, and at any rate for a time, the passing of Empire had left no lasting estrangement behind it. This was something that owed more to Mahatma Gandhi than to any other single man, for, long years before independence, he had looked the day when British and Indians, no longer rulers and ruled, but equals brought together by the chance of history might in equal friendship profit by the opportunity it had created. It is now for a later generation in Britain and in India to rise to the level of his perception.

The importance to Europe of India's political association with the Commonwealth may be exaggerated. It is by no means a determining fact in India's political life. None the less it has helped to continue India's association with peoples of western origin. There are more English people in India today than there were before independence. There are many Australians, Canadians and New Zealanders working on irrigation or other development projects such as would not have been found there before 1947. The Commonwealth is helping to serve this generation at least and even if its future is unpredictable—it is worth noting, however, that in the last session of the Council of the States no seconder was to be found for a motion that India should leave the Commonwealth—it has helped to keep open the door of opportunity for contact between East and West at a critical time in their relationship. This is particularly true in the field of culture and political ideas. It was not in England, nor for that matter in Ireland, that cinemas closed when Bernard Shaw died; it was in India. Not for nothing was Gandhi himself once described as the last of the Great Victorians. Though it is almost certainly the case that the future leaders of India will not be western-educated as have been some of those who have held office in the past decade, the consequences of this may not be so far-reaching as some suppose. Nehru was indeed a graduate of Trinity College, Cambridge, but of his famous colleagues in the struggle for freedom, neither Sardar Vallabhbhai Patel, nor Maulana Azad nor Rajendra Prasad, now President of India, went to western universities or other places of education. Yet whatever in consequence may have been their inward reservations, all worked with Nehru for the creation of a secular, democratic state, in which caste should have no recognized place, the Hindu religion no special and privileged position, but where all should be equal under the constitution and before the law as western precept and example taught.

Neither the passage of time, nor doubts about its future, should diminish our appreciation of the quite exceptional significance of the democratic experiment now, and in consequence, being attempted in India on a scale greater than in any other country on earth. It is upon the success or failure of this experiment in government that the prospect of fruitful dialogue with the West must very largely depend. It is indeed more than an essay in liberal democracy. It is itself a symbol of the attachment of India to some western ideas. The alternatives to democracy in India are communism or communalism and while the first in origin is also a western concept it would come to India by way, not of Moscow, but of Peking, and after having acquired some pronounced Asian characteristics *en route*. The emergence of communalism, a possibility not to be altogether discounted, would mean the end of the secular state, the triumph of an obscurantist Hinduism and a breach with western values. It is because these things are so that even in terms of a dialogue with the West the familiar question 'when Nehru goes?' has its relevance. He has been at once the principal artificer and the unwavering champion of the secular state and of the parliamentary system; he has set his face against caste and class distinction and his effortless leadership has given the system established in 1947 an air of assurance it could hardly otherwise have possessed. Today the party of the national revolution, still outwardly faithful to the teaching of the Mahatma, has acquired something of the air of an 'Establishment'. The impressive efficiency with which ministers long accustomed to office transact business or answer questions in the House of the People is coupled sometimes with a note of brusqueness, more often with a touch of condescension towards those less familiar than they with the conduct of affairs; in the states and the municipalities Congressmen are apt to assume, increasingly to their cost, that their past record alone entitles them to the indefinite indulgence of the electorate. Here indeed are many of the signs by which an 'Establishment' is to be known in the evening of its power. Yet even if the days of Congress rule are nearing their close it is far from certain that its term will be followed by some drastic transformation. It may be, that contrary to the opinion of almost all outside observers, there will emerge a strong successor government, neither Communist nor communalist, resolved to continue the liberal democratic experiment at home and friendly association with the Commonwealth and the western world. A condition of this, however, is some substantial measure of success for India's plans for economic development.

'The Congress is firmly wedded to the socialist goal.' So Nehru has asserted and so with some not unimportant qualifications it is, so long as he is at the helm. While the businessmen on the right of the Congress entertained anxieties diminished only by the thought that it will take the planners a long time to get there, some austere disciples of Gandhi wedded, as they are, to the master's belief in the village and the spinning wheel as a source of the good life, have been alienated by the thought of a western concept and western technocrats reshaping the pattern. Acharya Kripalani, notable among them as a former President of the Congress, indeed resigned in consequence from the Congress Party. But far more powerful than the fears of capitalists or the ideals of the austerely simple is the urge of the countless millions who are underfed, underhoused, underemployed to seek relief from their plight.

How are the living standards of so vast and so rapidly increasing a population to be raised? Is it by a social revolution, with ruthless planning imposed from above and sacrificing, if need be, one generation in the interests of those that are to follow? Or is it alternatively to be attempted by teaching and persuasion, by precept and example, by democratic means? This second alternative—a nation advancing by economically forced marches undertaken by the will of the majority of the people democratically expressed along the road the Chinese have travelled under the direction of a totalitarian regime—is the goal of the Congress. The challenge to them is not absolute but relative and is to be expressed in terms of that analogy, of keeping pace with China. If India succeeds in this great, even desperate endeavour, then some at least of the concepts of free western society will have acquired prestige such as should enable them to survive; should she fail then western notions of the free government of free society will be correspondingly discredited and the intellectual frontiers between India and the western world may close again as in the days before the great explorers travelled to the East. It is not therefore yet one more five-year plan that is at stake: it may be the future of cultural interchange between India and the West.

It may seem surprising that pride of place has been given not to language but to government and the nature of its social and economic aims. Yet for the multitudes who await the relief from want and suffering that was declared to be the first task of an independent India this would seem just. But assuredly language, too, has its importance. Originally it was conceived that Hindi should replace English as the official language and a deadline was fixed. But in 1958 as the time drew nearer, so much resistance emerged to any thought of the imposition of Hindi upon the south that the Congress, while emphasizing the need for making Hindi the 'linking language' among the fourteen recognized national languages of India, allowed that a not too rigid view should be taken about the deadline. The door was left open, therefore, for the continued use of English so long as it proved convenient and more generally it was laid down that in questions of language, potentially so divisive, there should be no imposition of the majority view upon the minority and that progress, here also, should be by agreement. Dissension between north and south as a result lost a good deal of its acrimony and for a long time to come the English language seems assured at least of a recognized place in India's political and intellectual life. The resolution of domestic differences on these lines should also, if incidentally, assist intellectual interchange and dialogue between India and the West.

Indians believe their country has a notable contribution to make to the intellectual and political thought of our day. They have a sense of greatness. When more extreme nationalists have sought to have the statues of India's former rulers removed from public places, when municipalities, as Calcutta, have wished to change indiscriminately the names of streets called after former British administrators they have more than once incurred reproof from India's Prime Minister. India, he tells them, is great enough to absorb all her past. And as she absorbs a past that embraces some things that Indians recall with pain as well as so much they remember with pride so, too, she absorbs a great deal from the western world without apparent fear of losing her identity. Her people for the most part, indeed, perhaps because of a lack of a deep or widespread sense of history, appear little concerned to weigh the possible consequences of so doing. Coherence may not be achieved; what is taken assumes an air of sufficiency even though incomplete. The system of responsible parliamentary self-government, the most notable of the imports from the West, strikes root, how deeply who knows as yet, while caste distinctions alien to its very spirit survive. India has many of the characteristics of a democracy, she has two at least of its great essentials, free elections and free discussion. But somehow to ask, is India, a country so large and so compounded of the traditional and the new, a democracy, seems inadequate and barely meaningful. As well ask the question that troubled some Congressmen at Gauhati: 'are elephants democratic?'[11]

*Comprendre* is a 'Revue de Politique de la Culture, et organe de la Société Européenne de Culture'. This article was part of the enquiry entitled 'L'Inde dans le Dialogue des Civilisations'.

# Index